Medieval History

This series includes pioneering editions of medieval historical accounts by eye-witnesses and contemporaries, collections of source materials such as charters and letters, and works that applied new historiographical methods to the interpretation of the European middle ages. The nineteenth century saw an upsurge of interest in medieval manuscripts, texts and artefacts, and the enthusiastic efforts of scholars and antiquaries made a large body of material available in print for the first time. Although many of the analyses have been superseded, they provide fascinating evidence of the academic practices of their time, while a considerable number of texts have still not been re-edited and are still widely consulted.

The Early Yorkshire Woollen Trade

A prominent philanthropist, landowner and politician near Halifax, John Lister (1847–1933) was dedicated to his community. He founded a Catholic school in Halifax and a reformatory trade school in the grounds of his ancestral home. A keen local historian, Lister became involved in the Yorkshire Archaeological Society, particularly in the later years of his life. Along with four other volumes, he edited for the Society this 1924 publication. Transcribing customs records from Hull and records made by royal officials in the fourteenth and fifteenth centuries, Lister describes in his introduction how the wool trade developed and became a central part of the livelihood and character of Yorkshire. He discusses imports and exports, the lives of merchant families, and how the merchandise itself evolved as wool-working developed. Illuminating the social impact of a historically significant industry, this work remains relevant to researchers interested in the medieval economy.

T0364285

Cambridge University Press has long been a pioneer in the reissuing of out-of-print titles from its own backlist, producing digital reprints of books that are still sought after by scholars and students but could not be reprinted economically using traditional technology. The Cambridge Library Collection extends this activity to a wider range of books which are still of importance to researchers and professionals, either for the source material they contain, or as landmarks in the history of their academic discipline.

Drawing from the world-renowned collections in the Cambridge University Library and other partner libraries, and guided by the advice of experts in each subject area, Cambridge University Press is using state-of-the-art scanning machines in its own Printing House to capture the content of each book selected for inclusion. The files are processed to give a consistently clear, crisp image, and the books finished to the high quality standard for which the Press is recognised around the world. The latest print-on-demand technology ensures that the books will remain available indefinitely, and that orders for single or multiple copies can quickly be supplied.

The Cambridge Library Collection brings back to life books of enduring scholarly value (including out-of-copyright works originally issued by other publishers) across a wide range of disciplines in the humanities and social sciences and in science and technology.

The Early Yorkshire Woollen Trade

Extracts from the Hull Customs' Rolls,
and Complete Transcripts of the Ulnagers' Rolls

EDITED BY JOHN LISTER

CAMBRIDGE
UNIVERSITY PRESS

CAMBRIDGE UNIVERSITY PRESS

Cambridge, New York, Melbourne, Madrid, Cape Town,
Singapore, São Paolo, Delhi, Mexico City

Published in the United States of America by Cambridge University Press, New York

www.cambridge.org
Information on this title: www.cambridge.org/9781108058520

© in this compilation Cambridge University Press 2013

This edition first published 1924
This digitally printed version 2013

ISBN 978-1-108-05852-0 Paperback

The Anniversary Reissue of Volumes from the Record Series of the Yorkshire Archaeological Society

To celebrate the 150th anniversary of the foundation of the leading society for the study of the archaeology and history of England's largest historic county, Cambridge University Press has reissued a selection of the most notable of the publications in the Record Series of the Yorkshire Archaeological Society. Founded in 1863, the Society soon established itself as the major publisher in its field, and has remained so ever since. The *Yorkshire Archaeological Journal* has been published annually since 1869, and in 1885 the Society launched the Record Series, a succession of volumes containing transcriptions of diverse original records relating to the history of Yorkshire, edited by numerous distinguished scholars. In 1932 a special division of the Record Series was created which, up to 1965, published a considerable number of early medieval charters relating to Yorkshire. The vast majority of these publications have never been superseded, remaining an important primary source for historical scholarship.

Current volumes in the Record Series are published for the Society by Boydell and Brewer. The Society also publishes parish register transcripts; since 1897, over 180 volumes have appeared in print. In 1974, the Society established a programme to publish calendars of over 650 court rolls of the manor of Wakefield, the originals of which, dating from 1274 to 1925, have been in the safekeeping of the Society's archives since 1943; by the end of 2012, fifteen volumes had appeared. In 2011, the importance of the Wakefield court rolls was formally acknowledged by the UK committee of UNESCO, which entered them on its National Register of the Memory of the World.

The Society possesses a library and archives which constitute a major resource for the study of the county; they are housed in its headquarters, a Georgian villa in Leeds. These facilities, initially provided solely for members, are now available to all researchers. Lists of the full range of the Society's scholarly resources and publications can be found on its website, www.yas.org.uk.

The Early Yorkshire Woollen Trade
(Record Series volume 64)

The editor of this volume, John Lister (1847–1933), prepared several publications for the Record Series, five of which are reissued in the Cambridge Library Collection. An obituary and bibliography of Lister, which can be found in the *Yorkshire Archaeological Journal*, 31 (1934), 423–6, records that he died 'at his ancestral home', Shibden Hall, Halifax, and that – like many of his colleagues in the Society – he was a member of the landed classes, and also a non-practising barrister. His obituary in *The Times* of 13 October 1933 reported that he was a founding member of the Labour Party in Halifax and had twice stood as a parliamentary candidate for the Independent Labour Party.

Lister was a pioneering researcher into the early history of the Yorkshire woollen industry. In the absence of documentation for production and trade inland, he made use of the records of royal taxation, both on exports, through customs accounts, and on domestic sale, through the ulnagers' accounts. His recognition of the value of the latter preceded the work of Herbert Heaton in his *Yorkshire Woollen and Worsted Industries* (Oxford, 1920; reprinted 1965). The first part of the present volume contains extracts from the customs accounts for the port of Kingston upon Hull for various years from 1304 to 1471, taken from the records of the King's Remembrancer: Particulars of Customs Accounts for Kingston upon Hull, which for this period now have the National Archives references E122/55/1 to E122/62/3. The second part of the volume contains extracts from the ulnagers' rolls for Yorkshire for various years between 1378 and 1478, taken from the records of the King's Remembrancer: Accounts Various, which for this period now have the National Archives references E101/345/15–24.

THE EARLY YORKSHIRE
WOOLLEN TRADE.

THE YORKSHIRE
ARCHÆOLOGICAL SOCIETY

FOUNDED 1863.   INCORPORATED 1893.

RECORD SERIES.
Vol. LXIV.
FOR THE YEAR 1923.

THE EARLY YORKSHIRE
WOOLLEN TRADE.

EXTRACTS FROM THE HULL CUSTOMS' ROLLS,
AND COMPLETE TRANSCRIPTS OF
THE ULNAGERS' ROLLS.

EDITED BY

JOHN LISTER, M.A.,

*Of Brazenose College, Oxford, and the Inner Temple,
Barrister-at-Law.*

PRINTED FOR THE SOCIETY.

1924.

INTRODUCTION.

The extracts and transcripts presented in this volume are intended to throw a little more light upon the yet somewhat obscure history of the development of the woollen industry in our county of York. They consist of (*a*) Extracts from the Rolls of the Collectors and Controllers of Customs at Hull, dating from the year 1304; and (*b*) Copies of the *Compoti* of the Ulnagers, *alias* Alnagers, who gathered the subsidy and ulnage on behalf of the Crown, laid and paid upon all cloths exposed for sale made in Yorkshire and elsewhere. These latter returns date from the year 1378.

HULL CUSTOMS ROLLS.

I do not think that any of these Rolls and *Compoti* have fully seen the light in print before, except one relating to the customs at Hull, produced in the original Latin in Frost's excellent book, *Notices relative to the Early History of Hull*, published in 1827.

Dealing firstly with the Customs Rolls, it may be useful to give a few facts relating to the early history of the custom due on cloths made in England intended for exportation abroad. This custom was included in the custom called the "New Custom," or "Little Custom," as Stubbs, in his *Constitutional History*, writes,[1] and which "New Custom," he states, was introduced by Edward I in 1303. But, *pace* so great an authority as Bishop Stubbs, although it does not seem to have applied to cloth, would appear to have originated earlier, for we have Rolls in the Record Office headed: "Rolls of the *New* Custom collected at Hull," beginning with the third year of the reign of the same King Edward, 1274–5,[2] down to the year 1304, in which year, among other merchandise,

[1] Stubbs' *Constitutional History*, ii, 524.
[2] K.R. Customs Accounts 55/1.

shipments of cloth from Yorkshire abroad seem first to be recorded. Wool and wool fells and hides, etc., only are included apparently in the rolls of the " New Custom " anterior to this latter date. In the first of our printed Rolls it will be noticed that the " New Custom " included general merchandise exported from the Port of Hull. Interesting as other goods then exported from our county may be and well worthy of being published, our extracts must only, with a few exceptions, be concerned with the export of, and custom charged on, cloth.

In the first of these Rolls (I) we find that the period covered is a very short one, extending only from the 4th of July, 1304, to the Michaelmas of the same year—three months less three days. This, as I have indicated, seems to have been the first occasion on which custom was laid on exported cloth, all the nine Rolls that precede it only dealing with wool and fells, etc. With these two items our Roll I does not deal. But, besides cloth, lead, cheese and salmon are accounted for. If this be the first instance of a custom being taken on cloth exported from Hull, it is not surprising, perhaps, to find that only two half cloths are mentioned as paying custom during the three months covered by the return. But one of these cloths was of the best quality, for it is described as being of scarlet, and the only "cloth in grain" exported. While the other half cloth is described as being *sine grano*, i.e. without grain.

It was under the provisions of the previous year, 1303, that the customs on exports of cloth were fixed at 2s. on "cloths of grain," 1s. 6d. on those of "half grain," and on those without "grain" in them at 1s.

But what, it may be asked, is the significance of the word "grain"? Samuel Maunder, in his *Scientific and Literary Dictionary* (1870), gives us, I think, the most concise definition. Under the term "Kermes," an equivalent for "grain," he writes: "Kermes [a little worm], of the genus *Coccus* of entomologists, found in the excrescences of oak trees, growing in the south of Europe. It is an article extensively used in dyeing, and is inferior to nothing but cochineal, as a means of producing scarlet. 'Kermes-grains,' as they are called, are the dried bodies of the female insects of the species *Coccus*

Ilicis, which lives upon the leaves of the *Quercus Ilex*, or prickly oak. It was formerly called *Vermiculus*, whence the French 'vermillon.' Kermes has been employed from time immemorial in India to dye silk, and was also used by the ancient Greeks and Romans for the same purpose; but since the introduction of cochineal, it has become an object of comparatively trifling importance."[1]

In these *Compoti*, therefore, we shall find scarlet cloths described as of "whole grain," and others in which a smaller portion of the scarlet dye was used as "cloths of the half grain," or cloths in which some "grain" was employed in the dye. Cloths with any "grain" in them paid more, as has been already noted, to the Custom House collectors than those from which it was absent.

There is in the Record Office a return made by Barton and Bedeford of imports, for the same period as that of the exports, by which we learn that from the 4th July to Michaelmas, 1304, the cloths imported at Hull were $3\frac{1}{2}$ cloths dyed in "grain," and 24 in which there was none of this dye.[2]

Coming to Roll II, 1305, we find that all the names of shipowners and exporters, with the exception of William of Tyndale and, possibly, that of John of Walthorp, are of foreign origin. This Roll covers a whole year—Michaelmas to Michaelmas. It enumerates 4 scarlet cloths and 57 "without grain," together with 16 pieces, of which pieces 11 were valued at the high figure of £15 12s. For the sake of comparison, let us refer to the imports of cloth at Hull for the same period. In this year, as will be noticed, they largely exceed the exports, cloths described as "mixed with grain" being 16 in number, and those without grain $392\frac{1}{2}$.[3] Pieces of cloth are valued mostly at 1s. the ell.

In Roll III it is to be noticed that all the exporters with the exception perchance of John Greyne, and the masters of ships, save Robert of Oxon, appear to be aliens. This Roll only covers a little over nine months, terminating on the 7th July,

---

[1] For further information see *A Manual of Dyeing*, by E. Knecht, C. Rawson, and R. Lowenttal (1893).

[2] K.R. Customs Accounts 55/16.

[3] K.R. Customs Accounts 55/17.

on the death of King Edward I. Only 3 scarlet cloths and 19 cloths without grain are accounted for, and in the returns of the same collectors for the period between the 7th July and Michaelmas no customs on cloths exported are recorded.

For the first year of Edward II, 1307–8, a *Compotus* of imports is preserved, which will be found printed in Appendix I. The number of foreign cloths imported was apparently 6 scarlet and 224 without grain. The return covers one whole year.

Roll IV, 1308–9, covers only a period of a little over ten months, as on the 20th August, 1309, the custom " ceased for a while in virtue of the King's Writ, under the provisions of the Statutes of Stamford." This custom was, however, frequently reimposed, and one meets with it again at Hull in 1310 The 1308–9 Roll, it may be noticed, purports to refer only to cloth and other merchandise exported by *alienigenæ* and *extranearii*.[1] What is the difference between these two terms ? *Extranearii*, i.e. strangers, probably means those who were not free of their city or town, nor members of a merchants' gild. In these medieval days men of different cities and places were mutually treated as strangers and foreigners. As Professor Ashley writes, the word foreigner is used for any non-burgess, whether English or alien; and it is sometimes not easy to determine which is meant. Regular official " customers "—Customs House officials as we should call them—were appointed in the days of Edward I some time before 1285.

The number of scarlet cloths exported in the ten months of 1308–9 is 12½, and of those without grain 92¼. Taking the imports and exports of cloth in both cases for a period of ten months we find that the imports amounted to about 191 cloths, and exports to 105. More scarlet cloths, we note, however, were exported than were imported.

In Roll V, A.D. 1310, which is the last account we have rendered by Robert of Barton and Gilbert of Bedeford, it is to be noted that there is reference to a few cloths shipped from Scarborough. This town had, like York, a monopoly for dyed cloth, and in the Hundred Rolls (*c.* 1274) we find it frequently

---

[1] The small custom after the 27 Edward III was levied only on aliens, they being alone permitted to export. See Hubert Hall, *Customs*.

stated that no cloth made there measured the breadth required by the law.

The export of cloths from Hull and Scarborough in 1310, covering a whole year, seems according to the *Compotus* to have been very small, and no ships are reported as sailing from those ports after the 24th July.

Between 1310 and 1324, when we meet with the next *Compotus*, there is a gap of fourteen years, and only two ships are named as carrying cloth abroad—cloths specially named " English cloths." The sworn value of those is for the first time given, though " pieces " had been valued in previous rolls.

Roll VI of 1324 introduces us to the De la Pole family— previously known as Atte-pole [? At the Pool]. This Richard of the *Compotus* is said to have been the eldest son of John de la Pole, *miles*, but about the knighthood there seems to be a little room for doubt.[1] Frost says that the observation made by Camden—*Mercatura non derogat nobilitati*—" may be applied with peculiar propriety to Richard and his brother, William de la Pole, whose commercial pursuits laid the foundation of all their future greatness."

This Roll VI would seem to be only a partial account of the cloth shipped in the year 1324–5. It will be noticed that the heading varies from the usual form, and purports vaguely to be " of money received from the New Custom." Some explanation seems needed regarding this account, as there appears to be something peculiar about it. Richard de la Pole continued in office until 1327.

Thirty years forward we reach the year 1354, Roll VII, when Walter Box and John of Northburgh were collectors of the custom. The period covered is from the 27th July of that year until Michaelmas in the following year, 1355. The reader will notice that the custom rates are altered—very considerably raised from those of the *Carta Mercatoria*. We meet with the explanation of this in the year 1361. In a Close Roll Writ, dated 8 February, 35 Edw. III, we find, under the heading *Pro mercatoribus*, an order directed to the Collectors of

[1] See Frost, *Memoirs of Hull*, p. 31.

the Custom on Woollen Cloths and on Worsted Blankets [*lecti de worstede*] that the King, after quoting the rates of custom imposed by his grandfather's—Edward I—charter, states that the alien-born merchants had been wrongfully charged by the collectors excessive custom dues on the pretext of a certain order made by the King and his Council, viz. 3s. 6d. for scarlet cloths and other cloths of whole grain; 1s. 9d. for cloths of half grain or intermixed with grain. These figures it will be noted are the same as those that occur in the *Compotus* of Walter Box and John of Northburgh, so far as alien merchants are concerned. "Cloths of Worstede" are, as we see, mentioned as subject to custom duty in this *Compotus* of 1354. The word "worsted" appeared in our extant Rolls for the first time in that of 1310 (No. V), where "sayes of worstede" are named, and cloths of this kind are scheduled in the Close Roll recently quoted of 1361. But what was a *simplex* and what was a *duplex lectus*? The Public Record translators sometimes render the word *lecti* as "beds," and sometimes, much more reasonably, I think, as "bed clothes." It appears to me that an even more correct rendering still would be "worsted blankets." In the Petition of the Commons in 1410[1] on behalf of the city of Norwich, mention is made of *les Worstedes appellez*, "Worsted-beddes," namely, "doubles et sengles." Surely blankets must be understood under this phraseology.

Unfortunately, the "Roll of Particulars" mentioned by the collectors of 1354, as having been delivered into the Treasury, does not appear to exist, and we only have the summary thereof. This states that there were 52 cloths without grain shipped by alien merchants at 21d. a cloth, and 8 cloths without grain by denizens [now permitted to export] at 14d. a cloth. No other cloths, scarlet, worsted, or double bed-blankets [*lecti*], were exported either by denizen or alien merchants.

That only 60 common cloths were shipped twenty-one years after the immigration of the Flemings does not say much in favour of their supposed vast influence on English weaving!

Roll VIII, 1363-4, is merely an account of cloths forfeited

[1] Ashley, *Economic History and Theory*, i, 248, note 64.

because those cloths were about to be shipped by a German merchant before the custom due had been satisfied. This is the first *Compotus* in which " strait cloths," i.e. probably kerseys, are named in these Rolls. The "fardels" contained, we are told, 1,288 ells, and were sold for £22 16s. 11d. The "*panni stricti*," i.e. strait cloths, were held each to be equal to one quarter of a whole cloth of assize, and were called " straits " as being less in breadth than the broad cloths were.

Rolls IX and X, 1380–1, are, as stated in our text, in a deplorably bad condition. I must here correct an error in my note on these documents. Careful investigation has proved that Thomas Flemyng, whose name appears in them, was controller, not a collector of the custom, and that both IX and X may be the remains of one *Compotus* for which Robert of Selby and Thomas of Wapplyngton were responsible as collectors.

This account is interesting as introducing us to the Hans merchants, but no further mention of them occurs until we reach Roll XIII, 1464. I do not understand why this should be so. The customs are stated in this *Compotus* of 1380–1 as apparently payable at different rates by (*a*) denizens; (*b*) by the Hans; (*c*) by aliens. The mutilated state of the return does not permit us to learn whether the duty paid by the Hans merchants differed from that charged on other aliens, but in Roll XIV, the fifth year of Edward IV, we find that, while " alienigenæ " paid 1s. 9d. a cloth, and denizens 1s. 2d., the Hans merchants were only charged at 1s.

The Hanseatic League Merchants, as it is affirmed, had other depots than the Steelyard, London. It was the chief, but they also had factories, we are told, in other ports, though I have seen no proof that they possessed such an establishment at Hull.

It is evident that the export of cloth by denizens in 1380–1 largely exceeded that of Hans and alien merchants.

Roll XI, 1391–2, is in a bad condition, and has cost a good deal of trouble to decipher, but yielding, as it does, in spite of its many *lacunæ*, very many most interesting particulars, I judged it wise to have it photographed and reproduce it in print. It gives us the names of ships and their owners, the names, too, of the exporters, the numbers of the various cloths, their value and the custom thereon. The custom duty is in this case and in subsequent *Compoti* an *ad valorem* one. It practically covers ten months.

For the first time in these accounts coverlets [*cooptoria*] are named. These are known, in our days, as bed-quilts or counterpanes. We also meet with " mantal clothes." In the Petition referred to already of the Norwich weavers, dated 1410, " Worstedes appellez mantelles " are enumerated, and are described as being of many various colours.

In regard to " coverlets," of which a very large number appear to have been exported in 1391-2, Roll XI, it is to be remembered, as Mr. Heaton notices,[1] that, " the weaving of coverlets for beds had long been an important branch of the York industry, but; although the weavers of the city claimed a monopoly of the trade, coverlet weavers were to be found in many places throughout the West Riding at the time of the Poll Tax Returns." Mr. Heaton, by the way, seems to have for the moment forgotten that the York monopoly only extended to dyed cloths, and that, moreover, the Weavers' Gild there seems to have encouraged, rather than otherwise, the admission of outside craftsmen to the privilege they themselves enjoyed, subject to their paying for that privilege.

The names of the ships forming the mercantile marine of this period are interesting, as also are those of the places to which they belonged.

Roll XII, 1401, as I have previously stated, is printed in its Latin form in Frost's *Appendix* to his *Memoirs of Hull*. It shows quite a large volume of trade for the short space of time covered between Easter, 1401, and the 7th July of the same year. In the heading are given not only the names of the collectors, but also that of the controller.

On p. 29 of our text we find that the purchase money of ships was sometimes taxed in the Customs Accounts, for Gilbert Neyse for the purchase of the moiety of the ship called *Pasdagh of Skiddam* had to pay a subsidy (?) of 5s. 6¾d. on a value of £8 6s. 8d.

---

[1] Heaton, *Yorkshire Woollen and Worsted Industries*, p. 55.

All the cloths shipped in this 1401 Roll appear to have been " without grain." No woollen cloths were coming from abroad.

Our next *Compotus*, XIII, is dated sixty-three years later. This only purports to cover forty-eight days. Only four ships are stated to have been freighted with cloth. The *Trinity of Hull* carried 365 cloths of denizens and 62½ cloths and 11½ yards of those of the Hans merchants. The *Marie Duras of Calais* carried 8 denizens' cloths. The *Peter of Hull* had 142 denizens' cloths, the *Mariflower of Hull* 7, and the *Mare of Hull* 144 of denizens'. All these cloths, as well those of the Hans as of denizens, were "without grain." The subsidy to be paid by the Hans merchants is not given in this Roll, but is stated to be found in the "Controller's Roll." Doubtless there was a tariff in regard to Hans merchants, which was left to the discretion of the controller. Unfortunately his Roll has not come down to us.

This Roll is followed by one (XIV) for half of the year 1465 and thirteen days, in which eleven ships are named as carrying cloth, exported by denizens, aliens, and Hans merchants. The number of cloths under these three heads are, aliens 74½, denizens 63, and Hans 29 and 3 yards. All are described as being without grain.

The last of these Customs *Compoti*, XV, is for a " quarter of a year and 12 days," and is dated 1471. The cloths shipped are all without grain, all freighted by denizens, and their total is 216.

COLLECTORS AND CONTROLLERS.

The officials who collected the dues at the port of Hull and elsewhere are generally described as the " Customers." I have taken some little pains to make a list of their names which will be found in Appendix II. The first roll of the collectors of the New Custom, 3 Edward I, has, unfortunately, no name attached to it, and only accounts for wool and wool fells, and it is not until the thirty-second year of Edward I that we find Robert of Barton and Gilbert of Bedeford named as receiving money on account of cloth either exported or imported. The collectors were supervised by a " controller," who, it appears, was expected to write out the rolls of the returns. The first of these controllers named is William of Wickkinggeston, Clerk.

The collectors and controllers seem, generally, to have been Hull or, at any rate, Yorkshiremen. Many rules were laid down from time to time in regard to their behaviour and manner of performing their duties. Regular " Customers " were first appointed in the early years of Edward I. According to the Statute 14 Ric. II, " no customer nor controller " was to have any ships of his own, nor meddle with the freight of ships. By Statute 11 Hen. IV, " no man "—to quote Rastall—" that holdeth any common Hosterie in any City or Borough of England, shall be Customer, Controller, finder nor searcher of the said Sovereign Lord the King, and that to eschew the dammage and losse, which thereof may happen, by the favour that such common hostlers may or will doe to Marchants, and other their hostes in the said offices."

The appointment on 12th November, 1397, of Thomas Percy to the office of Controller of the 3s. a tun custom on wine, and 12d. in the £ on other merchandise, was conditional that he wrote " the rolls with his own hand, and stay therein executing the office in person." In 1353 we learn that Walter Box, who appears as a collector in that year, was pardoned, on the payment of two marks, for selling wines before they were gauged, and taking corn and other victuals from England to Germany contrary to divers proclamations that had been made.

Ship Masters and Merchants.

The number of ship masters with English names in 1304, of any kind of merchandise, were two, those of John of Faxflete, John Shirlokes, and of masters with foreign names also two, viz. William of Hamburgh and Hermann Bukes. The number of English merchant exporters seems to be one, viz. Ralph of Dureem [? Durham], and of alien merchants three, viz. Walter de Feroun [or Feronn], Walter of Hamburgh, and Baldwin of Hamburgh.

In 1305 (Roll II) the names of both the owners (masters) and merchants with one exception, already noted, who exported cloth, appear to be those of aliens. In 1306–7 (Roll III) we find among five ships the names, apparently, of two English owners, viz. Robert of Oxon and William Heworth, the latter carrying 5 cloths for apparently an Englishman, one John Greyne. Reymond Geraud, whose cloths were shipped on Robert of Oxon's boat, also may have been an English merchant.

In 1308–9 (Roll IV) the names of all the ship-owners are those of aliens, and the merchants who freighted their ships I fancy are all foreigners. It is interesting to note that the Bishop of Osel exported from Hull on the ship of Englebright of Greffswold [?], 3 English cloths without grain, and paid the English Custom House officers 3s. duty for the same.

In 1310 (Roll V) all the cloths shipped at Hull were shipped in foreign vessels and by foreign merchants, but two ships sailed from the port of Scarborough, the same year, that were owned and freighted by English owners and shippers. In 1324–5, when Richard de la Pole was collector of customs at Hull, the two ships that sailed, having cloth thereon, were both owned and freighted by foreigners.

In 1391 (Roll XI) the aspect of things is quite different. This roll is (as has been noted) rather imperfect, but it shows the following ships as being owned by Hull masters, viz. the *Cuthberte of Hull* the *James of Hull*, the *George of Hull*, the *Trinity of Hull*, the *Cristofre of Hull*, the *Maudelyn of Hull*, the *Katherine of Hull*, the ship of John Kyrkeby called the . . . . . *of Hull*, another *Cutbert of Hull*, owned by a different master, another *Maudelyn of Hull* with a different master, the ship of John Blaktofft of Hull, the *Petre of Hull*, another *Trinite of Hull* with another owner. Several of the names of ships and masters are obliterated, but the list given shows thirteen Hull ships. Of other English ports we have the *James of Dartmouth*, the *Cristofer of Middleburgh*, the *Clement of York*, the *Seyntmarie bote of Barton*, the *Swan Ship of Barton*, the *Seynt marie shipp of Nottingham*.

Of foreign ships those of Campvere, now known as Vere in the Netherlands, were the most numerous. Their names were the *Maudelyn*, the *Seynt Mary Shipp*, the *Godberade*, and the *Marie-knyght*. Rotterdam owned the *Godbyrade*, the ship of Maynard son of Maynard, and the ship of Tydman Potter. Of

Dantzic were the *Trinity* and the *James*, of both of which the names of their masters are English. One ship is credited to Dordrecht, and one each to Bayonne, Menin, Koenisberg, Middleburgh, and Crotoy.

In the Roll for 1401 it will be seen that twelve Hull ships are named, one belonging to Newhaven, and one each to Dantzic, Middleburgh, Campvere, and Schiedam.

In Roll XIII, 1464, of the six ships named as shipping cloth, five are stated to be of Hull and only one as belonging to a foreign port, viz. Calais. It is to be noted that the Hans merchants' cloth was carried on a Hull ship, of which apparently an Englishman, John Brand, was master.

In the year 1465, Roll XIV there are six foreign ships and five English.

McCulloch tells us that "it is difficult to form any very accurate conclusion as to the state of mercantile shipping from the reign of Edward III to that of Henry VII, but the increase, if there was any, seems to have been very inconsiderable.[1] Our extracts from the Hull Customs Rolls seem to bear out to some extent his statement.

We have notices sometimes, but rather too rarely, of the perils that beset the merchants of the fourteenth and fifteenth centuries, both on the open sea and on the rivers that flowed towards it. In a Close Roll dated Oct. 24th, 1319, we learn from the proceedings of a suit instituted by the burgesses of Beverley and of other merchants of the realm, who had freighted three ships of Flanders at Kingston-on-Hull with cloth, that these ships, on their voyage to the Scheldt, were taken by Flemish pirates. Further, we learn that William de Bruntswik had on board of them "a robe and 2 whole pieces of Pers [i.e. blue] cloth of Beverley, of the value of £18 sterling, and that Gilbert Wadiator had 4 whole Beverley cloths of the value of £28 sterling." These prices, by the way, as Mr. Heaton remarks, indicate "a high standard of workmanship."[2]

If there were perils, many and various, to be encountered on the high seas, there were also dangers to be met with for the

---

[1] McCulloch, *History of Commerce*, p. 151.
[2] Heaton, *Yorkshire Woollen and Worsted Industries*, p. 4.

men and merchandise going down to the sea in ships, by the Ouse and its creeks and channels. In our Roll XI, viz. that of Robert Garton and John Colthorp—we have mention made of a ship owned by John Dandson[1] and of cloth freighted in another ship by a merchant named Robert Duffield. It appears that a ship owned, or freighted, with cloth by these two merchants and by another trader called Simon of Waghen, was totally lost on Wednesday, the 26th July, 1391, at Skelton Garth, on the north side of the Ouse. The ship and cargo were valued at £60. The cause of this loss and of that of many other ships is to be attributed to the existence of weirs, nets, and other obstructions by which the course of the river was perilously narrowed. An important presentment was made [circa 1394] by jurors of York, from which we learn the cause of the loss of John Dandson's and his fellow-merchants' ship, and that of many others.

I think part at least of the presentment, as given in the recently published volume of the Selden Society,[2] may be of interest. This presentment took cognizance of a number of offences from the 31 Edward III, a period of approximately thirty-seven years. The document begins: "Whereas the water of Ouse is a highway and the greatest of all the King's rivers within the kingdom of England, and is for the use of merchants in ships with divers merchandise from the high sea to the City of York and other places within the County, to the great increase of the kingdom and especially of the King's city of York and the County of York and of other counties, cities, boroughs, and towns in the northern parts of England, to wit, from the sea to the Humber, thence to the Trent, thence to the Ouse, and so to York. There are in the said water divers hindrances, stoppages, and weirs called fish-garths, and in the said weirs are divers spaces called ' rowmes,'[3] set strongly across the whole depth of the water with poles, stones, and hedges, whereby the common course of the said river and the carriage of merchandise as aforesaid was wholly stopped for a few years

---

[1] p. 23.

[2] Vol. II, *Public Works in Medieval Law*, Selden Society, xl, 253, 254.

[3] A " Room " seems to mean the space of one net (*spacium unius retis*).

now past and very often the said spaces were endangered and submerged." The jurors then proceed to affirm that "at Redewylyghe by Wystowstocches, Adam de Hatfield, late Bishop of Durham, and Adam Hugyn built a fishgarth and set it firmly with poles, stones, and hedges, on the north side of the said water in the 47th year of Edward III, and Walter de Skirlowe, now bishop, and the said Adam have maintained, enlarged and heightened the aforesaid obstruction from the 14th year of Richard II to the present day, so that no ship can pass in the summer season, to the undoing of the said city and country; and in the said weirs and 'rowmes' the said Adam has taken salmon and salmon fry with his nets during the close season, from the Nativity of the Virgin Mary to St. Martin's day, to wit, from the seventh year of Richard II; and fed his swine therewith; and that by reason of the obstruction aforesaid John Steer, merchant, on Tuesday, 26 July, 1390, lost two ships fully laden with woollen cloth to the value of £60, saving for himself nought of his ships or their cargo, to the great undoing of the said John and of the whole country of England in the northern part."

In regard to John Dandson & Co's ship it appears from a presentment made [*circa* 1348] that the weir or fishgarth at Skelton, which appears to have caused the casualty, was one of 18 "spaces," and belonged also to the Bishop of Durham, and had been set up in the 45th year of Edward III.

Skelton-garth certainly seems to have been a dangerous spot, for there are several presentments regarding vessels and men that perished there. Besides John Dandson's ship, on the 22nd September, 1377, John Spenser, we are told, lost three men unknown and his ship and cargo there to the value of £100; another ship and cargo was lost valued at £60 at the same place on the 5th October, 1375, and again three men were drowned. On the 25th June, 1376, "all by reason of the said obstruction at Skelton," John York, of Swinefleet, lost his ship with two Austin Friars and divers other merchandise [*sic*] to the value of £80. It is not surprising, after these cases of loss, to read in a presentment levelled at the Bishop of Durham in 1360, that Skelton-garth should be described as

" a very harmful weir." The Bishop of Durham at that time, by his attorney, came before the King at York and denied that he had weirs or stakes at Skelton. The case was tried and the jury found that the " rooms " at Skelton were set there *not* by the said bishop, but by four Skelton men, and the verdict, at any rate so far as this weir was concerned, was given in his favour, but was again contested, as we have seen, in later years. In a presentment made in 1348 it is stated that " the course of the river Ouse ought and is wont to be forty feet wide between York and the Humber, and a direct course unhindered by poles and weirs set in the said water or by nets and other engines."[1] It is " undeniable," writes Mr. Flower, the editor of vol. xl of the Selden Society, " that the condition of this river [the Ouse] and its tributary, the Derwent, was deplorable in the fourteenth century. All along its lower course encroaching fisheries impeded navigation."

YORKSHIRE ULNAGERS' ROLLS.

These Rolls, which throw so much light upon the development of the woollen industry, have been sadly neglected by our writers and lecturers on commerce and trade. I do not think any quotations from, or references to them are given in the books written by Professor Cunningham or Professor Ashley, or even by Mr. Hubert Hall. When, in the early eighties, I came across them in the P.R.O., I almost had presumption enough to consider myself their discoverer, or rather the discoverer of their great value in regard to the history of our early cloth industry. Since the period of my research these Rolls have, however, been utilised to good effect by Dr. Maud Sellers and Mr. Heaton.

The office of ulnager was one of considerable antiquity, and can be traced back to the early part of the reign of Edward I. Two men were appointed to view all cloths exposed for sale, whether home-made or of foreign manufacture, and to confiscate all wares not in accordance with the legal dimensions.[2] Shortly afterwards the work passed into the hands of one man

---

[1] Coram Rege Roll, Hil., 23 Edward III, 61.
[2] Patent Rolls, 7 Edward I, m. 3 (1270).

b

who was generally appointed for life. Perot le Tailleur had the ulnage of cloth " in the fairs of our realm " in the above monarch's time, and the King, on the occasion of Perot's having forfeited it, committed the office in 1298, by Writ of Privy Seal to Peter of Edelmeton. "This is the earliest documentary evidence of an office that existed until the reign of William and Mary," writes Professor Ashley in his *English Woollen Industry*. But we have, I find, an earlier appointment made in 1291 in connection with the Fair of St. Ives.[1]

On the 14th May, 1291, we read in the Rolls of the Fair Court of St. Ives that Hamon of Bury St. Edmunds " was the bearer of a letter patent from Sir Roger de Lisle, clerk of the Great Wardrobe, [ordering] that he should be admitted by the Keepers of the Fair of St. Ives to measure woollen cloths made in England, linen and canvas." The steward of the Court, we are told, would not admit Hamon to execute the said office, alleging that to do so would be to the disherison and prejudice of the abbot and convent of Ramsey and their bailiffs, and be contrary to the privilege granted by the charter of the King to the fair. However, Hamon yielded up his letter patent into the steward's hands, and " at the instance of the merchants, his letter patent having been renounced and annulled, he is admitted for the present."

In 1293 we find that Hamon, having with three others made oath in Court " to make honest measurement for sellers and buyers," was allowed to act as an ulnager.

From these proceedings we see that the King's Writ did not run at St. Ives' Fair in regard to the ulnaging of woollen cloth and canvas, and in a case tried in the Court of Exchequer, 19 Edward I, it is stated that it was customary for the merchants to measure canvas, and, it is to be supposed, also woollen cloths in fairs.[2]

In the 9th year of Henry III a statute was passed that there should be " one breadth of broad cloth, russets and haberjects, viz. two yards within the lists." According to

---

[1] *Select Cases concerning the Law Merchant*, edited by Chas. Gross for the Selden Society, i, 42.

[2] Exchequer Plea Roll, 16, m. 7d.

the statute of Richard I the carrying out of the assize, as it was called, was entrusted to four or six lawful men in every city or borough, supervised by the itinerant justices, who were to inquire whether the assigned keepers in each town were doing their duty. It seems that, as already stated, there was no royal officer, no ulnager appointed by the King until the early years of Edward I, when, as in 1291, we find, as we have noticed, Hamon of Bury St. Edmunds producing a writ to the keepers of the Fair of St. Ives, calling upon them to admit him to measure "woollen cloths made in England."

The words, "cloth made in England," is an interesting phrase, as showing that there was a distinction drawn between cloth imported from abroad and cloth made in England, Hamon, apparently, being only empowered to deal with the latter.

Hamon, two days previous to his exhibition of King Edward's writ, had been "attached for having been found measuring 60 ells of canvas in the booth of John of Boulogne, although he had not yet been sworn as an ulnager." At the instance of H. of Cottenham and other friends the amercements imposed upon the would be ulnager were remitted.

None of the Ulnagers' Rolls, in which Yorkshire is named, seem to be in existence prior to the appointment of Nicholas Shirlok in 1327.

At this date there was no subsidy paid on cloth, and the ulnagers then and thitherto and until the 27th year of Edward III, merely dealt with the sizes and sometimes with the qualities of the cloths made and exposed for sale. Cloths not equal to the standard assize were seized by them and forfeited to the King. Owing to this circumstance, viz. that English-made cloths were not taxed, it is impossible to judge the extent of the home manufacture, and it is not until we reach the Customs Roll for 1304 that we can glean anything to indicate the quantity exported from Yorkshire, or elsewhere. Nicholas Shirlok, in his Roll for the 2nd year of Edward III, merely reports the forfeiture he had made at York of two cloths found in the hands of the master of the market [d'ni m'cat'] in that city, which were forfeited because they were not "of the assize."

In his Roll, also, for 6 Edward III [1332–3], he accounts
for 1 cloth forfeited from a Lincoln merchant at Hull for being
of short measure, and of 3 cloths seized at York as forfeit. By
the description given of these elaborate cloths we may conclude
that they were of foreign manufacture.

The chief ulnagers of the realm employed deputies, and
Shirlok styles one Richard of Wynchecombe his "attorney."
Shirlok's successor, John Marreys, was ulnager for the realm
from 1348, apparently until 1365. There appear to be no Rolls
existing covering the period of his office. It will be seen from
our Appendix III that the names of several of his Yorkshire
deputies have come down to us.

John Marreys was ulnager when, in the 27th year of Edward
III [1353], the first subsidy on woollen cloth made in England
for sale was granted by Parliament. It is very disappointing
that none of his Rolls, after this event, have been apparently
preserved. They would have given us valuable information
as to the growth of the woollen industry in our county. On
the occasion of the grant of the subsidy on saleable woollen
cloth made in 1353, new powers were given to John Marreys,
and his tenure of office was renewed for life. For the ulnage
(i.e. for measuring it) of a whole cloth he was to take $\frac{1}{2}d.$, and
for half a cloth $\frac{1}{4}d.$ He was instructed to take nothing for any
cloth less than half a cloth, nor intermeddle in any way with
the ulnage of cloths other than those for sale.[1] Furthermore,
as ulnager he became collector of the new subsidy on English-
made cloth, granted by the Lords and Commons to the Crown.
Under this statute of 27 Edward III John Marreys, by virtue
of this statute, was empowered to collect 4$d.$ for every whole
cloth of assize wherein there was no "grain," and 2$d.$ for every
half such cloth; and for every "cloth of assize of scarlet" 6$d.$,
and half cloth 3$d.$ On cloths of the "half grain" 5$d.$ was to
be charged, and 2$\frac{1}{2}d.$ for every half such cloth. Cloths whose
measurement exceeded by three yards or more the standard
sizes of whole or half cloths were to pay after, i.e. according to,
the rate or subsidy which was payable for the whole cloth of
the same sort. Cloths exposed for sale, before the same had

---

[1] Patent Rolls, Nov. 3rd, 1353.

been measured, had paid the ulnage fee and the subsidy, and had been passed and sealed by the ulnager, Marreys, or his deputies or the bailiffs of a franchise, were to be forfeited. The ulnager or collector was not permitted to gather the subsidy money on any cloth but what was exposed for sale. He was not to tax cloth " which a man maketh for his own use to clothe him and his many," i.e. household.

It would appear that, although, in certain franchises, the local bailiffs or merchants had the privilege of measuring cloth, there were also royal officials appointed elsewhere to this duty. The first statute [Assize of Measures] dealing with the regulation of the manufacture of cloth is that of Richard I [1197, November 20th], by which it was enacted that wherever woollen cloths were made they should measure two ells in breadth, and should be equally good at the middle and the sides. All cloths made contrary to law were to be immediately burned, and all artifices to impose upon the buyer in the sale of cloths were strictly prohibited. But we are told, that licences to sell cloths of any breadth whatever were granted by Henry II, as exceptions probably to an older law.

By Statute 25 of Edward III, c. 1, we find that, in regard to cloth forfeited for deficiency of the assize measurement, the ulnager was to deal with the delinquency, " notwithstanding any franchise, usage, or privilege made to cities, boroughs, or to any person of the Realm of England to the contrary." Buyers under this Act of Parliament might measure the cloth they were purchasing, even though it had been measured and sealed by the ulnager, and were empowered to show any deficiency in the same to the mayors and bailiffs of the place, or to the keepers of the fair or market. If the complainant buyer proved his case, the cloth was to be forfeited to the King, seized into his hands and kept by the authorities just mentioned, who were to certify the Chancellor concerning the matter. The ulnager, if guilty of fraud or negligence in measuring, was to be " attainted before the keepers of the fairs and mayors and bailiffs where the cloth shall be bought," and to be imprisoned for one year, and put out of his office for ever. This explains the reference in the subsequent statute of the

27th Edward III to the seizing of forfeited cloth by mayors and bailiffs in addition to the powers granted to the ulnagers to measure, seal, and make forfeitures.

Nicholas Shirlok was appointed ulnager for England for the term of his life by Letters Patent in 1327.

In 1362 we find that the farming out, otherwise leasing, of the office of ulnager and collection of the subsidy on cloth had begun, and the King in that year let to farm that subsidy for London, the county of Southampton, and the counties of Surrey and Sussex. Also in the same year the farmers of the subsidy on cloth in Wiltshire, Somersetshire, and Dorset are mentioned. In 1365 we find that the subsidy had already been let in the counties of Worcester, Rutland, Norfolk, and Suffolk. Doubtless, at this date, though I have not found record of it, the subsidy was also let to farm by the Yorkshire ulnager. This practice, though sometimes suspended, continued apparently until the ulnager's office ceased in the time of William and Mary. The farmers were, we find, "never constrained to account to the King for the issues of the subsidy, but only for the rent at which they farmed it." It seems from a Close Roll of 1362 that many abuses had crept into the collection of the subsidy. False and counterfeit seals were current, at any rate in London. The seal of St. Michael, previously used in that city, was ordered to be made anew in 1365. The farmers and their deputies were bound to deliver all forfeited cloths to the sheriff of the counties where they were found, "by indenture between them made," i.e. between the farmers and the sheriffs. The latter were to answer to the King on their account, and by the indentures the ulnage farmers and deputies were discharged of their account, and were to have one-third part of the ulnage forfeitures for their trouble.[1]

In a great suit in the Exchequer Court, in 1637, between Thomas Lister, of Shibden Hall, and three other leading West Riding clothiers v. the royal ulnagers regarding ulnage, the latter officials allege in their answer to the Bill of Complaint, that this statute of King Edward III stimulated the cloth-makers of Yorkshire to make kerseys rather than broad cloths because the former, being made less than the assize measurement of

[1] See Appendix IV.

a half broad cloth, escaped free of taxation, "the makers of them conceiving that [under this statute] they might be made without paying to the King," and "the then makers of them were for their own private lucre and gain, and, in diminution of the King's subsidy and ulnage, encouraged rather to make kerseys than such cloths of assize as were only mentioned in the said statute of Edward III."

One is not surprised to learn this. It is just what we should expect from our shrewd, old Yorkshire forefathers. It will have been noticed that in the Customs Rolls the number of "straits," under which name kerseys were included, was large in proportion to the whole cloths of assize exported. Moreover, even in William Skipwith's ulnage and subsidy roll of the 17th Richard II, the "straits" or kerseys numbered 221 pieces, and the "cloths of assize," i.e. broad cloths, were 1,202 pieces and 9 yards.

In the statute of 27 Edward III we find that cloths not sealed before being exposed for sale might, as an alternative in certain cases, be seized and taken into the hands of the bailiffs of the town where such cloths were found. So it would appear that the King's ulnager had not even yet everywhere superseded the bailiffs in the performance of this duty. It is to be noted that in Shirlok's Roll, 6 Edward II, that indenture bonds were entered into between the Mayor of Hull, William de la Pole and the ulnager, and between the Mayor of York, Nicholas of Langeton, regarding the forfeitures of cloth in those two places, and these were delivered into the Treasury along with the Rolls themselves. In later times these bonds were made between the sheriffs and the ulnagers in regard to forfeitures.

The ulnagers were furnished, as we have noticed, in connection with the farming of the custom in London, with dies for seals to be affixed to the cloths exposed for sale. These are described as made of copper, and of lead at another, and were accounted for and passed on by each ulnager to his successor.[1] The number of these seals used in Yorkshire seems generally to have been eighteen; ten for the subsidy and eight for the ulnage.

[1] See Nos. 8 and 9, *Rolls of Ralph Byrnand.*

In 1378 we learn (from the Patent Rolls) that the counter-feiting of the ulnager's seal was not unknown in Yorkshire, for John of Pathorn, a deputy ulnager under William Hervy, Ulnager of England, for our county, suffered from this wrong-doing, and a Commission to Justices was issued to enquire by jury of the county of York to certify the charge of " counter-feiting of his seal and of the sealing several cloths with the false seals, and the cutting up of other cloths into small pieces." The deputies named in Appendix III at this time were generally appointed for the four northern counties of Yorkshire, North-umberland, Cumberland, and Westmorland.

In 1394 (November 25th) Thomas of Brounflete surrendered his office and received £20 a year compensation—the Patent Rolls for this date tell us—" in consequence of the ordinance of the Parliament lately held at Westminster touching the ulnage of cloth." This Act of Parliament was the notable one by which, according to the ulnagers, in the days of James I and Charles I, in their lawsuits with the West Riding clothiers, they conceived " that the devise and subtilltie of the makers of karsyes was . . . . . . well remedied." The reason why the ulnagers were of this opinion was, because unlike the statute of the 27th Edward III, in which only broad cloths of assize and half such cloths were taxed, the makers were allowed to make and put to sale cloths, as well kerseys as other cloths of such length and breadth as should please them, paying the ulnage, subsidy, and other duties, after the rate, whatever the length of their cloths might be, of the assize of cloth mentioned in the statute of Edward III.

The only Roll we can discover preserved for Yorkshire that gives a *Compotus* of the cloth taxed under the statute of Edward III, is that of Thomas Scorburgh, Ulnager for the East Riding, dated 1st November, 1378, which only covers about three months.[1] The number of cloths sealed during this period was 504½. It is to be noted that " strait " cloths, otherwise kerseys, are not named, and if there were any cloths at all less than half a broad cloth, i.e. less than 12 yards, they escaped

---

[1] This return for the East Riding, the earliest of all Yorkshire returns, is omitted in Mr. Heaton's excellent *Yorkshire Woollen and Worsted Industries.*

taxation and consequently do not appear in the Account. The ulnager tells us that no cloths in which there was any grain—any scarlet dye—were found by him exposed for sale, nor any cloths or pieces of cloths whereof the dozen exceeds the value of 13s. 4d. This last statement seems rather obscure, and there is no reference, that I can find, in the previous statutes to any custom being payable on a "dozen" cloth above this value. But, perhaps, it was an illegal charge imposed upon foreign merchants, for in the Close Rolls, 35 Edward III [1361], we find the King sending a writ to the collectors in the Port of Hull, on behalf of German merchants, in which it is stated that these "aliens" had been [illegally] charged, on the pretext of a certain order made by the King and his Council, with, among other illegal charges, "a custom of 3d. in the £ [de libra] on strait cloths and pieces of cloths." Thomas Scorburgh himself appears from his *Compotus* to have been a cloth merchant, and paid his contribution to the subsidy on 14½ "cloths of assize without grain."

The first ulnager's returns of cloths sealed under the statute of 17 Richard II, c. 2, are those of William Skipwyth and of John Raghton, the former for the county and the latter for the city of York and suburbs of the same. In the quaint leather pouch in which Skipwith's account is enclosed is enclosed with it the original of the Letters Patent appointing him to his office. This appointment the reader will find printed in this volume and prefixed to the *Compotus* of this ulnager

The names in Skipwith's Roll, it will be noticed, are arranged not under wapentakes but towns, and these town returns seem to include the inhabitants not only of the actual towns but also the makers or merchants of cloth in the honours or manors of which the towns were *chef lieux*. Thus, under Wakefield we find the names of several Halifax people, and the same circumstance may be found in regard to other towns.

It is somewhat curious to find mention made in Skipwith's Roll of the "daughter of the Vicar of Crayk" being taxed for a cloth she had made. Evidently she had woven that cloth for sale and not for her "many," i.e. household.

"Strait cloths" are named in this Roll, but they appear to have equalled half a broad cloth, i.e. 6 yards in length, so the kersey makers, it seems, who made cloth less than 6 yards still escaped or evaded taxation. The ulnager, it will be noticed, at the end of his account, states that "12 strait cloths of divers colours" had been seized as forfeitures because they had been set out for sale before the subsidy was paid, and the ulnager's seal attached. It is plain from the circumstance that these cloths were of "divers colours," that the cloths made in Yorkshire, outside the city of York and its suburbs, were in many cases dyed cloths, but in this Roll none of these dyed cloths had any "grain" intermixed in their colours.

It has to be remembered that Gross and Ashley were mistaken when they wrote that the monopoly of making cloth for Yorkshire—certain towns excepted—was granted by King Henry II, and confirmed by subsequent monarchs to the citizens of York. As Miss Sellers and, I think, Professor Cunningham have pointed out, what was granted was the monopoly of making dyed cloths.[1] The other Yorkshire towns named in the grant to which the privilege was granted were Beverley, Kirkby, Malton, Thirsk, Scarborough. But, besides these, to quote the Close Roll of Henry III, a similar privilege was conceded *aliis dominicis meis burgis*—"to other my demesne burgs." The term *burgus*, i.e. borough, as Miss Bateson in her Introduction to *Borough Customs* says, was somewhat loosely used in the Middle Ages,[2] and it is, I think, possible that burgs and manors, like Wakefield, held in ancient demesne, may have passed in the above grant under *alii mei burgi*.

If so, this may account for dyeing being carried on, for example at Halifax as early, at any rate, as the days of Edward I.

Dr. Maud Sellers in the *Victoria History* and Mr. Heaton in his book have very fully and admirably described the subsequent Ulnagers' Rolls, and I do not know that there is much to add to what they say about them. Roll No. III, the *Com-*

---

[1] Close Rolls, 4 Henry III.

[2] *Borough Customs*, Selden Society, i, lviii.

potus of John Raghton for the city of York, which has been photographed for me, is a splendid and perfectly preserved document. It gives us the number of cloths daily exposed for sale, the name of each vendor, and the number and colours of the cloth they sold. Perhaps one may be surprised in Raghton's summing up to find only 1 scarlet cloth mentioned, and that all the other cloths that paid the subsidy were free from " grain," i.e. the " kermes " dye.

In the *Compoti* that follow that of John Raghton, we note that the colours of the cloths are not stated, and all are reported as being without " grain."

In No. IV, the account of William Barker for the West Riding (1395–6), it is to be noted that Wakefield heads the list of cloths taxed with 173½, while Ripon closely follows with 168½ for a little over a year's space, Leeds coming third with 120 cloths. By Wakefield we must, I suppose, understand the manor or honour of that town.

In No. V the names of the places, unfortunately, are not given, but I think those I have inserted in brackets are about correct.

Between Nos. VI and VII there is, alas, a gap of seventy-one years, for which no returns seem to exist.

In No. VII the account rendered by Thomas Trigott, 1469–1470, the individual names, it will be noticed, of the makers or vendors are suppressed, and one or, as in the case of Pontefract, two of the principal merchants answer for their fellow-townsmen.

Thus, in the case of Doncàster, Thomas Pykborn accounts to the ulnager for cloths sealed and put on sale there. At the foot of or endorsed on the charter granted to Doncaster in 1467 by King Edward IV, we are informed that the " Letters [Patent] were sued out by *Thomas Pikburn* and John Trich." In Doncaster church there used to be many relics of stained glass with inscriptions and arms of the Pickburn family. In the middle aisle in the body of the church, among others, were their arms, viz. *Argent a fess sable between 3 paynnetts proper*, and underneath the words, " Pray for the soules of Thomas

Pickeburne and Isabell his wife."[1] This may or may not refer
to the man who answered for the cloth subsidy. The first
mayor of Doncaster, in 1493, was a Thomas Pigborne, who was,
perchance, the same individual.

Richard Symmes, who accounted for Barnsley cloth, was
a well-known man in his day and district. He was the father
of Richard Symmes, Vicar of Halifax. His will was proved
November 3rd, 1501, by Gerard Lacy, of Brearley, Halifax
parish.[2] Symmes was the founder with William Issot of a
chantry in Barnsley church. It is unnecessary to proceed
and show the importance of the other representatives of the
cloth trade in the rest of the towns that occur on these Rolls,
the two instances given above are sufficient examples.

In 1395–6 Wakefield, as we have seen, appears to have set
out for sale the largest number of cloths, and to have been
followed by Ripon in output, but in 1469–70 it is Ripon that
tops the list, followed closely by Halifax, which did not appear
by name, but was probably included under Wakefield some
seventy years earlier. The great drop in the later return for
Wakefield, after Halifax appears on the Rolls, seems to indicate
that this latter parish was so included in earlier days. Certain
local Halifax names entered under Wakefield also justify this
explanation. In the 1469–70 *Compotus* neither the city of
York nor Kingston-on-Hull are included, but in 1471–3 that
city and that town are entered. York had evidently greatly
fallen off in its output since former times, seeing that it only
paid £100 both for subsidy and ulnage, but it still outdistanced
Ripon and Halifax that contributed £35 11s. 4¼d. and £28
9s. 5¼d. respectively.

In the *Compotus* for 1473–5 we find York heads the Roll
with 2,346½ cloths, followed by Halifax with 1,493½ and Ripon
1,396½. In the return for 1475–8 the order is York, 2,288
cloths; Halifax, 1,493½ cloths; Ripon, 1,385½ cloths; leaving
all other places far behind.

The ulnager's *Compotus* of 1475–8 seems to be the last of
these Rolls in existence, for what one may call medieval times.

---

[1] Miller, *History of Doncaster*, p. 80.
[2] See *Yorkshire Deeds*, ii, 21.

Of course, there is a great wealth of documents, other than these, relating to the trade in more recent times. The Records of the Court of Exchequer—Bills, Answers, Depositions, etc.—will furnish those who in future make research into the history of our Yorkshire woollen trade with ample and most useful material.

Perhaps, I shall be expected in the light of the documents dealt with in this volume, to enter into the prickly controversy touching the influence of Flemish artizans on the weaving, fulling, and dyeing industries of our county. That the art of cloth-making was introduced in the days of Edward III into England—as stated by Rapin and subsequent historians who, sheep-like, followed in his footsteps, is, of course, no longer held. Nor do I think that the limited activities of those Flemings is now believed to have vastly, if at all, improved the quality of the cloth made in Yorkshire. The "coarse karseyes" that were made before these aliens arrived continued to be the staple manufacture, and the returns show that the exports of superior cloths lessened rather than increased after the arrival of John Kemp and his compatriots.

Cloths shipped abroad from Hull, whether made by Flemish or English craftsmen, all paid, as a rule, the same custom and the same subsidy. Had the qualities of the cloths made by the aliens shipped from Hull been vastly superior in quality to those made by Yorkshiremen, would not the customs due, in the interest of the King, have been higher? In the Customs Roll (No. XI), where the duty is an *ad valorem* one, there seems to be no evidence, so far as I can find, that this was the case. That, from the days of Henry II to those of Henry III and the Edwards, there had been a certain falling off in the manufacture of cloth in England may be conceded. In a dispute in the 10th year of Henry IV, viz. a suit between weavers who were not members of the Weavers' Gild in London and the Gild itself, the advocate for the former, Sir William Cokenage, submitted that the statute of 11 Edward III, c. 5, was made " by reason of the decay of woollen weaving and the paucity of cloth workers." The above was the statute that gave " safe conduct " to foreign clothworkers. Sir William did not gain his case, but this, I think, is the first reference we have in legal proceedings to the alleged decay in the woollen industry, and it occurs only seventy-one years after the foreigners were invited over. This evidence is better for the case of the Fleming advocates than that mid-seventeenth century testimony, which they are fond of quoting, of that fine word-spinner, Bishop Fuller, who tells us that our forefathers were " as yet ignorant of that art [clothing], as knowing no more what to do with their wool than the sheep that wear it, as to any artificial and curious drapery."

This is far from being the fact, for we know that " the cloths of Beverley and York "—as Mr. Heaton, in his book on the *Yorkshire Woollen and Worsted Industry*, writes, " were of no mean quality, and took their places alongside the high-class pieces produced at Lincoln, Stamford, and elsewhere, goods for which there was a big demand abroad." Spanish merchants were exporting pieces of scarlet cloth from York and Beverley to the continent in the reign of Henry II, and the *Beverley Bleu* and scarlet cloth of that place were especially famous both at home and abroad. The prices paid for these fabrics, as Mr. Heaton states, " indicate that these cloths were of the highest quality." It may have been noticed that, in the first Customs Roll printed in this volume, one of the only two pieces of cloth exported was of scarlet grain, on which the custom was twice that paid on the ordinary cloths that had no " grain " in them. It is interesting to note that these specimens of what Fuller styles " artificial and curious drapery," for example, the " Pers " or blue cloths of Beverley, were valued at a high figure, and that 4 cloths made there in 1319, as Mr. Heaton points out, were priced at 6s. a yard, or quite £4 10s. in modern money. That these high-priced cloths were made in Yorkshire in 1319, in a period when the art of cloth-making had fallen, according to some authorities, into decay, is a fact that does not much tell in favour of any great technical improvement introduced, as is asserted, by the Flemish aliens in the days of our third Edward. In company with Mr. Heaton I must confess my inability to accept Dr. Maud Sellers' conclusions in regard to the great importance of the migrations of Flemings, especially during the eleventh, twelfth, and fourteenth centuries.[1]

In conclusion I would sincerely thank all those friends who have aided me in the preparation of this volume, and, in particular, Mr. E. W. Crossley, Mr. H. Travis Clay, Mr. Charles Travis Clay, and Mr. Houseman. I am also under obligation to Mr. J. Bilson, to Mr. H. A. Learoyd, Town Clerk of Hull, and to the latter's record clerk, Mr. Stanewell, for their kind proffers of help in my research work. Above all others, however, the thanks of our Society, as well as my own, are especially due to the Rev. C. V. Collier for compiling an Index which must have cost him many hours of patient and toilsome industry. To the able copyists at the Record Office, and to the photographer who so skilfully photographed for me the Customs Roll XI and the Ulnager's Roll III it is my pleasing duty to record my gratitude.

[1] For Dr. Sellers' interesting discussion of this topic see *Victoria County History, Yorkshire*, ii, 436-440.

ERRATA.

Page 104, line 7.   *For* Him *read* him.

EXTRACTS FROM THE
CUSTOMS ACCOUNTS OF HULL,

―――――――――

I.

[Exchequer K.R. Bundle $\frac{55}{11}$]

ROLL OF ROBERT OF BARTON[1] AND OF GILBERT OF BEDEFORD,[2] Guardians and Collectors of the Small New Custom[3] of Merchandize shipped from the Port of Kingeston-on-Hull from the 4th day of July in the 32[d] year of the reign of [our] illustrious King of England, Edward, to the Feast of St. Michael next following.

The Ship of John of Faxflet[4] sailed from the Port of Hull on the 13th day of July.

. . . .

Walter of Ferour had [thereon] half a scarlet cloth for which he paid 12*d*.

Sum of cloth in grain[5] shipped from the realm at Hull from the 4th day of July in the Thirty-second year [of the King] to the Feast of St. Michael next following, half a scarlet [cloth], whereof the custom [amounted] to 12*d*.

[1] Robert of Barton was Bailiff of Kingston-on-Hull in the year 1301, and Frost, in the Appendix to his " Notices of Hull," gives from the Pipe Rolls, five *compoti*, in which the names of Robert of Barton and John of Hustweyt appear as the Collectors of the new custom on wool, fells, and hides, for the 23rd, 24th, 25th, 28th, and 31st years of King Edward I, 1294–1303.
In 1309 from the Patent Rolls we learn that a *Writ de Intendendo* was directed to the Sheriff of Yorkshire in favour of Robert of Barton & Gilbert of Bedford, as commissioners to levy " prest " customs upon all imports and exports above the ancient custom payable by merchants, strangers, and aliens, at Kingston-on-Hull and along the coast thence as far as Newcastle-on-Tyne.
Robert of Barton seems to have died in, or before, 1317, for in the Close Rolls there is an order, dated Nov. 3rd, 1317, to the Treasurer and Barons of the Exchequer to cause an allowance to be made to his executors, and to those of Richard Oysel for £800, paid by the said Robert and Richard, and by Master William Wykinston, when Keepers of the Customs at Hull, to the attorney of John le Cut, for the use of John de Brabant.

[2] Gilbert of Bedford held the office of Coroner at Hull, as proved—writes Frost—by an original charter. He was, apparently, the son of John of Bedford, who granted land with shops thereon to his said father, John, in 1303.

[3] The Small New Custom (see Introduction).

[4] John of Faxflete was, apparently, a merchant who served as a juror in an Inquisition *Ad quod damnum*, in connection with a ferry at Hull promoted by John Rotenheryng, who was Custos or Warden of the town in 1311. The Writ was tested Oct. 26th, 1308.

[5] " In grain," *i.e.* scarlet (see Introduction).

A

II.

$$\left[\text{E. } \frac{55}{20}\right]$$

1305

THE ROLL OF ROBERT OF BARTON AND GILBERT OF BEDEFORD, Guardians and Collectors of the " Small New Custom " of Merchandize shipped from the Port of Kyngeston-on-Hull, beginning from the Feast of St. Michael in the 33rd year of the reign of our Lord Edward, illustrious King of England, to the Feast of St. Michael next following.

The Ship of Reynbold of Strallesond[1] sailed from the Port of Hull on the 2nd day of October.
John Pape had 1 cloth without grain and paid 12d.
The Ship of John Dolman of Strallesond sailed, etc., on the same day of October.
Simon Moper of Gutteland[2] had 3 cloths without grain and paid 3s.
The Ship of Andrew del Dyke sailed the 13th day of October.
The same had 1 scarlet and 2 cloths without grain and paid 4s.
The Ship of Fris Bene of Friselond sailed, etc., the 14th day of October.
Henry of Grenyng[3] had 2 scarlet and 7 cloths without grain and paid 11s.
The Ship of Hulf of Norbergh[4] sailed, etc., the 17th day of October.
The same had one cloth without grain and paid 12d.
The same had 5 pieces of cloth without grain and paid 13½d.
The Ship of Guner of Norbergh sailed on the 8th day of Novr.
Serlo of Gutteland had 5 cloths and a half without grain and paid 5s. 6d.
Elias Clericus of Norwey had 4 cloths without grain and paid 4s.
The Ship of Gunne Bret of Tonesberwe[5] sailed on the 10th day of November.
The same had 2 cloths without grain and paid 2s.
William of Tyndale had 3 cloths without grain and paid 3s.
The Ship of John de Burgo sailed the 15th day of January.
Peter Reymond had 1 scarlet and 12½ cloths without grain and paid 14s. 6d.
Raymond Gribe had 5 pieces of cloth without grain, price £7 12s. 0d., and paid 23d.
The same had 8 cloths without grain and paid 8s.

---

[1] Strallesond—Stralsund, in North Germany, near Rostock, on the Baltic Sea.

[2] Gutland—probably Jutland.

[3] Grenyng—perhaps Groningen in the north of Holland.

[4] Norbergh. There is, in modern maps, a Norburg in Jutland.

[5] Tonesberwe—Tonsbirg, on the west side of Christiania Fjord.

The Ship of Warin Benedight sailed the 4th day of May.
John de Monte had 2 pieces of white cloth, price 50s., and paid 7½d.

The Ship of John of Walthcrp sailed the 9th July.
The same [John] had 1 cloth without grain and paid 12d.

The Ship of Simon Kerver of the Hok [Hook] sailed the 26th July.
The same had ½ a cloth without grain and paid 6d.

The Ship of Athelard of Stauer[1] sailed the 20th day of August.
The same [Athelard] had 1 cloth without grain and paid 12d.

The Ship of Radekyrn of Walderik[2] sailed the same day of August.
Pilegrinus of Stauer had 3 cloths without grain and paid 3s.
The same had 4 pieces of cloth, price £6 2s. 0d., and paid 18¼d.

The Ship of John of Stenebergh[3] sailed the 27th day of August.
Tydemanne Cote had 2½ cloths without grain and paid 2s. 6d.

III.
[E. $\frac{56}{2}$]

THE ROLL OF ROBERT OF BARTON AND GILBERT OF BEDEFORD, Guardians and Collectors of the New Small Custom of merchandize **1306** shipped at Kyngeston-on-Hull from the Feast of St. Michael in the 35th year of our illustrious lord Edward [the First] King of England **1307** to the 7th day of July next following.

The Ship of Henry Fretherick of Norbergh sailed the 7th December.
Magnus of Bergh had 2½ cloths without grain and paid 2s. 6d.

The Ship of Robert of Oxoñ sailed the 23rd Jany.
Reymond Geraud had 2 cloths without grain and 6 pieces containing 2½ cloths without grain and paid 4s. 6d.

The Ship of William of Teworth sailed the 5th day of April.
John Greyne had 2 cloths without grain and 3 scarlet and paid 8s.

The Ship of Simon of Carnesond sailed the 26th day of June.
The same had 1 cloth without grain and paid 12d.

The Ship of Walter, son of Arnald, sailed the same day of June.
Odo of Grenyng had 9 cloths without grain and paid 9s.

[In the account that follows of the same Collectors for the time between 7th July, 1 Edw. II, to Michaelmas, completing the year, no customs on cloth exported are recorded.]

---

[1] Staner or Stauer—? Stavoren, on the Zuyder Zee.

[2] Walderik—? Woldegk, in Mecklenburg-Strelitz.

[3] Stenebergh. Is this Steenbergen, near Rotterdam?

IV.

$$[\text{E. } \tfrac{57}{2}]$$

Concerning goods exported.

THE ACCOUNT OF ROBERT OF BARTON AND GILBERT OF BEDE-
FORD of the goods and merchandize of aliens and stranger merchants
at Kingeston-on-Hull, shipped from the Feast of St. Michael in the
1308–9 2nd year of the reign of our illustrious lord Edward, King of England,
son of King Edward, to the 20th day of August in the 3rd year of
our said lord King Edward, on which day the said Custom ceased[1]
in virtue of the King's Writ.

The Ship of William son of Peter sailed on the 22nd day of
November.
    Everard Pluckrose had 7½ cloths without grain, the custom
    whereon being 7s. 6d.

The Ship of Englebright of Gripperwold[2] sailed the 26th day of
February.
    John Brand had 2 "scharlet" [cloths]. Custom 4s.

The Ship of Thormode of Norweg sailed the 6th day of April.
    The same had 1½ cloth without grain, the custom whereon 18d.
    Seward of the same [Norweg] had 2 cloths without grain.
    Custom 2s.
    Enor of the same had 1 cloth without grain. Custom 12d.
    The same had 1¼ cloths without grain. Custom 15d.
    Serlo of the same had 4 cloths without grain. Custom 4s.
    Arnald of the same had 3 cloths without grain. Custom 3s.
    Episcopus Oselensis[3] had 3 cloths without grain. Custom 3s.

The Ship of Fretheric Wylde sailed the 8th day of May.
    The same had 6 cloths without grain. Custom 6s.

The Ship of Tidemann of Coyure [?] sailed the 19th day of May.
    Winand of Grenyng had 2 cloths without grain. Custom 2s.

The Ship of Albert of Coyure sailed the same day of May.
    Haricus [sic] of Loward had 2 "scharlet" [cloths]. Custom 4s.
    The same had 1 cloth without grain. Custom 12d.

The Ship of . . . guard of Hamburgh sailed the 8th day of June.
    John of . . . . . . had 1 cloth without grain. Custom thereon
    12d.

The Ship of Gerard of Hardewik[4] sailed the 27th June.
    Henry of Breme[5] had 7½ cloths of "scharlet." Custom 15s.
    The same [Henry] had 43 cloths without grain. Custom 43s.

---

[1] See Introduction.

[2] Gripperwold. Is this Greffswold, on the Baltic, near Stralsund ?

[3] *Episcopus Oselensis.* There is an island called Osel in the Gulf of Riga,
Baltic Sea.

[4] Harderwicke, Harderwyk, on the Zuyder Zee.

[5] Breme, *i.e.* Bremen.

The Ship of Adam of Hamborgh sailed the same day of June. Bernard the Brak' had 1 "scharlet" [cloth]. Custom 2s. The same had 16 cloths without grain. Custom 16s.

V.

$$[E. \frac{56}{14}]$$

Kingeston-on-Hull. Concerning things exported in the 4th year.

THE ACCOUNT OF ROBERT OF BARTON AND GILBERT OF BEDE-FORD of the goods and merchandize of alien (*alienigenarum*) and stranger (*estraneorum*) merchants shipped from the town aforesaid, **1310** from the Feast of St. Michael in the 4th year [of Edw. II] to the Feast of St. Michael in the 5th year.

The Ship of Arnald of Stanbergh sailed from the port of Hull on the 16th day of November.
> Radekyn of Greeng [? Grenyng'] had 2 cloths without grain, whereof the custom was 2s.

The Ship of Nankyn of Herderwik sailed from the port of Hull on the 30th day of May.
> The same Nankyn had 1 cloth without grain, the custom whereof being 12d.
> The same had Sayes of W[o]rtstede,[1] price £4, the custom whereof 12d.

The Ship of James of Hamburgh sailed from the port of Hull the 16th day of June.
> The same James had 2 pieces of cloth without grain, price 40s., whereof the custom was 6d.

The Ship of Cristian of Hamburgh sailed from the port of Hull the 24th day of July.
> The same had 1 cloth without grain. The custom 12d.
> The same had one piece of cloth without grain, price 22s., the custom thereof being 3¼d.

The Ship of Tydemann of Rostok[2] sailed from the port of Hull the same day of July.
> The same had 3 pieces of cloth without grain, price 100s., whereon the custom paid was 15d.
> The same had 2 pieces of cloth without grain, price 71s., the custom being 10¾d.

1310 Concerning merchandize at Scardeburgh shipped at the end of the fourth and beginning of the 5th year [of Edw. II].

---

[1] Sayes of worsted: Say is defined by Halliwell as a delicate serge or woollen cloth.

[2] Rostok—Rostock, an important trading port in Mecklenburg, on the Baltic, near Stralsund.

The Ship of Richard Cok of Jernemuth[1] sailed from the port of Scardebourg' the 12th day of May.

Nicholas Catel had 3 cloths without grain, the custom being 3s.

The Ship of William son of Walter of Muth sailed the 5th day of June.

The same had half a cloth without grain, the custom thereon 6d.

VI.

$$[E. \frac{56}{26}]$$

PARTICULARS OF THE ACCOUNT OF RICHARD DE LA POLE[2] of money received from the New Custom of our Lord the King at Kyngeston-on-Hull from the Feast of St. Michael in the 18th year [of Edw. II] to the same Feast in the 19th year.

1324-5

The Ship of Simon of Bardewyk[3] sailed from the Port of Hull the 19th day of May [18th year].

1325

Lympeld of Emse[4] had an English cloth of the sworn price of £13, the custom whereon was 3s. 4d.

The Ship of Boydewyn Devoll [or Deuoll] sailed from the Port of Hull 10th Sept., in the 19th year.

Nicholas of Grenyng had 2 English cloths, price per oath £8, whereon the custom was 2s.

---

[1] Jernemuth—Yarmouth.

[2] Richard de la Pole. One of the distinguished family of that name, son of Sir William de la Pole, knt.

We find from the Patent Rolls that a *Writ de Intendendo* dated July 30th, 1317, was issued for Richard-atte-Pole and William-atte-Pole [his brother], whom Stephen of Abingdon, the king's serjeant and head butler (*pincerna*), had appointed to be his deputies at Kingston-on-Hull, in connection with the duty of purchasing wine for the royal cellar. Let us note how the plebeian *Atte-Pole* was superseded for ever by the *De la Pole*.

In 1318 a writ of aid for Richard de la Pole going [from London ?] to Hull was issued in July, 1318. In 1324 (perhaps also as Frost states, in 1322) he was collector of the customs at Hull.

In 1326 he was appointed by the King Warden (*custos*) of the town of Hull, in place of Robert of Hastanges, to whom the King had lately granted the same. The latter, we are told, was broken by age and debility, and could not attend personally to the office. Robert of Hastanges was to pay a reasonable fee to Richard de la Pole for being relieved. In 1327 the Patent Rolls inform us that Richard de la Pole and Master John Barton were the "late Collectors" of the customs in Hull. On account of loans advanced by them to the King, in that year, Richard and his brother, William de la Pole, were granted a charge laid upon the customs towards the reimbursement of their money. In subsequent years many other charges on the customs were granted in consideration of loans to Richard and his brother William.

In 1336 Richard de la Pole was the king's chief butler in the port of London. He was knighted in 1340, died in 1345, and was buried in the Trinity Church, Hull.

[3] Bardewyk—Berwick ?

Emse—Ems ?

VII.

[E. $\frac{58}{10}$]

THE ACCOUNT OF WALTER BOX[1] AND OF JOHN OF NORTHBURGH, Collectors of the Custom and subsidy in the Port of Kingeston-on-Hull and in single (*singulis*) places elsewhere along the sea coast from on one side as far as Grimesby and the other as far as Whyteby, and that place itself (*et ibidem*), in accordance with a Writ of the King [Edward III] under the Great Seal resting
1354 in their hands given on the 30th day of July, in the 27th year [of his reign] whereby the King appointed the aforesaid Walter and John [to collect] the subsidy aforesaid [arising] from all woollen cloths made in the Realm of England to be exported out of the said realm, to wit [a custom] of 14*d*. [to be paid] by denizens (*indigeni*) and 21*d*. by aliens on every cloth of assize and 3*s*. 4*d*. by denizens and 3*s*. 6*d*. by aliens on every scarlet cloth and every cloth of whole grain dyed [*integro grano*], and a moiety of this custom on every cloth of the half grain in which [but] little grain shall have been intermixed; and also the same custom's rate on every cloth more or less, as it [the cloth] shall be larger or less, according to the proportionate size thereof. Also of clòths of Worstede to be exported out of the said realm, to wit [a custom] of 1*d*. from denizens, and from aliens 1½*d*. for a whole cloth; and from denizens 5*d*. and from aliens 7½*d*. for one single bedblanket; and from denizens 9*d*. and from aliens 13½*d*. for a double bedblanket (*lecto dupplic'*), for the use of the King as those cloths were anciently charged under the penalty of the forfeiture of the same. And they [*i.e.* the collectors] are to answer the King in regard to the income arising from the same Custom and Subsidy from the 30th day of July in the 27th year until the Feast of St. Michael next following; in the 28th year beginning, by the view and testimony of Adam Punde[2] controller of the same subsidy and custom, from which Feast verily the said Walter and John have to render their account thereof.

The Small Custom on cloths. The same [*i.e.* collectors] render account of £4 11*s*. 0*d*. arising from the subsidy and custom on 52 cloths without grain in the Port of Kingeston-on-Hull shipped by alien merchants from the aforesaid day of July to the Feast of St. Michael next following in the 28th year, to wit for every cloth of assize 21*d*. as is contained in the Roll of Particulars that has been delivered into the Treasury, and of 10*s*. 4*d*. from the subsidy and custom arising from 8 cloths without grain in consideration of the custom on merchandize shipped from the aforesaid port during the aforesaid time; to wit for every cloth 14*d*. as is contained

---

[1] Walter Box was a Bailiff of Hull in 1341, 1342, 1349, also in 1362, and was Mayor in 1351. In 1353 he received, on paying a fine of 4 marks, a pardon from the king, in company with John Upsale and Robert of Selby, burgesses of Hull, for selling wines before they had been gauged, and also taking corn and other victuals from England to Germany.

[2] Adam Punde was a Bailiff of Hull in 1345, and Mayor in 1352 and 1368.

[stated] therein. And they do not render account of any custom relating to other cloths, scarlet ones, cloths of Worsted or double bedblankets (*lectis dupplic'*) because none of these have been shipped from the said port either by denizen merchants or alien ones, during the time aforesaid, as they say.

Sum of receipts 101s. 4d.

[The above is scored through and altered in various ways, presumably on enrolment. It is marked as enrolled.]

VIII.

[E. $\frac{58}{11}$]

Particulars of the Account of Thomas of Wapplynton[1] and of John of Middleton,[2] Collectors of the Custom and Subsidy of our lord the King in the Port of Kyngeston-on-Hull, under the King's Writ Patent [sealed] with the Great Seal, given on the 18th day of February in this 37th year, concerning the forfeitures of strait cloths there, from the same 18th day of February in the 37th year to and finishing on the 2nd day of October in the 38th year.

1363–4

The same answer for 2 fardels[3] of short cloths containing 1288 ells of strait cloths, found in the hands of Henry Dartewyn, German merchant, in the port aforesaid about to be shipped to foreign parts without paying the custom, and for that reason forfeited to our Lord the King. These cloths, by the King's Writ dated 12th April, 38th year [of the King], were to be sold.

The same [collectors] answer for £22 16s. 11d. received for the said 2 fardels of strait cloths sold, according to the King's Writ, and by view and witness of Geoffrey of Hamby, supervisor.

IX and X.

[E. $\frac{58}{14}$]

[These Rolls, or rather this Roll, for two *compoti* are contained in one Roll, are in a deplorably bad state of condition, and the name "Robert" is only legible as the Christian name of one of the collectors, and the words "Hull" and "to and from the 5th August." In No. IX the full names, however, as given from some other source, by the compilers of the P.R.O. Calendar, are Robert of Selby and Thomas of Wapplyngton. The date, which is

---

[1] An order was made, on Dec. 30th, 1384, that an Enquiry should be made as to what goods Thomas of Waplyngton, late one of the Collectors of Customs and Subsidies, had in the county of York at the time of his death, and that such goods should be taken into the king's hands (Patent Rolls). This Collector was appointed, or reappointed, a Collector, along with Ralph Crust and Robert Selby, on May 25th, 1382, for the Port of Hull and all places between Grimsby and Scarborough.

[2] John of Middleton was one of the Hull Bailiffs in 1364.

[3] Fardels, *i.e.* burdens, or packs. " Who would fardels bear."—*Hamlet.*

1380-1 also illegible, is assigned to the years 3 and 4 of Richard II, and the term covered by the *compotus* ended, as faintly appears on the original title, on August the fifth, 1381. At the end of the first *compotus* [IX] are written two "sums total of these three rolls," meaning, I suppose, membranes, though of these only two seem to have survived. These totals are (*a*) the amount of the value of the exports, and (*b*) the value of goods imported as well as exported. The totals are as follows:—]

" Part of sum of these three rolls ":

Value of exports	. £51 6s.8d.
Cloths of denizens without grain . . .	78½
Cloths of the Hans without grain . . .	34
Cloths of aliens without grain . . .	49½
Single bedblankets of denizens . . .	10
Single bedblankets of aliens	2

Then we have the

" Sum total of these three rolls."

Value of goods and merchandize both exported
and imported:

Wax	. 5 lbs.
Cloths of denizens without grain . . .	1000
Cloths of the Hans without grain . . .	244
Cloths of aliens without grain . . .	91
Single bedblankets of denizens . . .	246
Single bedblankets of aliens . . .	4

The total sum of money received for exports and imports is set down at £148, and then we are told that an "allowance was made to the aforesaid Collector of £9 3s. 7¾d. out of the said sum of the cloths of the Hans; to wit for each cloth 9d."

[*Compotus* X on membrane 3 has only the heading, "Roll of the time of Thomas Flemyng," and consists of two membranes. Flemyng appears to have succeeded Selby and Wapplyngton in office. At the end of this account the following partial summary of the value of the merchandize exported and the number of cloths and bedblankets is given as below.]

Value of exports	£47 15s. 0d.
Cloths of denizens without grain . .	78½
Cloths of the Hans without grain . .	34
Cloths of aliens without grain . .	49½
Single bedblankets of denizens . .	10
Single bedblankets of aliens . . .	2

And underneath is written:

Sum total in the time of Thomas Flemyng . . . . . .

[This latter sum total, unfortunately, is illegible. The figures given above only refer apparently to the entries on one of the membranes.]

XI.

$$[E. \frac{59}{22}]$$

PARTICULARS OF THE ACCOUNT OF ROBERT GART[ON][1], CLERK,
AND JOHN [COLTHORP].[2] . . . .
in the Port of the Town of Kyngeston[-on-Hull] . . . . . . to wit
1391-2 from the . . . . . . 8th day of December in 15th year until the Feast
of St. Michael . . . .

[Beyond the words " Ship of Simon " the first entry is illegible.]

The Ship of Thomas Skarburgh, called the *Cutberte of Hull*,
sailed the same day.

William Warde for ½ a cloth and 3 dozens of strait cloths.
Value 26s. 8d. Subsidy 16d.

. . . . . . of the Crosse, 1½ cloth. Value 70s. Subs. 3s. 6d.

. . . . . . of Holme, 1 cloth and 1 coverlet. Value 30s. Subs. 18d.
Sum: Values . £7 16s. 3d.
Subs. . 7s. 10d.

The Ship of Wisse Clark [?] . . . . . .
The same Wisse, 2½ cloths. [Value £4 10s. 0d. Subs. 4s.]
Sum: Value . £4 10s. 0d.
Subs. . ' 4s. 0d.

The Ship of Henry Roll, called the *Maudelyn of Camifer*,[3] sailed
the same day.

Robert Ward, ½ a cloth, 15s.; 103 dozen of *mantal clothes*,
100s.; 3 dozens of strait cloths, 10s. 6d.; 132 stones of fat,
£4 8s. 4d. Value £10 13s. 10d. Subs. 10s. 8½d.

John . . . . . . 11 cloths. Value £15. Subs. 15s.

John of the Hill, 16¼ cloths. Value £22 13s. 4d. Subs. . . . . . .

[The rest of the freight of this ship consisted of other articles of
merchandize.]

The Ship of John Parow, called the *Shenkwyn of* . . . . . . [sailed]
the same day.

John Rose [?], 3 cloths. [Value £5 6s. 8d.] Subs. 5s. 4d.

John of the Hill, 6 cloths. . . . . . .

John Spaldyng, 7 cloths. . . . . . .

The Ship of William Cole, called the *James of Dertmouth*, sailed
the 4th day of February.

Thomas of the Gare, 82 dozens of strait cloths. Value
£14 6s. 8d. Subs. 14s. 4d.

---

[1] Robert Garton, clerk. In an Enquiry *re* lands of this individual, directed
to be held in Nov., 1398, he is described as a late " Customer " of the king at
Hull for the custom and subsidy of wool freighted there (Patent Rolls of this
date).

[2] John Colthorp is mentioned on July 29th, 1389, as a Collector of the subsidy at Hull in conjunction with William Ponde; Thomas Paule, chaplain,
being at that date appointed their " Controller " (Patent Rolls).

[3] Camifer, or more correctly Campvere, is the town now known as Vere, in
the island of Walcheren in the Netherlands.

Walter Mannynge, 20 dozens strait cloths. Value 76s. 8d.
   Subs. 3s. 10d.
               Sum: Values . £18 3s. 4d.
                     Subs.   .   18s. 2d.

The Ship of John Arnald, called the *James of Hull*, sailed the
same day.
   William Rolleston, 5 cloths, £7 10s. 0d.; 80 quarters of corn,
      £14 13s. 4d. Value £22 3s. 4d. Subs. 22s. 2d.
   John Seyrby, ½ a cloth, 13s. 4d.; 4 quarters of corn, 16s. 8d.
      Value 30s. Subs. 18d.
   Robert Kylyngholme, 2 cloths. . . . . . .

[The next entry is of a ship, whose name and date of sailing are
obliterated, but it was evidently freighted entirely by York mer-
chants. The roll begins, where next legible, with:]
   The same Everard [*i.e.* the man named as master of the ship],
      11 cloths. . . . . .
   Henry Mustre, 10½ cloths. . . . . . . Subs. 16s.
   John Wynck, 20 cloths. Value £22. Subs. 22s.
   Henry Wyman, 20½ cloths, £30 15s. 0d.; 2 bedblankets (*lecti*),
      13s. 4d. Value £31 8s. 4d. Subs. 31s. 5d.
   Robert Warde, 8½ cloths and 1 coverlet (*cooptorium*). Value
      £13. Subs. 13s.
   Richard Wolston, 24 cloths. Value £36. Subs. 36s.
   William Denyas, 22 cloths. Value £33. Subs. 33s.
   John Newby, 60½ cloths. Value £92. Subs. £4 12s. 0d.
   Thomas Toth, 21 cloths, £33; 4 dozens of strait cloths, 15s.;
      3 bedblankets, 20s.; Value £34 15s. 0d. Subs. 34s. 9d.
   William Palmer, 33 cloths. Value £51 4s. 0d. Subs. 51s. 2d.
   John of Bolton, 56 cloths. Value £84. Subs. £4 4s. 0d.
   Richard Sourby, 20 cloths. Value £31. Subs. 31s.
   Thomas [?] Osbaldwyk, 11½ cloths. Value £16 5s. 0d. Subs.
      16s. 4d.
   John Schay, 37 cloths. Value £55 10s. 0d. Subs. 55s. 6d.
   John Plumtre, 73½ cloths, £110 5s. 0d.; mantelclothes [quan-
      tity not stated], 100s. Value £115 5s. 0d. Subs. 115s. 3d.
   . . . . . . Taverner, 3½ cloths, £4 13s. 14d.; 200 strait cloths,
      66s. 8d. Value £8. Subs. 8s.
   William Hillom, 16 cloths. Value £24. Subs. 24s.

[A hiatus follows, which corresponds with the freight of some
ship, the particulars of whose name, master, and cargo are obliterated.]
   The Ship of Henry Blaktofft, called the *George of Hull*, sailed
the same day.
      . . . . . , 5½ cloths without grain, £8 5s. 0d.; 300 strait cloths,
         108s.; 160 quarters of corn, £30. Value £43 12s. 0d. Subs.
         43s. 8d.
      . . . . . , 14 dozens of strait cloths, 50s.; 30 quarters of corn,
         £6 15s. 0d. Value £9 5s. 0d. Subs. 9s. 3d.

. . . . . , 80 quarters of corn, £18; 600 strait cloths, £10 16s. 8d.
Value £28 16s. 8d.   Subs. 28s. 10d.
. . . . . , 59 quarters of corn, £13 5s. 0d.; ½ a cloth . . . . . .
[There are 7 other entries relating apparently only to corn.]
The Ship of Peter . . . . . , called the *Cristofer of Middleburgh*,
. . . . . .
. . . . . , 5 cloths . . . . . .
The Ship of John . . . .
[This ship was apparently entirely laden with corn.]
The Ship of William Johanson, called the *Seynt Mary shipp of
Camifer*, sailed . . . . . .
. . . . . . of the Hill. [No cloth.]
Sum: Value . 66s. 8d.
Subs. . 3s. 4d.
The Ship of Erbold, son of John, called the *Goldenbergh of Fley-
thinge*, sailed the same day.
[The names of the consignors and nature of the freight are
destroyed, except the word " pann.," *i.e.* cloths.]
The Ship of Edmund of . . . . . , called the *Mighell* . . . .
Henry Braken, 19½ cloths. Value £28 10s. 0d. Subs. 28s. 6d.
. . . . . . Aglion, 30 cloths. Value £45. Subs. 45s.
. . . . . . Dandson, 11 cloths. Value £15. Subs. 15s.
John . . . . . , 10 cloths. Value £13 6s. 8d. Subs. 13s. 4d.
William Burton, 10 cloths, £15 10s. 0d.; 5 doz. strait cloths,
16s. 8d.; 3 single bedblankets (*lecti*), 18s. Value £17 4s. 8d.
Subs. 17s. 3d.
William . . . . . , 39 cloths. Value £58 10s. 0d. Subs. 58s. 6d.
. . . . . . , 13 cloths. Value £19 10s. 0d. Subs. 19s. 6d.
. . . . . . , 13 cloths. Value £19 10s. 0d. Subs. 19s. 6d.
William Calton, 11 cloths. Value £16 10s. 0d. Subs. 16s. 6d.
. . . . . . Rayner . . . . . , 37 cloths, £55 10s. 0d.; 14 coverlets,
42s. Value £57 12s. 0d. Subs. 57s. 7½d.
John West, 21 cloths. Value £31 10s. 0d. Subs. 31s. 6d.
Hugh Spendluffe, 37 cloths, £55; 1 doz. strait cloths, 4s.
Value £55 4s. 0d. Subs. 55s. 2½d.
Thomas Waghen, 10 cloths, £15; 3 doz. strait cloths, 25s.
Value £16 5s. 0d. Subs. 16s. 3d.
John Barker, 4½ cloths. Value £6. Subs. 6s.
John Frost, 9 cloths . . . . . .
William Bol . . . , 2 cloths . . . . . .
William of the . . . . . .
Thomas . . . . . .
Thomas Doncastre . . . . . .
John Wharton, 25 cloths . . . . . .
Thomas Barbour, 12 cloths . . . . . .
John . . . . . . , 52 strait cloths, ...; 3 coverlets, 13s. 4d.
. . . . . .
William Denyas, 10 cloths, ...   Subs. 14s.

William Palmer, 11 cloths, ...   Subs. 16s. 6d.
Henry Brigge, 32 cloths, £49 13s. 4d.; 3 coverlets, 13s. 4d.
    Value £50 6s. 8d. Subs. 50s. 4d.
John Carleton, 12 cloths. Value £18. Subs. 18s.
Thomas Colyngham, 17 cloths, £26 6s. 8d.; 6 doz. of strait
    cloths, 20s.; 8 coverlets, 33s. 4d. Value £29. Subs. 29s.
Edmund . . . . . , 3 cloths. Value £4. Subs. 4s.
Robert Kylinholme, 3½ clotns. Value £8. Subs. 8s.
John S . . . . . , 6 cloths, 100 strait cloths. Value £9 15s. 0d.
    Subs. 9s. 9d.
John Hedon, 7 cloths, £9 6s. 8d.; 100 strait cloths, 35s. Value
    £11 and 20d. Subs. 11s. 1d.
Robert Duffeld, 40½ cloths, £61 0s. 0d.; 10 coverlets, 30s.
    Value £62 10s. 0d. Subs. 62s. 6d.
John Schay, 10 cloths, £15; 2 coverlets, 6s. 8d. Value
    £15 6s. 8d. Subs. 15s. 4d.
John Langton, 5 cloths. Value £9. Subs. 9s.
William Eseby, 3 cloths . . . . . .
John . . . . . , 2½ cloths . . . . . .
William Bingham [?], 17½ cloths . . . . . .
Robert Ward, 8½ cloths . . . . . .
Hugh Sleford, 6 cloths, £8; 18 dozens of strait cloths . . . . . .
Thomas Sleford, 15½ cloths . . . . . .
The same Robert Ward, 8 cloths. Value £12. Subs. 12s.
John . . . . . , 4 doz. strait cloths. Value 13s. 4d. Subs. 8d.
John Derfeld, 24 coverlets. Value 72s. Subs. 3s. 6½d.
John of Bolton, 6 cloths. Value £10 10s. 0d. Subs. 10s. 6d.
John Harpham, 9½ cloths, £14 5s. 0d.; 6 coverlets, 20s. Value
    £15 5s. 0d. Subs. 15s. 3d.
John Stokyng, 3 cloths. Value 106s. 8d. Subs. 5s. 4d.
John Wragby, 19 cloths, £25; 200 strait cloths, 60s. Value
    £28. Subs. 28s.
William Midelham, 14 cloths. Value £18. Subs. 18s.
William Rawdon, 9 cloths. Value £13 10s. 0d. Subs. 13s. 6d.
John Birkyn, 6 cloths. Value £7 10s. 0d. Subs. 7s. 6d.
. . . . . . Sauere, 4 cloths. Value 100s. Subs. 5s.
John [?] of Hedon, ½ a cloth without grain. Value 15s.
    Subs. 9d.
The Ship of John W . . . .
John Dandson, 4 cloths . . . . . .
John [?] of Bedale, 4½ cloths without grain, ... £6 9s. 0d.
    . . . . . .
John Pilkyngton, 1000 strait cloths. Value £15. Subs. 15s.
John . . . . . , 400 strait cloths. Value £7. Subs. 7s.
Robert Ward, 300½ strait cloths, £6 2s. 6d. Subs. 6s. 1½d.
John Warnur [?], 9 cloths. Value £12. Subs. 12s.
John Buklond, 200 strait cloths, 70s.; 40 manttall [cloths], £6.
    Value £9 10s. 0d. Subs. 9s. 6d.
[John Piper, the same John Warnur, and Thomas Barber make
up the rest of the freight with corn.]

. . . .
[Name of Ship perished.]
    John Dandson, 6 cloths . . . . . .
    William Burton, 30 cloths . . . . . .
    . . . . . . strait cloths . . . . . .
    The same John Wisdom, 18 [?] cloths. . . . . . . Subs. 24s. 4d.
    Richard Batte, 12 cloths, £16; . . . strait cloths . . . . . . ;
      2 coverlets, 6s. 8d. Value £20 11s. 8d. Subs. 20s. 7d.
    William Bridd, 26 cloths. Value £39. Subs. 39s.
    William Belesby, 3 cloths. Value £4. Subs. 4s.
    William of the Hill, 10 cloths. Value £15. Subs. 15s.
    Thomas Doncastre, 10 cloths. Value £15. Subs. 15s.
    Richard Aglion, 12 cloths. Value £18. Subs. 18s.
    William Asliott, 1 cloth. Value 26s. 8d. Subs. 16d.
    Adam Brigge, 11 cloths, £17 10s. 0d.; . . . dozens of strait
      cloths, 35s.; 6 coverlets, 20s. Value £20 5s. 0d. Subs.
      20s. 3d.
  The Ship of John Suyt . . . .
    Thomas Howme, 10 cloths, and . . . [dozens] of strait cloths,
      £10 10s. 0d. . . . . . .
    Roger Burton, 12 cloths, £16; . . . . stones of calf skins, 6s. 4d.
    Value £16 6s. 4d. Subs. 16s. 5d.
    John Rauston, 30 cloths, £36. Subs. 36s.
        Sum [total]: Values . £77 18s. 4d.
             Subs. . 77s. 11d.

  The Ship of Arnald Jacobson, called the *Godbyrade of Roterdam*,
sailed the same day.
    Peter Johnson, 3½ cloths. Value £4 18s. 0d. Subs. 4s. 11d.
    The same Peter for 100 stones of calf skins. Val. 10s. Subs. 6d.
        Sum: Values . 108s.
          Sub. . 5s. 5d.

  The Ship of Richard Megson called the . . . .
    The same Richard, 4½ cloths . . . . . .
    William Bridde, 23 cloths . . . . . .
    William of Walton, 16 cloths . . . . . .
    Walter Chery, 10½ cloths, . . . ; 6 dozens of strait cloths, 20s.
    Robert Squier, 18½ cloths. Value £27 15s. 0d. Subs. 27s. 9d.
    John Stalker, 5 cloths. Value £13 6s. 8d. Subs. 13s. 4d.
    William Pund, 8 cloths. Value £12. Subs. 12s.
    William Burchon, 8½ cloths. Value £13 3s. 4d. Subs. 13s. 2d.
    William Huggatt, 10 cloths and 2 coverlets. Value £15 6s. 8d.
      Subs. 15s. 4d.
    Robert of the Hill, 1½ cloths. Value 40s. Subs. 2s.
        Sum: Values . £164 and 20s.
          Subs. . £8 4s. 1d.

  The Ship of William Blakeney, called the *Trinity of Hull*, sailed
the same day.
    Richard Chaundeler, 50 cloths, £65; 10 coverlets . . . . . .
    John Bakker, 1 cloth, ... Subs. 20d.

Richard of Sourby, 10 cloths without grain, ... Subs. 15s.
The same William Blakeney, ... Subs. 3s. 0d.
William Witton. [Other names and figures illegible.]

The Ship of Richard Cotes, called the *Cristofre of Hull*, sailed the same day.

[The whole of the lading of this ship consists of corn and other goods, save 40s. worth of linen cloth, and 1¼ woollen cloth, the latter shipped by William Brydd, value 40s., with subsidy thereon of 2s.]

[The particulars of the lading of the next ship of John . . . . . . are nearly obliterated. The following two names are decipherable:]

John Derfeld, 14 cloths. Value £18 13s. 4d. Subs. 18s. 8d.
John Buklond, 4 dozens of strait cloths. Value 13s.4d. Subs.8d.

Sum: Values . £42 10s. 0d.
Subs 42s. 6d.

The Ship of Robert Rayner, called the *Clement of York*, sailed the same day.

John Buklond, 4 cloths, 106s. 8d.; . . . strait cloths, 35s.;
10 " mantilclothes " . . . . . .

The Ship of Thomas P[arkour] . . . . . .
Thomas Parkour, . . . cloths . . . . . .
William Marchard [?], 5 cloths . . . . . .
Thomas F . . . . . , 12 cloths . . . . . .
William Boteler, 3 cloths . . . . . .
William Raudon, 5½ cloths. Value £7. Subs. 7s.
William Thornelay, 4½ cloths, ...; 100 strait cloths, 30s.
Value £7 15s. 0d. Subs. 7s. 9d.
Henry Braken, 6 cloths, £9 2s. 0d.; . . . . . Value £9 4s. 0d.
Subs. 9s. 4d.
William Terry, 16 cloths without grain, ... Subs. 24s.
Robert Ward, 8 cloths, £12 [6s. 8d.?]; 4 dozens strait cloths,
13s. 4d. Value £13. Subs. 13s.
Richard Chace, 18½ cloths. Value £28. Subs. 28s.
William of Lescham, 31 cloths, ...; 400 strait cloths.
Laurence . . . . . .
John Witte [?], 1½ cloth . . . . . .
Henry Wyman, 40 cloths, £60; 4 coverlets, 13s. 4d. [?].
John Wyncke, . . . cloths, £28 10s. 0d.; 2 coverlets, 6s. 8d.
Value £28 16s. 8d. Subs. 28s. 10d.
John Granby, 16 cloths, £22 8s. 4d. Subs. 22s. 8d.
John Spalding, . . cloths, ... Subs. 16d.
John Candeler, 20½ cloths, ...
John Bolton, 16 cloths, £24; 6 coverlets, 20s. . . . .
William Worsopp, 16½ cloths, £26; 3 dozens strait cloths, 10s.
. . . . . . Subs. 26s. 6d.

. . . .
Henry Preston, 11 cloths, £14 13s. 4d. . . . . . .
Robert Louth, 28 cloths, £42 13s. 0d. [?].
Thomas of the Gare, 20 cloths, ...; 3 doz. strait cloths

Robert Duffeld, .. cloths ......

Robert ....., 2½ cloths ......

The Ship of Henry Rolle, called . . . .

John Duffeld, 10 cloths ......

Robert Warde, 40 stones of fat (*cepi*), ...; 5 doz. " mantilclothes," 40s. ......

Peter Ruksy, 5 cloths ......

Richard Russell, 100 calf skins ......

Robert Ingram, 4½ cloths.

Sum: Values . £33 and 20d.

Subs. . 33s. 1d.

The Ship of John Blaktofft, of Hull, sailed the same day.

The same John Blaktofft ......

John Smyth, 4 cloths ......

William Hillom [?], 10 cloths ......

The Ship of John Flaymburgh, called the *Seynt mari* [*shipp* ?],
sailed the same day.

Thomas Foutteney [?], 30 quarters of corn ......

The same John Flaymburgh ......

[The rest of the lading of this ship was corn, except 86 stones of
fat (*cepi*).]

The Ship of Gerard Pierson, called the *Chrystofre of Sluys*, sailed
the same day.

Reginald Ward, 5 cloths, £6; 100 stones of fat (*cepi*),
£4 10s. 0d. Value £10 10s. 0d. Subs. 10s. 6d.

The same Reginald for 300 calf skins. Value £55. Subs.
55s. 9d. [?].

William of Melburn, 2 cloths, 66s. 8d.; 100 calf skins, 16s. 8d.
...... Subs. 4s. 2d.

The same William Melburn, 1 cloth. Value 26s. 8d. Subs.
16d.

The Ship of John Roulott, called the *Maudelyn of Hull*, sailed
the first day of April.

John Roulott, 2½ cloths. Value 70s. Subs. 3s. 6d.

Robert of Kilyngholme, ½ a cloth without grain. Value 10s.
Subs. 6d.

John of Knolles, 16 cloths without grain. Value £20. Subs.
20s.

[Hiatus.]

John ......

Walter Dymelton, 6 cloths ......

Thomas Swan, 6 cloths, ...; 80 stones of fat (*cepi*), 60s.;
6 dacres of calf skins ......

Sum: Values . ...

Subs. . 30s. 2d.

The Ship of Peter Hayn, called the *Cristofre of Middelburgh*,
sailed the same day.

Henry Preston, 9 cloths. Value £11. Subs. 11s.

Robert Warde, 3 cloths, £4; 250 strait cloths, £4 7s. 6d.

Value £8 7s. 6d.   Subs. 8s. 4½d.
   Sum: Values . £19 7s. 6d.
     Subs. . 19s. 4½d.

The Ship of John Pirson, called the ....
Richard Aghen, 10 cloths ......
Henry Feght, 7 cloths ......
Albert Wyse, 200 stone of calf skins ......
Richard Bridsall, 4 cloths ......
   Sum: Values . £31 4s. 8d.
     Subs. . 31s. 3d.

The Ship of Giles, son of Peter, called the *Godberade of Camifer,* sailed the same day.
 Robert of the Hill, 6½ cloths, £8 12s. 0d.; 10 stone of feathers, 8s. 4d. Value £10 and 16d. Subs. 9s. 1d.
 William of Stade, 24 stone of fat (*cepi*), 20s. 5d.; 24 stone of feathers, 21s.; 11 stone of goat skins, 6s. 10d.; 450 stone of calf skins, £4 6s. 8d. Value £6 15s. 11d. Subs. 6s. 9¾d.
 The same John [*sic*] of the Hill, 200 calf skins ...... Value 33s. 8d.

The Ship of Mark Williamson ....
[No cloths.]

The Ship of Robert Beane [?], called the *Seyntmariebote of Barton,* sailed the same day.
 The same Robert, 8 chaldron of coals. Value 26s. 8d. Subs. 16d.
   Sum: Value . 26s. 8d.
     Subs. . 16d.

The Ship of William van Buske, called the *Cristofre of Durdraght,* sailed the same day.
 John of the Hill, 80 stones of fat (*cepi*). Value 66s. 8d. Subs. 3s. 4d.

The Ship of John Lacye, called the *Trinite of Danesic,* sailed the 2nd day of May.
Thomas Standissh, 80 quarters of corn ......
John Palmer ......
John of B ......
John of Knolles, 30 quarters of corn, £6 0s. 0d., [&] 1½ cloths, 40s. Value £8. Subs. 8s.
   Sum: Values . £36.
     Subs. . 36s.

The Ship of Thomas Symes [?], called the *Swan Ship of Barton-on-Humbre,* sailed the 12th of May.
[The freight was only corn, beans, and pease, the name of the consignors being Thomas Standissh and Thomas Symes.]

The Ship of John Wetherby, called the *Katherine of Hull,* sailed the 20th day.
 Peter Steller, 60 quarters of corn, £10; 200 strait cloths, 70s. Value £13 10s. 0d. Subs. 13s. 6d.

Thomas Parcour, 203 " dozans " of strait cloths.   Value £4.
Subs. 4s.

Magister [the master] and his mates (socii), 40 quarters of corn.
Value £8 6s. 8d.   Subs. 8s. 4d.

Sum: Values . £100 3s. 4d.
Subs.   .   £4 19s. 2d.

The Ship of Robert Utlawe, called the *James of Dansic* [?],
sailed the 24th day of May.

James of Bramham, 480 quarters of corn, £100; 60 quarters of
beans and pease, £8; 66 quarters of oats, £6.   Value £120.
Subs. £6.

The Ship of John Deneson, called the ....

The same John, 5 cloths, £6 13s. 4d.; 5 dacres of calf skins, 10s.

Sum: Values . £7 3s. 4d.
Subs.   .   7s. 2d.

The Ship of John Longe, called the *Katharine of Bayon,* sailed
the 28th of May.

[The freight of this ship consisted entirely of corn, save 96 stones
of fat (cepi)].

The Ship of Herman ....
[A hiatus.]

....., 6 coverlets, 20s.......

The same German [sic], 10 cloths without grain.   Value
£16 13s. 4d.   Subs. 16s. 8d.

William Ruston, 22 cloths, £33; 4 dozens of strait cloths,
13s. 4d.   Value £33 13s. 4d.   Subs. 33s. 8d.

John Whittgyft, 8 cloths, £12; 2 coverlets, 6s. 8d.   Value
£12 6s. 8d.   Subs. 12s. 4d.

Thomas Awebergh, 20 cloths, £33 6s. 8d.; 4 coverlets, 13s. 4d.
Value £34.   Subs. 34s.

Robert Dodyngton, 12 cloths, £20; 6 coverlets, 20s.   Value
£21.   Subs. 21s.

William Drinckleton, 4 cloths.   Value 106s. 8d.   Subs. 5s. 4d.

Thomas of the Gare, 15 cloths, £22 10s. 0d.; 2 coverlets, 6s.8d.
Value £22 16s. 8d.   Subs. 22s. 10d.

George Piper [?], 10 cloths.   Value £15.   Subs. 15s.

Robert Ward, 6½ cloths, £8 16s. 4d.; 100 strait cloths, 30s.
Value £10 8s. 4d.   Subs. 10s. 4d.

John Wragby, 150 and 1 quarter strait cloths.   Value 60s.
Subs. 3s.

Richard Wolston, 65½ cloths, 10 coverlets, 60s.   Value ......
Subs.......

Thomas Braken......

[Three or four names follow obliterated.]

The Ship of John ....

John Portier, 2 cloths......

Sum: Value . £2 10s. 0d.
Subs.   .   2s. 6d.

The Ship of William Johanson, called the *Seyntmarieshipp of Camifer*, sailed the same day.

> Thomas Hawme, 400 strait cloths. Value £8. Subs. 8s.
> > Sum: Value . £8.
> > Subs. . 8s.

The Ship of Stephen Hales, called the *Maudeleyn of* . . . . . , sailed the same day.

> William Maltby, 38 cloths . . . . . .
> Thomas Doncastre, 15 cloths . . . . . .
> John Roulet, 5½ cloths . . . . . .
> Robert Hakenall . . . . . .
> Thoms Kyrkeby, 4 cloths . . . . . .

The Ship of John Kyrkeby, called the . . . . . . *of Hull*, sailed the same day.

> John Parkour, 2½ cloths, 60s. . . . . . . Value 75s. Subs. 3s. 9d.
> . . . . . . Billeson, 2 dozens of strait cloths, 6s. 8d. Subs. 4d.
> > Sum: Values . £4 and 20d.
> > Subs. . 4s. 1d.

The Ship of Maynard son of Maynard, called the . . . . . . *of Roterdam*, sailed the same day.

> The same Maynard, 4 cloths, 106s.; . . . calf hides, 13s. 4d.
> Value. . . . . . .
> > Sum: Value . £6 0s. 0d.
> > Subs. . 6s.

The Ship of John Chapman, called the *Cutbert of Hull*, sailed the same day.

> Robert Midelton, for 6 cloths. Value £7 10s. 0d. Subs. 7s. 6d.
> > Sum: Value . £7 10s. 0d.
> > Subs. . 7s. 6d.

[The Ship] of Symon Johanson, called the *Skenwyke of Durdraght*, sailed the 12th day of June.

> 505 dickers of calf skins. Value 100s. Subs. 5s.
> > Sum: Value . 100s.
> > Subs. . 5s.

. . . .

[All particulars of a certain Ship obliterated.]

The Ship of Henry Roll, called the *Maudelayne of Camifer*, sailed the same day.

> Robert Warde, 4 cloths, 100s.; 100½ strait cloths, 56s. 4d.;
> 7 dozens of mantilclothes, 65s. Value £9 18s. 4d. Subs. 9s. 11d.
> The same Robert, . . . dacres of calf skins. Value £6 15s. 0d. Subs. 6s. 9d.
> Thomas of the Gare, 200 strait cloths. Value 73s. 4d. Subs. 3s. 8d.   Sum: Values . £21 6s. 8d.
> > Subs. . 21s. 4d.

The Ship of Thomas Danson, called the *Maudelayn of Hull*, sailed the 20th day of June.

John Roulott, 3½ cloths.   Value £4 and 20d.   Subs. 4s. 1d.
Robert Hokenale, 30 dacres of calf skins. Value 40s. Subs. 2s.
Sum: Values . £6 and 20d.
Subs. . 6s. 1d.

The Ship of Simon Johanson, called the *Skenkwwyn of D[urdraght]*, sailed the same day.
William Redhode, 5 cloths . . . . . .

The Ship of Nicholas Goldsmyth, called the *Marie knyght of* . . . . , sailed the first day of July.
The same Nicholas, 10 cloths.   Value £15.   Subs. 15s.
. . . . . , 3 cloths.   Value £4 10s. 0d.   Subs. 4s. 6d.
Thomas [?] Trompe, 3 cloths, . . . strait cloths.   Value £4 10s.
Subs. 4s. 6d.
John . . . . . . , 20 cloths.   Value £30.   Subs. 30s.
John [?] Wyman, 18 cloths . . . . . .

The Ship of John . . . .
[All the freight of this ship corn.]

The Ship of Peter . . . . . , [sailed] the same day.
. . . . . . Warde, 2 cloths . . . . . .
[About 6 more entries obliterated.]

The Ship of Adam Walker [?], ...
Robert Simmes, 200 strait cloths . . . . . .
John Topcliffe, 5½ cloths.   Value £7 6s. 8d.   Subs. 7s. 4d.
Sum: Values . £10 13s. 4d.
Subs. . 10s. 8d.

The Ship of Tydmann Potter, called the . . . . . . *of Roterdam*, sailed the . . . . . .
John Haukesworth, 102 dozens of strait cloths, 66s. 8d., [and
other merchandise].   Value £4 16s. 8d.   Subs. 4s. 10d.
[Other items are for coal, etc.]

The Ship of John Clerk, called the *Petre of Hull*, sailed the same day.
The same John for 3 cloths.   Value £4.   Subs. 4s.

The Ship of Robert Rayner . . . .
John Barkesworth . . . . . .
Sum: Value . 100s.
Subs. . 5s.

The Ship of Everard Medryk, called the . . . . *of Meinynge*, sailed the first day of August.
Andrew van Ruchen, 18 cloths.   Value £24.   Subs. 24s.
The same Everard, 25 cloths.   Value £35.   Subs. 35s.
Herman Malkyn, 7½ cloths.   Value £11 5s.   Subs. 11s. 3d.
Thomas Toth, 29½ cloths.   Value £49 3s. 4d.   Subs. 49s. 1d.
Tydeman Unkhorn, 1½ cloth.   Value 50s.   Subs. 2s. 6d.
Sum: Values . £121 18s. 4d.
Subs. . £6 and 23d.

The Ship of John Suyt, called the *Seynt marie shipp of Notyngham*, sailed the same day.

John Byngley, 2 cloths. Value 60s. Subs. 3s.

The Ship of John Bakker, called the . . . .

John Carleton, 11 cloths . . . . . .

John Stalker, 21½ cloths. Value £32 10s. 0d. Subs. 32s. 6d.

John Broun, 2 cloths. Value 66s. 8d. Subs. 3s. 4d.

. . . . . . Aglion, 16 cloths. Value £24 0s. 0d. Subs. 24s.

Thomas Paye, 1½ cloth. Value 45s. Subs. 2s. 4d.

John Tuckar, 8 cloths. Value £15. Subs. 15s.

Henry of Cassell [?], ½ a cloth. Value 20s. Subs. 12d.

Robert Howme, 60 cloths, £82 10s. 0d.; 4 dozens of strait cloths, 13s. 4d. Value £83 3s. 4d. Subs. £4 3s. 2d.

Sum: Values . £179 11s. 8d.

Subs. . £8 19s. 8d.

The Ship of John Ricard, called the *Cristofre of* . . . . . , sailed the same day.

The same John, 23 cloths, ...; and 3 " dozans " of strait cloths, 10s.

Sum: Value . £28.

Subs. . 28s.

The Ship of Godfry Malet, called the *Seynt Christofre of Crotay*, sailed the same day.

Roger . . . . . , 18½ and 1 quarter cloths. Value £32 10s. 0d. Subs. 32s. 6d.

Sum: Value . £32 10s. 0d.

Subs. . 32s. 6d.

The Ship of Oluf Henston [?], called the *Marieknyght of Gonesbergh*,[1] sailed the 10th day of August.

The same Oluph [*sic*], 1 cloth, 38s. 8d.; 6 coverlets, 18s. Value 56s. 8d. Subs. 2s. 10d.

Peter Johnson, 10 cloths. Value £15. Subs. 15s.

Godhard Ollyfson, 5 cloths, £7; 6 coverlets, 20s. Value £8. Subs. 8s.

Sum: Values . £25 16s. 8d.

Subs. . 25s. 10d.

[At foot of this membrane is written the total, viz.: Values £1680 17s. 0d. Subs. £84 0s. 10½d.]

The Ship of Giles, son of Peter, called the . . . . , sailed the same day.

William Munkton, 24 cloths. Value £32 15s. 0d. [?]. Subs. 32s. 9d.

Robert Hokenal, [hides] . . . . . .

The Ship of James Raynesberke, called the *Marieknyght of Camfer*, sailed the same day.

Andrew van Ruchen, 26 cloths. Value £36 10s. 0d. Subs. 36s. 6d. Sum: Value . £36 10s. 0d.

Subs. . 36s. 6d.

---

[1] Gonesbergh. Can this be Königsberg, on the Baltic, in East Prussia ?

The Ship of Peter Hayne, called the *Cristofre of Midelburgh*, sailed the 10th day of August.

Robert Ward, 303 dozens of strait cloths, 120s.; 6 stones of calf skins. Value £10 15s. 0d. Subs. 10s. 9d.

John Buklond, 200½ strait cloths . . . . . .

Robert Hokenall, . . . [hides] . . . . . .

William Godyff, 6 cloths without grain . . . . . .

Symon Palmyer, 5½ cloths . . . . . .

Robert Howme, 200 strait cloths . . . . . .

Henry Thurkeld, 11 [?] cloths . . . . . .

John Knolles, 7½ cloths, £10; and 5 dozens of strait cloths, 17s. 6d. Value £10 17s. 6d. Subs. 10s. 10½d.

Walter of Dymelton, 3 cloths. Value 75s. Subs. 2s. 9d.

William Melburne, 3½ cloths. Value £4 0s. 0d. Subs. 4s.

Sum: Values . £76 15s. 0d.

Subs. . 76s. 9d.

The Ship of John P . . . . , called the *Trinite of Hull*, sailed the 22nd [?] day of August.

Andrew Preston, [corn].

The Master (*magister*) and his mates (*socii*), [among other goods] 3 dozens of strait cloths. Value 10s.

John Foxstre, 1000 strait cloths. [Value £15.] Subs. 15s.

William Sallay, 402 dozens of strait cloths . . . . . .

The Ship of Symon Johanson, called . . . .

William Godife, 7 cloths, £8 15s. 0d.

William Aslot, 12½ cloths. Value £14 11s. 8d. Subs. 14s. 6d.

William Donyour, 10 cloths, £12.

Robert Ingram, 4½ cloths. Value 105s.

Robert Hokenall, 2½ cloths, 55s.

Thomas Doncastre, 16 cloths, £19 5s. 0d.; 2 coverlets, 7s.; 100 strait cloths, 35s.

Thomas of the Gare, 400 strait cloths, 105s.; 4 dozens of " mantilclothes," 25s.

Thomas Chery, 7 cloths . . . . . .

Robert Ward, 2 cloths . . . . . .

[About 6 names missing.]

John Preston, 2 dozen . . . . . .; 4 " mantill " [*sic*], 13s. 4d.

Sum: Values . £113 0s. 10d.

Subs. . 113s. 0¾d.

The Ship of Robert Rayner, called the *Clement of York*, sailed the first day of September.

John Apelton, 8 cloths without grain, £10 12s. 4d.; 200 strait cloths, 70s.; 2 dozens of " mantelclothes," 18s.; 6 " mantell " [*sic*], 20s.; 6 coverlets, 30s. Value £17 and 16d. Subs. 17s. 2d.

Robert Warde, 16 cloths . . . . . .; 200 strait cloths, 70s. Value . . . . . . Subs. 24s. 10d.

John Leversege, 6 coverlets. Val. 20s.

Robert Hokenall, ½ a cloth. Value 13s. 4d. Subs. 12d.

Sum: Values . £43 11s. 4d.
    Subs. .

The Ship of Thomas of P . . . .
[Eight items obliterated.]
. . . . . . of Bokyngham, 21 cloths . . . . . .
. . . . . . Parcour, 200½ strait cloths. Value £4 6s. 8d. Subs.
    4s. 4d.
John Symon, senr., 40 cloths, £60; 4 dozens of strait cloths,
    13s. 4d. Value £60 13s. 4d. Subs. 60s. 8d.
John Symon, junr., 14½ cloths and 2 dozens of strait cloths.
    Value £22 and 20d. Subs. 22s. 1d.
John Tutburye, 21½ cloths, £32; 6 coverlets, 40s. Value £34.
    Subs. 34s.
William Boukland, 1 cloth and a quarter. Value 30s. Subs.
    18d.
Henry Moustre, 22 cloths. Value £33. Subs. 33s.
Thomas Waghen, 12 cloths . . . . . . Subs. 18s.
Richard Aglion, 15½ [?] cloths . . . . . .
John Langton, 3 cloths . . . . . .
Henry Lakensmyth, 3 cloths . . . . . .
Henry Wyman, 6 cloths . . . . . .
William . . . . . , ½ a cloth . . . . . .
. . . . . , 8 cloths . . . . . .
. . . . . . of Malton, 3 cloths . . . . . .
John of the Hyll [?], 2½ cloths . . . . . .
William Ch . . . . . , 2 cloths . . . . . .
            Sum: Values . £519 12s. 4d.
                Subs. . £25 19s. 7½d.

[A considerable hiatus occupied by the freight of one ship.]

The Ship of John Dandson, ...
John Newby, 48 cloths, £62 5s. 0d.; and [?] strait cloths,
    16s. 8d. . . . . . .
Thomas Parcour, 10 cloths, £14 14s. 4d.; 200 strait cloths,
    70s. Value £18 10s. 0d.
John Gregge, 26½ cloths. Value £35 6s. 8d. . . . . .
William Godiffe, 4 cloths. Value £6. Subs. 6s.
John Dandson, 5½ cloths, £7 15s. 0d. Subs. 7s. 9d.
John Wisdom, 3½ cloths, £4 8s. 4d.; and 100 strait cloths, 35s.
    Value £6 3s. 4d. Subs. 6s. 2d.
John Wayt, 15 cloths . . . . . .

The Ship of Henry Rolleston [?], ...
John of Houden, 400 [strait] cloths . . . . . .
Robert Sauvage, 200 strait cloths . . . . . .
John Derfeld, 40 cloths. Value £53 6s. 8d. Subs. 53s. 4d.
John of Hull, 1 cloth. Value 25s. . . . . . .
Nicholas Waren, 1½ cloth. Value 35s. Subs. 35s.
Robert Ward, 200½ strait cloths. . . . . . . Subs. 3s. 2d.
William Mydelham, 8½ cloths. . . . . . . Subs. 11s. 4d.
Henry Rolle, 4 chaldrons of sea coal. . . . . . . Subs. 8d.

William Donyour, 1 cloth, 23s. 4d. . . . . . .
Richard of Hewik, 10 cloths. Value £12. Subs. 12s.
John Spaldynge of York, 10 cloths. Value £15. Subs. 15s.
Godfrey Upstall, [hides].
John Bromton, ½ a cloth. Value 10s. Subs. 6d.
Thomas Barbour, 6 cloths. Value £9. Subs. 9s.

[There is evidently something missing from the end of this compotus, as no total summing up appears.]

XII.

[E. $\frac{60}{2}$]

Printed
in Latin
in Frost's
Hull,
where the
imports
also are
given.

PARTICULARS OF THE ACCOUNT OF JOHN LEVERSEGG[1] AND JOHN
TUTTEBURY,[2] Collectors of the subsidy of our Lord the King; to wit,
of 8d. in the £ from the Feast of Easter in the 2nd year of King
Henry IV, to the 7th day of July next following in the year aforesaid,
by the view and witness of William Pound,[3] Controller there for the
same term.

1401
The Ship of John Bele, called *Marishipp of Midelburgh*, sailed
9th day of April.
    From Thomas Spicer, for 3 cloths without grain, val. 60s.,
    subsidy 2s.
    From Robert Ingrame, for 5½ cloths without grain, val. 110s.,
    subsidy 3s. 8d.
    From Dionisia Biset, 2 cloths without grain, val. 40s., subsidy
    16d.
    From John Anton, for ½ a cloth without grain [and] 9 stone
    of " thrommes " [thrums], val. 20s., subsidy 8d.
        Sum of values £11 10s. 0d., subsidy 7s. 8d.

The Ship of Edmund Thorne, called *Laur' of Hull*, sailed the 17th
day of April.
    From Robert Clark, for 1½ cloth without grain and ½ ell of
    strait cloth, value 45s., subs. 1s. 6d.
    From John Elys, for 20 cloths without grain [and] 5½ single
    coverlets, value £30, subs. 20s.
    From John Stillyngflete, for 8 cloths without grain [and] 3
    single coverlets, value £13, subs. 8s. 8d.
    From Henry Wyman for 21½ cloths without grain, value
    £32 5s. 0d., subs. 21s. 6d.

---

[1] John Leversegg or Liuersege, was one of the king's Customers and paid to
the Commonalty of the town of Hull 200 marks in two years, viz., 20th and
21st Ric. II, being in payment of 100 marks per annum, granted by the king
to the same Commonalty, to be taken annually out of the Customs. He was
Mayor of Hull in 1395 and 1397.

[2] John of Tuttebury was an eminent merchant and took an active part in
public affairs. Frost has a long note regarding him, p. 149. He was a Bailiff
of Hull in 1395, and Mayor in 1399.

[3] William Pound was Controller of the Subsidy at York, as we see, in 1399,
and had been a Bailiff of Hull in 1388. He was Mayor in 1396.

From John Sprowe, for 26 cloths without grain, value £39, subs. 26s.

From Thomas Swanland, for 30 cloths without grain, value £45, subs. 30s.

From Thomas Alkebarowe, for 4 cloths without grain [and] 3 single coverlets, value £6 16s. 8d., subs. 4s. 6¾d.

From John Wilton, for 10 cloths without grain [and] 3 dozen ells of strait cloth, value £15 10s. 0d., subs. 10s. 4d.

From Thomas Rillyngton, for 16 cloths without grain, value £24, subs. 16s.

From William Wrenchill, for 11 cloths without grain, value £16 10s. 0d., subs. 11s.

From the same Thomas Rillyngton, for 30 cloths without grain, value £45, subs. 30s.

From John Lofthous, for 35 cloths without grain, value £52 10s. 0d., subs. 35s.

From John Sprowe, for 10 cloths without grain, value £15, subs. 10s.

From Richard Bate for 20 cloths without grain, value £30, subs. 20s.

From Henry Preston, for 10 cloths without grain, value £15, subs. 10s.

From Robert Warde, 4 cloths without grain, value £6, subs. 4s.

From Richard Wigan, for 11 cloths without grain and 7½ single coverlets, value £18 6s. 8d., subs. 12s. 2¾d.

From William Eseby, for 4 cloths without grain, 3 dozen ells of strait cloth and 1 single coverlet, value £7, subs. 4s. 8d.

From the same [aforesaid] Richard Bate, for 10 cloths without grain, value £15, subs. 10s.

From the same John Lofthous, for 4 cloths without grain, value £6, subs. 4s.

From William Walton, for 2 cloths without grain, value 70s., subs. 2s. 4d.

Sum of values £437 13s. 4d.

Subs. £14 11s. 9½d.

The Ship of Richard Pirle called *Christopher of Hull*, sailed the same day.

From Stephen of the Dale, for 4 cloths without grain, value £6, subs. 4s.

The Ship of Robert Thorne, called *Bartholomew of Hull*, sailed the 20th day of April.

From the same Robert, for 200 ells of strait cloth, value 60s., subs. 2s.

The Ship of Robert Meleton, called *Jonet of Hull*, sailed the 26th day of April.

From William Terry, for 4 cloths without grain [and] 3 ells of strait cloth, value £9, subs. 6s.

The Ship of Robert Maisterson, called *George of Hull*, sailed on the 4th May.

From William Terry, for 6 cloths without grain, value £8, subs. 5s. 4d.

From John White for 2½ cloths without grain, value 66s. 8d., subs. 2s. 2¾d.

From John Gull, for 5 cloths without grain, value £7, subs. 4s. 8d.   Sum of values £18 6s. 8d.
Subsidy 12s. 2¾d.

The Ship of John Engson, called *Petre of Hull*, sailed the 6th day of May.

From John Rotse, for 16 cloths without grain [and] 40 'wagh'[1] of salt, value £22 13s. 4d., subs. 15s. 1½d.

From William Rolleston, for 8 cloths without grain and ½ single bedblanket, value £10 10s. 0d., subs. 7s.
Sum of values £33 3s. 4d.
Subsidy 22s. 1½d.

The Ship of Robert Johnetson, called *Gabriel of Hull*, sailed the 9th day of May.

From John Tuttebury, for 6 cloths without grain, value £6 10s. 0d.

The Ship of Peter Hayneson, called *Christopher of Camfer*, sailed the 18th day of May.

From Robert Ferriby, for 5 cloths without grain, value £6 10s. 0d., subsidy 4s. 4d.

From William Selander, for 1½ cloth without grain and 236 calf haired fells [hides], value 75s., subs. 2s. 6d.

From Nicholas Brabant, for ¼th of a cloth without grain, value 10s., subs. 4d.

From Baldwin Van Trude, for 100 stones of thrums, value £7 10s. 0d., subs. 5s.

The Ship of John Dobson, called *Godsknight of Newhaven*, sailed the same day.

From the same John for 4½ cloths without grain, 120 haired calf fells, 4 chaldrons of sea coals [and] 2 stone of feathers, value £9 1s. 4d., subs. 6s. 0¾d.

From John Lamson for 2 cloths and 2 quarters and ½ without grain [and] 1 single coverlet, value 73s. 4d., subs. 2s. 5½d.

The Ship of John Hury, called *Christopher of York*, sailed the 27th May.

From William Melburn for 13 cloths without grain, value £17 6s. 8d., subs. 11s. 6¾d.

The Ship of Nicholas Umbelampe, called *Christopher of Camp'ver*, sailed the 29th May.

From the same Nicholas for 1 cloth without grain, value 30s., subs. 12d.

---

[1] Wagh=weigh, a denomination of weight still used in the Orkney and Shetland Isles, equal to 1 cwt., as "a weigh of fish."   See Jamieson's "Scottish Dictionary."

The Ship of Ludkin Onberdstons, called *Mariknight of Dansk* [Dantzic], sailed the 6th day of June.

From the same Ludkin, for 1 cloth without grain, value 40s., subs. 16d.

From Tidemañ Rodehous, for 14 cloths without grain, value £28, subs. 18s. 8d.

The Ship of Nicholas Rotormund, called the *Mariknight of Breme[n]*, sailed the 7th day of June.

From John Amolonk, for 8½ cloths without grain, value £14 18s. 0d., subs. 9s. 11½d.

From Claus' [? Claudius] Scape, for 5½ cloths without grain, value £10, subs. 6s. 8d.

From Tidman Hemell, for 5 cloths without grain, value £10, subs. 6s. 8d.

From Leofard Van Camynade, for 10½ cloths without grain, value £18 10s. 0d., subs. 12s. 4d.

From the above Tidman Hemell, for 1 piece of "wersted," value 15s., subs. 6s.

Sum of the values £54 3s. 0d.
Subs. 36s. 1½d.

The Ship of William Johnson, called *Christopher of Camfer*, sailed the 12th day of June.

From John Waghen, for 3 cloths without grain, value 60s., subs. 2s.

From William Burton, for 2 cloths without grain, value 40s., subs. 16d.

The Ship of William Robynson, called *Myghell [Michael] of Hull*, sailed the 14th day of June.

From Liffard Van Campynad, for 20 cloths without grain, value £40, custom 6s. 8d.

From Henry Vanderbek, for 11 cloths without grain, value £20, subs. 13s. 4d.

From the same Henry, for 1 single coverlet, value 10s., subs. 4d.

From Gerwin Duñe, for 20 cloths without grain and 2 single coverlets, value £40 13s. 4d., subs. 27s. 0¾d.

From William Burton, for 5 cloths without grain, value £6, subs. 4s.

From John Sessay, for 10 cloths without grain, value £15, subs. 10s.

From Robert Clerk, for 3 cloths without grain, value 60s., subs. 2s.   Sum of values £125 3s. 4d.
Subsidy £4 3s. 5½d.

The Ship of Thomas Hayneson, called *Leonard of Hull*, sailed the 16th day of June.

From Gerwin Duñe, for 12 cloths without grain [and] 1 single coverlet, value £24 6s. 8d., subs. 16s. 2¾d.

From Robert Atte Wode, for 7½ cloths without grain, value £10, subs. 6s. 8d.

From William Burton, for 5 cloths without grain, value £6,
subs. 4s.

From John Sessay, for 10 cloths without grain, value £15,
subs. 10s.

From Thomas White, for 5½ cloths without grain, value
£8 5s. 0d., subs. 5s. 6d.

From Richard Thoresby, for 11½ cloths without grain, value
£17 5s. 0d., subs. 11s. 6d.

Sum of values £80 16s. 8d.

Subsidy £53 0s. 10¾d.

The ship of Henry Evardson, called *Seint Johnsknight of Weryng*,
sailed the 15th June. [No cloth.]

The Ship of Arnald Spekels, called *Mariknyght of Dansk'*, sailed
the same day.

From Gerwin Duñe, for 10½ cloths without grain [and] 1 single
bedblanket, value £21 6s. 8d., subs. 14s. 2½d.

From the same Arnald Spekels, for 21 cloths without grain,
value £42, subs. 28s.

From Henry Yhager, for 9 cloths without grain [and] ½ a single
bedblanket, value £17 3s., subs. 11s. 5¼d.

From Martin Wyt, for 8½ cloths without grain, value £16,
subs. 10s. 8d.

From John Flowell, for 2 cloths without grain, value £4,
subs. 2s. 8d.

From William Symondson, for 100 ells of strait cloths, value
35s., subs. 14d.

From Bernard Doweman, for 7½ cloths without grain, value
£15, subs. 10s.

From Henry Wyman, for 11 cloths without grain [and] 1 single
bedblanket, value £16 15s. 0d., subs. 11s. 2d.

Sum of values £133 19s. 8d.

Subs. £4 9s. 4d.

The Ship of Henry Chaumpaigne, called *Trinite of Hull*, sailed
the same day.

From John Wisdom, for 100 ells and ½ an ell of strait cloth
[and] half a single bedblanket, value 47s., subs. 19d.

From William Burton, for 5 cloths without grain, value £6,
subs. 4s.

From Henry Braken, for 8 cloths without grain, value £12,
subs. 8s.

Sum of values £20 7s. 0d.

Subs. 13s. 7d.

The Ship of Thomas Scardeburgh, called *Kateryn of Hull*, sailed
the 17th June.

From John Humbilton, for 3½ cloths without grain, value 70s.,
subs. 2s. 4d.

The Ship of James Pierson, called *Garderote Van Gose*, sailed the
18th day of June.

From William Stokes, for 6½ cloths without grain [and] 6 single bedblankets [and] 60 quarters of oats, value £18 15s. 0d., subs. 12s. 6d.

From the same James Pierson, for ½ cloth without grain, value 17s., subs. 17d.

From John Goode, for 2½ cloths without grain [and] 22 stones of fat, value 74s., subs. 2s. 5¾d.

Sum of values £23 6s. 0d.

Subsidy 15s. 6¾d.

The Ship of John Lewe, called *Pasdagh of Skiddam*, sailed the same day.

From John Touneley, for 1 cloth without grain, value 37s., subs. 15d.

From Gilbert Neyse for the purchase of half [the moiety] of the said ship, value £8 6s. 8d., subs. 5s. 6¾d.

Sum of values £10 3s. 8d.

Subsidy 6s. 9¾d.

The Ship of Hugh Marflete, called *Mighell of York*, sailed the 24th day of June.

From Thomas Friston for 3 cloths without grain and 1 single bedblanket, value 66s. 8d., subs. 2s. 2¾d.

The Ship of John Shildon, called *Eleyn of Hull*, sailed the 6th day of July.

From John Dranfeld, for 1 cloth [and] a quarter and half a quarter (1 *qr't di'*) without grain [and] 7 fother of lead in 40 pieces, value £30, subs. 20s.

Sum of this roll. Values £113 10s. 2½d. Subs. 75s. 9d.

XIII.

[E. $\frac{62}{5}$]

Issues
Kynges-
ton-super-
Hull.

1464 PARTICULARS OF THE ACCOUNT OF JOHN DEY,[1] Collector of the Customs and Subsidy of our Lord the King in the port of the town of Kyngeston-on-Hull; to wit, from the Feast of St. Michael the Archangel, in the fourth year of the reign of King Edward the Fourth (before which feast John Dey and John Grene will have to account) until the 16th day of November, then next following; To wit, for 48 days, by view [supervision] of Thomas Blount, Controller there during the same time.

The Ship of John Brand, called the *Trenyte of Hull*, sailed the second day of October in the 4th year aforesaid.

The same [mentioned before in connection with lead] Thomas Beverlay, a denizen, 16 cloths without grain.

The same John Kent, a denizen [mentioned before in connection with lead], 14 cloths without grain.

[1] John Deye in 1463 was Sheriff of Hull, and in 1466 and also in 1469 Mayor of that town.

The same William Todd, a denizen [mentioned before in con-
nection with lead], 12 cloths without grain.
Thomas Wrangish, denizen, 16 cloths without grain.
William Brounflete, denizen, 16 cloths without grain.
Thomas Scotten, denizen, 12 cloths without grain.
Robert Taylour, denizen, 13 cloths without grain.
John Gaunt, denizen, 40 cloths without grain.
John Tong, denizen, 14 cloths without grain.
William Tole, denizen, 13 cloths without grain.
John Challowe, denizen, 12 cloths without grain.
William Welles, denizen, 13 cloths without grain.
John Michell, denizen, 39 cloths without grain.
Michael Holgate, denizen, 12 cloths without grain.
John Hogeson, denizen, 6 cloths without grain.
Robert Pyllett, denizen, 6 cloths without grain.
John Scalstorn, denizen, 6 cloths without grain.
John Holme, denizen, 7 cloths without grain.
Edmund Copyndale, denizen, 5 cloths without grain.
William Lorymer, denizen, 8 cloths without grain.
Ralph Langton, denizen, 4 cloths without grain.
Richard Symson, denizen, 4 cloths without grain.
William Thorp, denizen, 12 cloths without grain.
William Brompton, 9 cloths without grain.
The same John Michell, denizen, 22 cloths without grain.
The same William Brompton, denizen, 5 cloths without grain.

Hans

Henry Wynsty, Hans, 20 cloths without grain.   Value £40.
Subsidy in Controller's Roll.
Hans Towler, Hans, 15 cloths without grain and 4 yds. Value
£30. Subs. [*blank*].
Andrew Sarder, Hans, 12 cloths without grain. Value £24.
Subs. [*blank*].
Hans Harswyk, Hans, 15½ cloths and 7½ yds. without grain.
Value £31. Subs. [*blank*].
Thomas Stevenson, denizen, 18 cloths without grain.
Robert Jakson, denizen, 12 cloths without grain.
Sum of this Ship:
Cloths of denizens without grain, whereof 365 cloths.
Customs £21 0s. 7d.
Cloths of the Hans without grain, 62½ and 11½ yds.
Customs £8 13s. 2½d.

The Ship of John Hayles, called the *Marie Durras* of Cales,
sailed the same day.
Peter Gyle, denizen, 8 cloths without grain.
The same Peter, denizen, 5 dacres of tanned hides.
Sum of this Ship:
Denizens, 8 cloths without grain. Customs 9s. 4d.
Value of merchandize of denizens, £4. Subs. 4s.

The Ship of Clement Hyll, called the *Peter of Hull,* sailed the 16th
day of November.

John Redesdale, denizen, 13 cloths without grain.
Robert Jakson, denizen, 8 cloths without grain.
Thomas Dalehous, denizen, 7 cloths without grain.
Robert Brian, denizen, 7 cloths without grain.
William Ratlyff, denizen, 6 cloths without grain.
John Chester, denizen, 12 cloths without grain.
John Gylyott, denizen, 20 cloths without grain.
John Whitfeld, denizen, 8 cloths without grain.
Robert Taylour, denizen, 12 cloths without grain.
John Michell, denizen, 12 cloths without grain.
William Lematon, denizen, 11 cloths without grain.
Nicholas Halpley, denizen, 12 cloths without grain.
John Gaunt, denizen, 14 cloths without grain.
The same John Redesdale, denizen, 1 fother of lead.
    Sum of this Ship:
        Cloths of denizens without grain, 142 cloths.
        Customs £8 5s. 8d.

The Ship of Robert Spofford, called *Mariflower of Hull*, sailed the same day.
    John Hadylsey, denizen, 7 cloths without grain.
    Sum of this Ship:
        7 cloths without grain of denizens.
        Customs 8s. 2d.

The Ship of Peter Jacobson, called the *Gabriel of Weststowe*, sailed the same day.
    [Freighted only with lead.]

The Ship of John Porter, called *Mare of Hull*, sailed the same day.
    John Kent, denizen, 25 cloths without grain.
    Thomas Beverlay, denizen, 18 cloths without grain.
    John Gyllyott, denizen, 12 cloths without grain.
    William Lematon, denizen, 10 cloths without grain.
    William Welles, denizen, 4 cloths without grain.
    John Fereby, denizen, 7 cloths without grain.
    John Chellowe, denizen, 10 cloths without grain.
    William Brounflete, denizen, 12 cloths without grain.
    Richard York, denizen, 10 cloths without grain.
    William Lambe, denizen, 12 cloths without grain.
    John Tong, denizen, 12 cloths without grain.
    William Stansteley, denizen, 12 cloths without grain.
    Sum of this Ship:
        Cloths of denizens without grain, 144.
        Customs £8 8s. 0d.

XIV.

[E. $\frac{62}{7}$]

PARTICULARS OF THE ACCOUNT OF JOHN DEYE AND JOHN BRYDDE,
Collectors of the Customs and Subsidy of the King of wool, hides,

1465

etc., in the Port of the Town of Kyngeston-on-Hull in the 5th year of the King aforesaid [Edward IV], from the 18th day of March until the Feast of St. Michael then next following, To wit for half a year and 13 days.

The Ship of Peter Tolle, called the *Mawdeleyne of Cawmfer*, sailed the 16th day of May in the aforesaid year.

Clawys Molner, Hans, for 1 cloth without grain.

Sum of cloths: 1 cloth.   Customs 12*d*.

The Ship of Cornelius of Grave, called the *Mary of Hull*, sailed the 20th day of May in the year aforesaid.

Cloths without grain : denizens.

John Darrys, denizen, 10 cloths without grain.

John Kent, denizen, 7 cloths without grain.

Sum of cloths without grain 17.   Customs 19*s*. 10*d*.

The Ship of John Atthaye, called *Mary of Pisco*[1] of Spain, sailed the 20th day of May in the year aforesaid.

Cloths of aliens without grain.

John Russe, alien, 7 cloths and 2½ yds. without grain.

John Perych, alien, 3½ cloths and 8 yds. without grain.

Nicholas of Pusco, alien, 1½ cloth and 1½ yds. without grain.

Stephen Spanyerd, alien, 2½ cloths without grain.

Ramus of Spayne, alien, 4 cloths and 3½ yds. without grain.

Martin of Kenterya, alien, 2 cloths without grain.

John Bretayne, alien, 3 cloths and 5 yds. without grain.

The same John for 4½ cloths without grain.

Sum of cloths, 28½ and 8½ yds.   Customs 79*s*. 4¼*d*.

The Ship of John Thomas, called the *Trinite of Corukirnoll*, sailed the 26th day of May in the year aforesaid.

The same John, alien, 11 cloths without grain.

Sum of cloths, 11.   Customs 30*s*. 3*d*.

The Ship of Henry Scrowder, called *Mary of Dansk*, sailed the 29th day of May in the year aforesaid.

The same Henry Scrowder, Hans, 1 cloth without grain.

Laurence Grote, Hans, 1 cloth without grain, value 20*s*.

Peter Streinkynder, Hans, 1 cloth without grain, value 20*s*. 4*d*.

Claus Harskyn, Hans, 1 cloth without grain, value 20*s*. 8*d*.

John Court, Hans, 2½ yds. without grain, value 2*s*. 6*d*.

Sum of Hans cloths, 4 cloths 2½ yds.   Customs 3*s*. 1¼*d*.

Hans cloths not certified, 3 cloths and 2½ yds. Customs above 12*d*. charged above, 5*s*. 5¼*d*.

Subs. 3*s*. 2*d*.

Value of said 3 cloths 2½ yds., for subsidy, 63*s*. 3*d*.   Subsidy 3*s*. 2*d*.

The Ship of Michael Kykebus, called the *Cristofer of Dansk*, sailed the 11th day of June in the year aforesaid.

Jeremyas van Rode, Hans, 22 cloths without grain.

Sum of this Ship, 22 cloths.   Customs 22*s*.

---

[1] *Pisco*. Is this intended for Biscay, a port in the north of Spain, on the gulf of the same name ?

Aliens'
cloth
without
grain.

The Ship of John Potter, called the *Maryfloure of Hull*, sailed the 30th day of June in the year aforesaid.

John Ducheyn, alien, 30 cloths without grain. Customs £4 2s. 6d.

Denizens'
cloth
without
grain.

The Ship of Henry Stabyll, called the *Cristofer of Hull*, sailed the 12th day of July in the year aforesaid.

Nicholas Rysworth, denizen, 7 cloths without grain.
Sum of denizens' cloths, 7. Customs 8s. 2d.

Denizens'
cloth
without
grain.

The Ship of William Swan, called the *Trinite of Flambergh*, sailed the 2nd day of September in the aforesaid year.

John Chester, denizen, 8 cloths without grain.
Sum of cloths of denizens, 8. Customs 9s. 4d.

Denizens'
cloth
without
grain.

The Ship of Thomas Jonson, called the *Trinite of York*, sailed the 12th day of September in the year aforesaid.

Nicholas Riseworthe, denizen, 31 cloths without grain. Customs 36s. 2d.

The Ship of Colyn of Bretan, called the *Remest of Deipe*, sailed the same day [12th July].

Jeny Coyt, alien, 5 cloths without grain.
Sum of cloths, 5. Customs 13s. 9d.

XV.

[E. $\frac{62}{14}$]

Kynges-
ton-on-
Hull.

1471

PARTICULARS OF THE ACCOUNT OF WILLIAM SWELYNGTON AND THOMAS ALCOK,[1] Collectors of both the Great and Little Customs of our Lord the King, and also of the Subsidies, from the 18th day of June, in the 11th year of the reign of King Edward the Fourth, after the Conquest of England, until the Feast of St. Michael then next following, for a quarter of a year and 12 days.

The Ship of John Van Caliote, called the *Jesu* [?] *of Camifere*, sailed the 28th day of June, in the 11th year of the reign of King Edward IVth.

Giles Englissh, denizen, 26 cloths without grain.
Thomas Beverlay, denizen, 8 cloths without grain.
John Skelton, denizen, 12 cloths without grain.
Thomas Gaunte, denizen, 12 cloths without grain.
Robert Alcok, denizen, 4 cloths without grain.
John Gilliott, denizen, 22 cloths without grain.
The same John Skelton, denizen, 8 cloths without grain.
John Wilson, denizen, 12 cloths without grain.

---

[1] Thomas Alcock was son of William Alcock, of Hull, a wealthy merchant there. Thomas was brother (to quote Canon Raine) " of the pious and munificent Bishop John Alcock, of Ely." Another brother, Robert, a merchant, in his will (1483) bequeaths to John Alcock, his brother Thomas's son, the fourth part of a ship called the *George*. Thomas Alcock the Collector of Customs was executor along with the widow of his father William Alcock's will. Thomas Alcock was mayor of Hull in 1478.

C

William Sherparowe, denizen, 3 cloths without grain.
William Eland, denizen, 10 cloths without grain.
Roger Bussell, denizen, 6 cloths without grain.
John Recard, denizen, 4 cloths without grain.
John Herper, denizen, 10 cloths without grain.
William Goldsmyth, denizen, 3 cloths without grain.
John Robynson, denizen, 4 cloths without grain.
The same William Goldsmyth, denizen, 2 cloths without grain.
Nicholas Rysshworth, denizen, 8 cloths without grain.
Edmund Gryngley, denizen, 5 cloths without grain.
The same Roger Bussell, denizen, 3 cloths without grain.
Robert Bower, denizen, 5 cloths without grain.
John Herde, denizen, 6 cloths without grain.
William Whyte, denizen, 4 cloths without grain.
Sum of cloths of denizens without grain, 176.
Customs £10 5s. 4d.

The Ship of Hayn Willmson, called the *Marie of Westersorwe*, sailed the same day.

Cloths without grain of denizens.

Giles Englissh, denizen, 6 cloths without grain.
Mariona Kentt, denizen, 11 cloths without grain.
John Skelton, denizen, 12 cloths without grain.
The same Mariona Kentt, denizen, 11 cloths without grain.
Sum of cloths of denizens without grain, 40.
Customs 46s. 8d.

ULNAGERS' ROLLS FOR YORKSHIRE.

I.

Ulnager's Roll for cloths in East Riding

[Exchequer Accounts, 101, Bundle $\frac{345}{21}$]

Estrith.   PARTICULARS OF THE ACCOUNT OF THOMAS SCORBURGH, Ulnager of the King, in the " Estrithinge," in the County of York, the City of York excepted, as well within Liberties as without, by patent Writ of the King, dated the first day of November in His second year, remaining in the hands of the said Thomas; to wit, regarding the subsidy and ulnage, and forfeitures of cloths there from the **1378,** aforesaid first day of November in the second year, until the 23ᵈ **1378-9** day of January then next following.

Of Roger Ailsy, for 7 cloths of Assize
without grain.   Subs. 2s. 4d.   Ulnage 3½d.
,, John Aslaby, 5 of these cloths.   Subs. 20d.   Ulnage 2½d.
,, John Waynflete, 4 of these cloths.   Subs. 16d.   Ulnage 2d.
,, William Ake, 4½ of these cloths.   Subs. 18d.   Ulnage 2¼d.
,, William Knolles, 3 of these cloths.   Subs. 12d.   Ulnage 1½d.
,, James Flemyng, 1½ of these cloths.   Subs. 6d.   Ulnage ¾d.
,, John Burton, 3½ of these cloths.   Subs. 14d.   Ulnage 1¾d.
,, Katerina Wrangill, 6 of these cloths.   Subs. 2s.   Ulnage 3d.
,, Ingelram Ducheman, 5 of these cloths.   Subs. 20d.   Ulnage 2½d.
,, Robert Bysett, 4 of these cloths.   Subs. 16d.   Ulnage 2d.
,, Thomas Goldsmyth, 1 of these cloths.   Subs. 4d.   Ulnage ½d.
,, Thomas Flour, 1½ of these cloths.   Subs. 6d.   Ulnage ¾d.
,, Simon Grymesby, 6 of these cloths.   Subs. 2s.   Ulnage 3d.
,, Walter Dymelton, 4 of these cloths.   Subs. 16d.   Ulnage 2d.
,, John Merflete, 5 of these cloths.   Subs. 20d.   Ulnage 2½d.
,, Matilda of Thorne, 6 of these cloths.   Subs. 2s.   Ulnage 3d.
,, William Batte, 7½ of these cloths.   Subs. 2s.   Ulnage 3¾d.
,, William Terry, 9 of these cloths.   Subs. 3s.   Ulnage 4½d.
,, William Chery, 8 of these cloths.   Subs. 2s. 8d.   Ulnage 4d.
,, John Battey, 4 of these cloths.   Subs. 20d.   Ulnage 2½d.
,, Robert Standyn, 8½ of these cloths.   Subs. 2s.10d.   Ulnage 4¼d.
,, John Anlaby, 11 of these cloths.   Subs. 3s. 8d.   Ulnage 5½d.
,, John Legett, 5 of these cloths.   Subs. 20d.   Ulnage 2½d.
,, John Saundreson, 6 of these cloths.   Subs. 2s.   Ulnage 3d.
,, John Browne, 4½ of these cloths.   Subs. 18d.   Ulnage 2¼d.
,, John Godisman, 4 of these cloths.   Subs. 16d.   Ulnage 2d.

Of Agnes Capett, 9 of these cloths.   Subs. 3s.   Ulnage 4½d.
,, Richard, servant of Robert, 19 of these
    cloths.   Subs. 6s. 4d. Ulnage 9½d.
,, Simon Bedale, 22½ of these cloths. Subs. 7s. 6d. Ulnage 11¼d.
,, William of Cotyngham, 3½ of these
    cloths.   Subs. 14d.   Ulnage 1¾d.
,, Thomas Swanland, 21 of these cloths. Subs. 7s.   Ulnage 10½d.
,, Thomas Scorburgh, 14½ of these cloths. Subs. 4s. 8d. Ulnage 7¼d.
,, John Duke, 1½ of these cloths.   Subs. 7d.   Ulnage ¾d.
,, William Ithun, 7 of these cloths. Subs. 2s. 4d. Ulnage 3½d.
,, Thomas Autays, 18 of these cloths. Subs. 6s.   Ulnage 9d.
,, John Huntyngton, 14 of these cloths. Subs. 4s. 8d. Ulnage 7d.
,, Walter Dunham, 2 of these cloths. Subs. 8d.   Ulnage 1d.
,, William Wylkoo, ½ a cloth of this
    kind.   Subs. 2d.   Ulnage ¼d.
,, Nicholas Chamberlayn, 4 of these
    cloths.   Subs. 16d.   Ulnage 2d.
,, Thomas of Lokyngton, 5 cloths [sic]. Subs. 20d.   Ulnage 2½d.
,, John Chamberlayn, 5 of these cloths. Subs. 20d.   Ulnage 2½d.
,, John Kelstern, 1 of these cloths. Subs. 4d.   Ulnage ½d.
,, Robert Scherman, 3 of these cloths. Subs. 12d.   Ulnage 1½d.
,, William Malton, 1 of these cloths. Subs. 4d.   Ulnage ½d.
,, Stephen Lekenfeld, 2 of these cloths. Subs. 8d.   Ulnage 1d.
,, Thomas Marchall, 7 of these cloths. Subs. 2s. 4d. Ulnage 3½d.
,, Richard Schirburn, 7 of these cloths. Subs. 2s. 4d. Ulnage 3½d.
,, William Rolston, 30 of these cloths. Subs. 10s.   Ulnage 15d.
,, William Maliard, 31 of these cloths. Subs. 10s.4d. Ulnage 15½d.
,, Richard Aglion, 29 of these cloths. Subs. 9s. 4d. Ulnage 14½d.
,, Robert Cotyngham, 3 of these cloths. Subs. 12d.   Ulnage 1½d.
,, Roger Bedford, 5 of these cloths. Subs. 20d.   Ulnage 2½d.
,, William Bird, 17 of these cloths. Subs. 5s. 8d. Ulnage 8½d.
,, Richard Cokeram, 1 of these cloths. Subs. 4d.   Ulnage ½d.
,, John Boles, 2 of these cloths.   Subs. 8d.   Ulnage 1d.
,, Thomas Jolyff, 7 of these cloths. Subs. 2s. 4d. Ulnage 3½d.
,, Nicholas Waren, 5 of these cloths. Subs. 20d.   Ulnage 2½d.
,, Roger Ailsy, 9 of these cloths. Subs. 3s.   Ulnage 4½d.
,, Richard Lokynton, 4 of these cloths. Subs. 16d.   Ulnage 2d.
,, William Potyger, 4 of these cloths. Subs. 16d.   Ulnage 2d.
,, Richard Brunby, 4 of these cloths. Subs. 16d.   Ulnage 2d.
,, Robert Dodyngton, 1 of these cloths. Subs. 4d.   Ulnage ½d.
,, Thomas Alkebare, 4 of these cloths. Subs. 12d.   Ulnage 1½d.
,, Henry Watton, 1 of these cloths. Subs. 4d.   Ulnage ½d.
,, John Walkyngton, 5 of these cloths. Subs. 20d.   Ulnage 2½d.
,, William Melburn, 3 of these cloths. Subs. 12d.   Ulnage 1½d.
,, Robert Skypwyth, 2 of these cloths. Subs. 8d.   Ulnage 1d.
,, Thomas Skypwyth, 2 of these cloths. Subs. 8d.   Ulnage 1d.
,, William Burton, of Hedon, 4 of these
    cloths.   Subs. 16d.   Ulnage 2d.
,, William Merflete, 2 of these cloths. Subs. 8d.   Ulnage 1d.
,, John Dandson, 3 of these cloths. Subs. 12d.   Ulnage 1½d.

Of William Mason, of Bridlyngton, 2 of these cloths.	Subs.	8d.	Ulnage	1d.
,, Thomas Bedforth, 5 of these cloths.	Subs.	20d.	Ulnage	2½d.
,, William Wrenchell, 1½ of these cloths.	Subs.	6d.	Ulnage	¾d.
,, William Arcylot, 10 of these cloths.	Subs.	3s. 4d.	Ulnage	5d.
,, William Howson, 6 of these cloths.	Subs.	2s.	Ulnage	3d.

He does not answer for any profit arising from the subsidy or ulnage of scarlet cloths, or cloths of half grain, or in which some grain is intermixed, or for the forfeiture of any cloths or pieces of cloth whereof the dozen exceeds the value of 13s. 4d. exposed for sale there not sealed in the seal appointed for this purpose, during the aforesaid period of this account, because no cloth of this kind has been exposed for sale there during this period, as he says upon his oath.

Sum: Of cloths 504½
Subs. £8 8s. 2d.
Ulnage 21s. 0¼d.

II.
Letters Patent,
18 Ric. II.

1394   Richard, by the grace of God, King of England and France, and Lord of Ireland, To All to whom these present letters shall come, Greeting. Know that inasmuch the Magnates and Commons of our kingdom of England, in the Great Council of lord Edward, late King of England, our grandfather, lately held at Westminster, by the request of the same made in regard to the forfeitures to him belonging in connection with the ulnage of cloths within the same kingdom, Granted to the same our grandfather a certain subsidy on every vendible cloth, as well of one colour as of another within our said Kingdom of England, in addition to the customs thereof due, to be received from the vendor; that is to say, 4d. for every cloth of assize in which there shall be no grain, and 2d. for the half of a cloth of this sort, and 6d. for every scarlet cloth of assize, and 3d. for the half of this sort of cloth, and 5d. for every cloth of assize of half grain, and 2½d. for a half cloth of this kind. And for every cloth or half a cloth of assize, exceeding 3 ells or more, that shall not equal a cloth of assize, and for every cloth exceeding a whole cloth of assize by 3 ells or more shall be paid proportionately to the rate of the subsidy on a whole cloth of the same sort, to be paid and received for Our use. Provided, however, that nothing of this subsidy shall be required to be paid for any cloths that anyone shall cause to be made for their own clothing and that of their own family, and no demand shall be made or payment made for cloths sealed with the seal of the Collector of the Subsidy aforesaid, already once paid by the seller, whatever be the hands into which those cloths thus sealed shall come to be sold or otherwise. And that all cloths exposed for sale before they shall have been sealed with the aforesaid seal shall be forfeited to Us, and seized into Our hands by the said Collector or Ulnager, or the Bailiffs of the town where vendible cloths of this sort shall happen to be found unsealed. And also in the same Council it was ordained that the King's Ulnager should cause to measure with an ell yard, and sign by a certain sign, whereby a man may know how much a cloth of this kind contains in itself, and that the King's ulnager take one halfpenny for every whole cloth so measured, to wit from the seller, and one farthing for half a cloth, and that the same ulnager shall not meddle in the ulnage of other than cloths that are vended. And, moreover, whereas in divers statutes it is contained that a cloth of Ray shall be 28 ells in length measured by the list and of 5 quarters in breadth and that a coloured cloth be 26 ells measured by the back, and at least 6 quarters in width, and that a half cloth, whether it be of Ray or colour have the length and width aforesaid proportionately. And now by Statute passed in our last Parliament it is allowed that any man of our realm may make cloths of Kerseys as well as others, of such length and breadth as may please him, and expose for sale and sell the same cloths paying ulnage, subsidy and other money; to wit, for every cloth and piece of cloth according to the rate [proportionately], any statute, ordinance, proclamation, restriction or prohibition to the contrary made notwithstanding. And that no one sell any cloths, or expose them for sale before they be measured by an ell yard by our ulnager, and sealed with the seal appointed for this purpose, under the penalties contained in the statutes promulgated relating thereto. We willing that responsibility for the aforesaid ulnage and subsidy aforesaid be undertaken in the County of York, and trusting in the fidelity of William Skypyth, have appointed the same William Our ulnager by himself and his capable deputies to measure and seal with the seal appointed for the ulnage all and singular the cloths and pieces of saleable cloths in the County of York aforesaid, as well within liberties as without, Our City of York excepted, hitherto called cloths or pieces of cloth whether they be sold or exposed for sale therein, or carried outside the County aforesaid. Moreover, we have appointed the same William to levy, collect and receive the money from the sellers arising from this ulnage, as is aforesaid, as well as the subsidy aforesaid, in the County aforesaid, as well within liberties as outside of them, the aforesaid City of York excepted, by himself and his capable [sufficientes] deputies, for whom he may will to answer, regarding all and singular vendible cloths and pieces of cloths thus ulnaged and sealed with the ulnager's seal, for Our Use, according to the form of the Statute in our last Parliament enacted, and that he faithfully answer to Us concerning the money and subsidy aforesaid in our Exchequer [Court]. And when the subsidy shall have been paid on all these cloths and pieces of saleable cloth they are to be sealed with the seal appointed for the purpose. Moreover, he shall cause proclamation to be made, in such places within the County aforesaid, as well within as without Liberties, as shall seem to him best, that no one, native or foreigner, expose any cloths or pieces of cloths for sale, or carry them outside the County aforesaid before the money arising from this ulnage and the aforesaid subsidy shall have been paid and the seal for the ulnage and that for the subsidy affixed, under penalty of the forfeiture of the same cloths. And [he is appointed] to search all dwellings and shops and other places in the County aforesaid, both within and without liberties, the City of York excepted, where cloths of this kind and pieces of vendible cloths may be found, and to seize all such cloths and pieces of cloths exposed for sale, and not sealed with the seals aforesaid into Our hands, as forfeited, and, under the supervision of the Sheriff of the County aforesaid for the time being, according to Indenture thereto relating now duly to be made between the said William and the afore-said Sheriff, to sell and out of the money thereout arising faithfully answer likewise to Us at our Exchequer. Also [he has power] to arrest rebels in this matter, and commit them to Our prisons, until we otherwise determine their punishment. We will also that our Trea-surer for the time being make and pay according to his discretion, competent remuneration to the aforesaid William, according to his merit and labour in this behalf. We give strict orders moreover, to the Sheriff of Our County aforesaid for the time being, also to Mayors, Bailiffs, Constables, Officers, and other Our faithful subjects of the County aforesaid, both within Liberties and outside them, that they obey and pay attention to the same William and his deputies in doing and executing the premises. In Testimony whereof We have caused these Our letters patent to be made. Witness Myself at Westminster the 20th day of July, the eighteenth year of Our reign.

$$[E. \frac{345}{15}]$$

Yorkshire. PARTICULARS OF THE ACCOUNT OF WILLIAM SKIPWYTH, Collector of the Ulnage and Subsidy of saleable cloths and forfeitures of the same in the County of York, the City of York excepted, to wit, from **1394** the 20th day of July in the 18th year [Ric. II] until the 4th day of **1395** November in the 19th year.

Ponte-fract, Houdon, and Selby	From John Lewse, of Pontefract, 8½ cloths	16d.
	William Scryyveyne, of the same, 1½ cloths	6d.
	Thomas Chaundeler, of the same, ½ a cloth	2d.
	Matilda Northfolk, 1 cloth	4d.
	Richard Akworth, ½ a cloth	2d.
	Thomas Fynell, ½ a cloth	2d.
	John Guderede, ½ a cloth	2d.
	John Chuttok, ½ a cloth	2d.
	Thomas Stamford, ¾ths of a cloth	3d.
	John of Banke, ½ a cloth	2d.
	William Layland, 1½ cloth	6d.
	Thomas of the Stones, of Pontefract, 2 cloths	8d.
	John, son of the same, 1½ cloth	6d.
	Roger of Prisos, of Wakefeld, 3 cloths	12d.
	John Lewes, of Pontefract, 12 cloths	4s.
	John of Lepton, 6 pieces of strait cloth, containing 36 yards of assize	6d.
	John of Kendale, 1 pack of 12 pieces of strait cloths, contain-ing 72 yds. of assize	12d.

John Wylkynson, 24 pieces of strait cloths, containing 144
    yds. of assize . . . . 2s.
John Mylnthorp, of Appelby in Westmarland, 10 cloths . 3s. 4d.
William Nype, 2 fardels, containing 6 cloths . . 2s. 0d.
John of Kendale, 1 pack of strait cloths, containing 12 pieces
    of cloth, containing 62 yds. of assize . . . . 12d.
Matilda of Wath, 1½ cloth . . . . . . 6d.
William Wastell, 1¼ cloth . . . . . . 5d.
Robert Ploughman, 1½ cloth . . . . . 6d.
Alice Sayvell, 1¼ cloth . . . . . . 5d.
John Akworth, 1½ cloth and 3 yds. . . . 6½d.
Isabel Holman, 2 cloths . . . . . . 8d.
John Taillour, of Moulhill, Pontefract, 5 cloths . . 20d.
Of the same, 2½ cloths and 3 yds. . . . . 10½d.
Richard Rayner, of Carleton, 3 cloths . . . 12d.
John Lauerall, 4 cloths . . . . . . 16d.
Thomas Hosyer, 1 cloth and 3 yds. . . . 4½d.
Alice Tableter, 1½ cloth . . . . . . 6d.
John of Scraford, 1 cloth . . . . . 4d.
Robert Johnson, of Kendall, 1 pack containing 4 cloths . 16d.
Henry Bradeley, 6 cloths . . . . . 2s.
Robert of Whiteby, 1½ cloth and 3 yds. . . 6½d.
Robert of Wragby, 1½ cloth . . . . 6d.
Richard of Darthyngton, 5½ cloths and 3 yds. . . 22½d.
William of Wragby, taillour, 6 cloths . . . 2s.
John Annotson, of Berneslay, 2 cloths . . . 8d.
John of Hesill, 1 cloth and 3 yds. . . . . 4½d.
Richard of Dene, 23 pieces of strait cloths, containing 238 yds.
    of assize . . . . 23d.
Thomas Horne, 4½ cloths . . . . . 18d.
Richard Lyster, of Balne, 1¾ cloth . . . . 7d.
Robert of Lancaster, 3¾ cloths . . . . 15d.
Thomas Herrison, 5½ cloths . . . . 22d.
Robert Malson, 4 cloths . . . . . . 16d.
Matilda Hode, of Pontefract, 3 cloths . . . 12d.
Of the same, 1¾ cloth . . . . . . 7d.
John Bokeland, 1¼ cloth . . . . . 5d.
Peter Walker, 1¾ cloth . . . . . . 7d.
Alice Hipram, of Pontefract, 2¾ cloths and 3 yds. . 11½d.
John Belacys, 1½ cloth . . . . . . 6d.
Thomas Fyney, 2¼ cloths . . . . . 9d.
William Northfolk, 4 cloths . . . . 16d.
John Goderede, walker, 4¼ cloths . . . 17d.
William Walker, of Pontefract, 2¼ cloths . . 9d.
John of Cafe, walker, of the same, 4¾ cloths . . 19d.
Robert of Buseby, of the same, 3 cloths . . . 12d.
Thomas Fenell, glover, of the same, 1 cloth and 2 yds. . 4½d.
John of Okelay, 1½ cloth . . . . . 6d.
Alice of Pathorne, of Pontefract, 2¼ cloths . . 9d.
John of Carleton, 1 cloth . . . . . 4d.

	John Goldesmyth, 4¼ cloths	17d.
	Richard of Bronby, 3¼ cloths	13d.
	Thomas Draper, of Wakefeld, 6 cloths	2s.
	John Lewes, of Pontefract, 13½ cloths	3s. 2d.
	Richard Rayner, 3 quarters	3d.
Wake-	Henry of Brodlo [? Brodle], 10 cloths	3s. 4d.
feld,	John Walerd, 9 cloths	3s.
Ledes,	Richard Deyne, 6 cloths	2s.
and	Robert Waweyn, 6 cloths	2s.
Doncas-	Robert Draper, of Wakefeld, 6 cloths	2s.
ter	William Torwer, 5 cloths	20d.
	Roger Prisowe [or Pusowe], 9 cloths	3s.
	John of Milthorp, 6 cloths	2s.
	John of Kendale, 6 cloths	2s.
	William Gnype, 5 cloths	20d.
	John Moyser, 6 cloths	2s.
	Robert Stanley, 8 cloths	2s. 8d.
	John Donbiggyng, 4 cloths	16d.
	John Thorpe, 3 cloths	12d.
	Simon Flemyng, 3 cloths	12d.
	John of Kent, 2 cloths	8d.
	William of Topclyff, 2 cloths	8d.
	John of Burgh, 2 cloths	8d.
	Thomas Sadeler, 2½ cloths	10d.
	Henry of Worthyngton, 1 cloth	4d.
	Robert Bull, 2 cloths	8d.
	William Allecame, 2 cloths	8d.
	Robert Heryll, 2 cloths	8d.
	John of Freyston, 1 cloth	4d.
	William Egson [? Ogson], 1 cloth	4d.
	John Golley, 1 cloth	4d.
	John of Branden, ½ a cloth	2d.
	John Marshall, 1 cloth	4d.
	John Claworth, 6 cloths	2s.
	John Cotgrave, 6 cloths	2s.
	John Waweyn, 1 cloth	4d.
	John Wright, 3 cloths	12d.
	William of the Wode, 3 cloths	12d.
	Thomas Megson, 6 cloths	2s.
	William of Thornes, 1½ cloth	6d.
	Elena Pyper, ½ a cloth	2d.
	The daughter of the Vicar of Crayk, 1 cloth . .	4d.
	Thomas Anson, 1 cloth	4d.
	Henry Neuland, 1½ cloth	6d.
	William Prentys, 6 cloths	2s.
	William Ottelay, 5 cloths	20d.
	Thomas of Bare, 6 cloths	2s.
	Robert Taillour, 3 cloths	12d.
	Richard of Burbrygg, 1¼ cloth	5d.

Thomas Westwod, 1¼ cloth	5d.
Thomas Chapman, 2 cloths	8d.
Alice Taillour, 3 cloths	12d.
Alice Smythwyff, 1 cloth	4d.
William Colston, 2½ cloths	10d.
William Webster, 3 cloths	12d.
Thomas . . . . . . 1½ cloth	6d.
John Gardener, 2½ cloths	10d.
Matilda Colyn, 3 cloths	12d.
Margaret Barker, 4 cloths	16d.
Robert Legg, 3 cloths	12d.
Richard Brynnand, 3 cloths	12d.
Adam of Assheton, 4 cloths	16d.
Helena Wattes, 2 cloths	8d.
Roger Chapman, 3 cloths	12d.
Agnes Wranghill, 1½ cloth	6d.
Ellen Kirtlyngton, 3 cloths	12d.
John Goldsmyth, 4 cloths	16d.
Thomas Aleynson, 2 cloths	8d.
Robert of Newyk, 2½ cloths	10d.
Agnes Payley, 3 cloths	12d.
John Castelyn, 4 cloths	16d.
John Clerc, 2 cloths	8d.
Alice Nalson, 1½ cloth	6d.
John Dernbrok, 3 cloths	12d.
Thomas Norton, 4 cloths	16d.
Thomas Walker, 2 cloths	8d.
John Hamstwayt, 1 cloth	4d.
Henry Taillour, 3 cloths	12d.
Agnes Warde, 2 cloths	8d.
Robert of Kirkeby, 3 cloths	12d.
Katerine Mallom, ½ a cloth	2d.
Thomas Colyn, ¼th of a cloth	1d.
John Whitheved, ½ a cloth	2d.
Thomas of Fulford, ¾ths of a cloth	3d.
Thomas Lokyngton, ½ a cloth	2d.
Thomas Draper, 1 cloth	4d.
Magota Horner, ½ a cloth	2d.
Richard Coke, ½ a cloth	2d.
John Horne, 1 cloth	4d.
Joan of the Water, 1 cloth	4d.
Robert of Wetherby, 1½ cloth	6d.
Richard of Balderby, 1½ cloth	6d.

Ryche-	John of Kendale, ½ a cloth	2d.
mond,	John of Rande, of Bedall, 3 cloths	12d.
Bedall,	Robert Raner, 3 cloths	12d.
and	John of Hill, 4 cloths	16d.
Allerton	Thomas Walker, 2 cloths	8d.
	Thomas Bryan, 1½ cloth	6d.

Peter Lytster, 5 cloths	20d.
William Kateryk, 2 cloths	8d.
Alan Taillour, 5 cloths	20d.
William of Myddelton, 2 cloths	8d.
William of Ryton, 3 cloths	12d.
Robert of Stabell [or Scabell], 1½ cloth	6d.
John of Kendale, 10 cloths	40d.
Thomas Smyth, 9 cloths	3s.
Henry Couper, 3 cloths	12d.
John Mayser, of Kyrkeby, 10 cloths	40d.
Thomas Yhole, 3 cloths	12d.
John of Garton, 9 cloths	3s.
William Riche[mond ?], 2 cloths	8d.
John Garton-man, 3 cloths	12d.
John Thornton, 4 cloths	16d.
John of Holme, 3 cloths	12d.
John Stalker, 1½ cloth	6d.
Richard Hagland, 3 cloths	12d.
William of Rolston, 5 cloths	20d.
John Kelke, 4 cloths	16d.
William of Wymster, 2 cloths	8d.
Robert Webster, 1½ cloth	6d.
William Walker, 3 cloths	12d.
Adam Taillour, 1¾ cloth	7d.
Geoffrey Taillour, 1 cloth	4d.
John Stevenson, 2 cloths	8d.
Richard of Langtoft, 3½ cloths	18d.
Geoffrey Taverner, 2½ cloths	10d.
Nicholas Cordwaner, 4 cloths	16d.
Geoffry Webster, 2 cloths	8d.
Thomas Smyth, 3¾ths cloths	15d.
Peter Glover, 2¼ cloths	9d.
Henry Glover, 2 cloths	8d.
Thomas Horsher, 3 cloths	12d.
John Mercer, 2 cloths	8d.
Adam Milner, 1½ cloth	6d.
John Candeler, 3½ cloths	14d.
Robert Marshall, 1½ cloth	6d.
William Lorimer, 1 cloth	4d.
Thomas Patynmaker, ½ a cloth	2d.
John Irynmongher, 1 cloth	4d.
Adam Bower, 2 cloths	8d.
William Glovemaker, 1 cloth	4d.
John Mustardmaker, 4 cloths	16d.
William Carter, 3 cloths	12d.
Thomas Penner, 6 cloths	2s.
John Balster, 8 cloths	2s. 8d.
Thomas Draper, 10 cloths	3s. 4d.
John Sherman, 6 cloths	2s.
John Flesshewer, 4 cloths	16d.

John Buk, 5 cloths . . . . 20d.
Thomas Parchemenmaker, 6 cloths . . . . . 2s.
William of Holme, 8 cloths . . . . . . 2s. 8d.
John Sadeler, 6 cloths . . . . 2s.
Geoffry Porter, 5 cloths . . . . 20d.
Adam Horners, 6 cloths . . . . 2s.
Thomas Ponderas, 10 cloths . . . . . . 3s. 4d.
William Lavermaker, 7 cloths . . . . . . 2s. 4d.
John Pouchemaker, 6 cloths . . . . . . 2s.
Geoffry Skynner, 8 cloths . . . . . . 2s. 8d.
Adam Brewster, 5 cloths . . . . . . 20d.
Nicholas Mason, 9 cloths . . . . . . 3s.
John Lytster, 5 cloths . . . . . . 20d.
William Barker, 6 cloths . . . . . . 2s.
Thomas Bokeler, 5 cloths . . . . . . 20d.
Geoffry Goldsmyth, 4 cloths . . . . . . 16d.
Adam Taverner, 6½ cloths . . . . . . 2s. 2d.
John Spether, 4 cloths . . . . 16d.
William Wryter, ½ a cloth . . . . . . 2d.
Thomas Gyrdeler, ¾ths of a cloth . . . . . 3d.
Geoffry Cardemaker, 1 cloth . . . . . . 4d.
Adam Plasterer, 2 cloths . . . . . . 8d.
Nicholas Goldsmyth, 3 cloths . . . . . . 12d.
William Skynner, 4 cloths . . . . . . 16d.
Adam Raper, ½ a cloth . . . . . . 2d.
Geoffry Barbour, ¼ of a cloth . . . . . . 1d.
John Wyrdrawer, 1½ cloth . . . . . . 6d.
Adam Skynner, ¼ of a cloth . . . . . . 1d.
John Kamesmyth, 1½ cloth . . . . . . 6d.
William Capmaker, 2 cloths . . . . . . 8d.
Thomas Lytster, 1¼ cloth . . . . . . 5d.
William Tepell, 5 cloths . . . . . . 20d.
Thomas Swanland, 3 cloths . . . . . . 12d.
John Catton, 2 cloths . . . . . . 8d.
Joan Hertylpole, one cloth . . . . . . 4d.
Alice Lokton, ½ a cloth . . . . . . 2d.
The wife of Robert Glover, ½ a cloth . . . . 2d.
Thomas Lokyngton, 8 pieces of strait cloth, containing 48 yds.
    of assize . . . . 8d.
Robert Penreth, 6 pieces of strait cloth, containing 36 yds.
    of assize . . . . 6d.
Roger Haylso, 3 pieces of strait cloth, containing 18 yds. of
    assize . . . . 3d.
Robert Archer, ½ a cloth . . . . . . 2d.
William Brygg, of York, 1 cloth . . . . . 4d.
John Taillour, of Rypon, 6 pieces of strait cloth, containing
    36 yds. of assize . . . . 6d.
John Fouler, 1 cloth . . . . 4d.
John Taillour, of York, 1 cloth . . . . . 4d.
William Sybson, 3 quarters of a broad cloth . . . 3d.

	John Johnson, 4 pieces of strait cloth, containing 24 yds. of assize	4*d.*
	Thomas Wylson, 1 cloth	4*d.*
	John Keuse, 1 cloth	4*d.*
Rypon, Borough-brigg	Margaret Lynton, 1½ cloth	6*d.*
	Joan Mason, 1 cloth	4*d.*
	John Goldesmyth, 6 yds.	1*d.*
	John Rayar, ¾ths of a cloth	3*d.*
	John Taillour, ½ a cloth	2*d.*
	Henry Webster, ½ a cloth	2*d.*
	Robert Hungate, ½ a cloth	2*d.*
	Robert Webster, ½ a cloth	2*d.*
	William Thorton, ¾ths of a cloth	3*d.*
	William Taillour, 1½ cloth	6*d.*
	William Spycer, 1 cloth	4*d.*
	Robert Byrsall, 1 cloth	4*d.*
	John Scolmayster, ½ a cloth	2*d.*
	William Kirby, ½ a cloth	2*d.*
	Alesota Bullok, ½ a cloth	2*d.*
	William Greff, ½ a cloth	2*d.*
	John Braban, ½ a cloth	2*d.*
	John Hartessor, 1 cloth	4*d.*
	John Morton, 6 yds. of cloth	1*d.*
	Simon Glover, ¾ths of a cloth	3*d.*
	Richard Hewyk, ½ a cloth	2*d.*
	John Gryston, ½ a cloth	2*d.*
	John Setryngton, ¼th a cloth	1*d.*
	John Gasgyll, ¼th a cloth	1*d.*
	William Russell, ½ a cloth	2*d.*
	Nicholas of Sendall, ½ a cloth	2*d.*
	John Kerby, ½ a cloth	2*d.*
	Robert Taillour, ½ a cloth	2*d.*
	John Kendell, 2½ cloths	10*d.*
	John Draper, ½ a cloth	2*d.*
	William Eryom, 1 cloth	4*d.*
	Peter Milner, ¼th a cloth	1*d.*
	William Draper, 2⅓ cloths	10*d.*
	Richard Cadby, 1 cloth	4*d.*
	William Buryan, 6 cloths	2*s.*
	Elizabeth Lewe, 6 cloths	2*s.*
	Richard of Clyfton, 4 cloths	16*d.*
	Robert of Stranger, 10 cloths	3*s.* 4*d.*
	Richard Bate, 6 cloths	2*s.*
	John Schewe, 12 cloths	4*s.*
	John Merflet, 8 cloths	2*s.* 8*d.*
	Robert Retherby, 4 cloths	16*d.*
	Nicholas of Belton, 2 cloths	8*d.*
	Ralph of Hull, 2 cloths	8*d.*
	John Wytheved, 8 cloths	2*s.* 8*d.*

John Merflete, 1 cloth . . . . 4d.
John Stocwyth, 6 cloths . . . . 2s.
John Flecher, 1 cloth . . . . 4d.
Richard Taillour, 1 cloth . . . . . . 4d.
Alice of Beverley, 2 cloths . . . . . . 8d.
William Bawston, 1 cloth . . . . . . 4d.
Robert Sherman, 6 cloths . . . . . . 2s.
John Wrawby, 4 cloths . . . . . . 16d.
Thomas of Gren, 2 cloths . . . . . . 8d.
Nicholas Chamerlay, 4 cloths . . . . . 16d.
Alice of Waweyn, 12 cloths . . . . . 4s.
Alice Southbrwer, 1 cloth . . . . . . 4d.
William Chery, 7 cloths . . . . . . 2s. 4d.
Thomas Chery, 4 cloths . . . . . . 16d.
John Stirop, 12 cloths . . . . . . 4s.
Robert Sumpter, 9 cloths . . . . . . 3s.
John Warrener, 18 cloths . . . . . . 6s.
Astell of Malton, 14 cloths . . . . . 4s. 8d.
John Tudber, 6 cloths . . . . . . 2s.
Richard Puell, 1 cloth . . . . . . 4d.
William Yerkelay, 18 cloths . . . . . 6s.
John Raxby, 8 cloths . . . . . . 2s. 8d.
John Burton, 17 cloths . . . . . . 5s. 8d.
William Berd, 10 cloths . . . . . . 3s. 4d.
Stephen of Denton, 4 cloths . . . . . 16d.
Robert Cogsale, 6 cloths . . . . . . 2s.
John of Berden, 6 cloths . . . . . . 2s.
Nicholas Laske, 2 cloths . . . . . . 8d.
John Arcybot, 10 cloths . . . . . . 2s. 4d.
Symon of Bedall, 18 cloths . . . . . 6s.
John Bate, 10 cloths . . . . . . 3s. 4d.
Nicholas of Wainell, 6 cloths . . . . . 2s.
William Sherman, 2 cloths . . . . . . 8d.
Edward Deyorn, 6 cloths . . . . . . 2s.
Robert of Croxet, 6 cloths . . . . . . 2s.
Thomas Sherman, 11 cloths . . . . . 3s. 8d.
Peter Steller, 10 cloths . . . . . . 3s. 4d.
Robert Clerk, 5 cloths . . . . . . 20d.
John Sherman, 2 cloths . . . . . . 8d.
Roger Cox, of Herlse, 4 cloths . . . . . 16d.
Thomas Berkeys, 5 cloths . . . . . . 20d.
Stephen Sherman, 2 cloths . . . . . . 8d.
Robert Freman, 8 cloths . . . . . . 2s. 8d.
Agnes of Chapell, 10 cloths . . . . . 3s. 4d.
Richard Freston, 10 cloths . . . . . . 3s. 4d.
John Brundholme, 57 pieces of strait cloth, containing 342
   yds. of assize . . . . 4s. 9d.
John Koke, 24 pieces of strait cloth, containing 216 yards of assize 3s.
John Welflet, 6 cloths . . . . . . 2s.
John Demelyn, 3½ cloths . . . . . . 14d.

Sum total of pieces of strait cloth, 221, containing 1,326 yds. of a cloth of assize that make 51 cloths of assize. Whereof the subsidy [is] 18s. 5d.

Sum total of cloths of assize, 1202 cloths and 9 yds. [Thereof the] subsidy is £20 0s. 10d., to wit, on every cloth 4d.

He is charged on his account for 52s. 2¾d. received from the ulnage on the cloths aforesaid, to wit, on every cloth one halfpenny, and on the half of such a cloth, one farthing.

He does not answer for any profits arising from the subsidy on Scarlet Cloths of assize, or of cloths of half grain, because none of this cloth was exposed for sale during the same time [i.e. of his office], as he says upon his oath.

But he does answer for 60s. and 2d. received for forfeitures of 12 strait cloths of divers colours exposed for sale before the subsidy thereon was paid, and sealed with the seal appointed for this purpose, and for that cause forfeited to the King, as appears and is contained in a certain Indenture concerning this matter made between Robert Conestable, High Sheriff of the County aforesaid, and delivered along with this Account.

Sum of Receipts, £26 . 11 . 7¾.

[In the Exchequer K.R. Accounts [Bundle $\frac{345}{15}$] is a Writ dated 4th Nov., 19 Ric. II, directed to William Skipwyth, late ulnager in Co. York, instructing him to deliver the seals of his office to Richard Agylton, appointed ulnager for the East Riding, William Ledes of Ripon for the North Riding, and William Barker of Tadcaster for the West Riding, the City of York excepted.

In the same bundle are two parts of an Indenture, dated 30 Sept., 19 Ric. II, between Robert Conestable, Sheriff of York, and William Skipwith, collector of the ulnage and subsidy on cloth in the said County as to sale of cloth arrested for being exposed for sale before the subsidy was paid, and the cloth sealed.

William Skipwith was appointed ulnager by letters patent, dated 20th July, 18 Ric. II.]

III.

[E. $\frac{345}{16}$]

PARTICULARS OF THE ACCOUNT OF JOHN RAGHTON,[1] Ulnager of the King, of saleable cloths in the City of York and suburbs of the same exposed for sale, sealed with the seal that is appointed [to be used] for this purpose, and Collector of the money arising from for-

[1] John of Raghton, " draper " was admitted a freeman of York in the 6th year of the reign of King Richard II, the 2nd of February, 1382-3, and ten years later, February 2nd, 1392-3, was elected one of the three Chamberlains, otherwise Bailiffs, of the City. He married Alice, daughter and heiress of John of Braithwaite, who was Mayor of York in 1391-2. After John de Raghton's death his widow, Alice, married Edmund de la Pole. John of Raghton, by his wife, Alice, had a son, John of Raghton, merchant, Chamberlain of York in 1423-4; Sheriff in 1428-9; and Master of the Merchants' Guild in 1435.

1394

feitures of the same, under the Writ patent of the King, given the 20th July in [His] 18th year resting in his hands, to wit: of this collection of the subsidy, ulnage, and forfeitures of the above cloths, there, from the Sunday next before the Feast of the Nativity of Blessed Mary, occurring on the 6th day of September in the same 18th year, on which day he first received the said Writ of the King for exercising his office in this regard; as he says upon his oath, until the Feast of St. Michael in the 19th year, as appears below.

Money received

Imprimis, on the 6th day of September, in the 18th year aforesaid.

Of Robert of Merston[1] for 2½ ' blewe ' cloths . . . 10d.
Of Andrew Junour for two red cloths [rubei] and 2 ' blewe ' cloths and 1 ' sangwyn ' cloth and 1 ' ruset ' cloth and ½ a ' plonket ' cloth . . . . 2s. 2d.
Of William of Merton[2] for ½ a cloth of ' meld ' . . 2d.

Sum: Cloths . 10½
      Subsidy . 3s. 2d.
      Ulnage . 4¾d.

The 7th day of the same month.

Of Thomas of Sorby for 2 ' blewe ' cloths and 1 white cloth 12d.
Of John Passelewe[3] for 1½ ' blewe ' and ½ of ' meld ' . . 8d.
Of Alice Barbour for ½ a white cloth . . . . 2d.
Of Robert of Selby[4] for 1½ ' blewe ' cloth [and] ½ a ' russet ' cloth 8d.
Of Henry Lakyn for 2 white cloths . . . . 8d.
Of John Thorneton[5] for ½ a red [rubeo] cloth without grain 2d.

Sum: Cloths . 10
      Subs. . 3s. 4d.
      Ulnage . 5d.

The 8th day of the same month.

Of Thomas Whitik[6] for 1½ white cloths . . . . 6d.
Of Nicholas Baynbrige for 1½ white cloths and 1 ' blewe ' . 10d.

Sum: Of Cloths 4 cloths.
      Subs. . 16d.
      Ulnage . 2d.

The 9th day of the same month.

Of John of Barton for ½ a ' russet ' cloth . . . 2d.
Of Agnes Calthorn for ½ a ' blewe ' cloth . . . . 2d.
Of the same Agnes for 11 ells of ' blak ' . . . . 1¾d.
Of Margaret Hukester for 7 ells of white . . . . 1d.
Of Alice Hukester for ½ a ' plunket ' cloth . . . 2d.

[1] Robert of Merston, " merchant," was elected a freeman of York in 1367–8.
[2] A William of Marton, " draper," was elected a freeman of York in 1385–6.
[3] A John Passelew, " merchant," was elected a freeman in 1392–3.
[4] Robert of Selby, " marchaunt," was elected a freeman in 1387–8, and a Robert Selby was a member of the Corpus Christi Guild in 1411–2. Alice, the latter's wife, is named in the Guild " Obituary " in 1413–4.
[5] A John son of William of Thorneton, "mercer," was admitted a freeman in 1365, and a John of Thorneton, " draper," in 1366–7.
[6] Thomas Wittyk, " merchant," was admitted a freeman in 1386–7.

Of John Gerard[1] for 2 'blewe' cloths . . . . 8d.
Sum: Of cloths 4½ and 5 ells.
Subs. . 18s. 0¾d.
Ulnage . 2½d.

The 10th day of the same month.

Of Laurence Lovell for 1½ red cloth . . . . 6d.
Of Alice Bothe for ½ a 'plunket' cloth . . . . 2d.
Of Mariota of Barton for ½ a 'blewe' cloth . . . 2d.
Sum: Of cloths 2½
Subs. . 10d.
Ulnage . 1¼d.

The 11th day of the same month.

Of John Tang for 1½ 'blewe' cloth . . . . 6d.
Of John Spaldyng for ½ a 'blewe' cloth . . . . 2d.
Of Alice Otryngton for 7 ells of red cloth . . . 1d.
Of Agnes Hukester for 3 ells of 'meld' cloth . . . ½d.
Sum: Of cloths 2 cloths and 10 ells.
Subs. . 9½d.
Ulnage . 1¼d.

The 12th day of the same month.

Of Margaret Hukester 6 ells of white and 6 ells of red. . 2d.
Of John Dandson ½ a 'plunket' cloth . . . . 2d.
Of John Stanelay[2] 6 ells of 'russet' . . . . 1d.
Sum: Cloths . 1 and 5 ells.
Subs. . 5d.
Ulnage . ¾d.

The 14th day of the same month.

Of Margaret Boweland ½ a 'blewe' cloth . . . . 2d.
Of John Ottelay[3] 1 'blewe' cloth . . . . 4d.
Of John Candelere ½ a white cloth . . . . 2d.
Sum: Cloths . 2
Subs. . 8d.
Ulnage . 1d.

The 15th day of the same month.

Of Edmund Cariour 6 ells of white . . . . . 1d.
Of Thomas Smyth 2 'russet' cloths . . . . 8d.
Sum: Cloths . 2 and 6 ells.
Subs. . 9d.
Ulnage . 1¼d.

The 16th of the same month.

Of John Coke ½ a 'blewe' cloth . . . . . 2d.
Of John of Raghton one 'blewe' cloth . . . . 4d.
Of Richard of Calton ½ a white cloth . . . . 2d.

---

[1] John Gerard, "webster," was admitted a freeman in 1377-8.

A John of Stanlay, "girdeler," was elected a freeman in 1351-2, and a John of Staynlay, "marchaunt," was elected in 1386-7. Probably the latter is the man mentioned in the ulnage roll.

[3] John of Ottelay, "merchant," was elected a freeman in 1386-7.

D

Sum: Cloths . 2
Subs. . 8*d.*
Ulnage . 1*d.*

The 17th day of the same month.

Of John of Lynton ½ a white cloth	2*d.*
Of the same John 6 ells of 'blewe'.	1*d.*

Sum: Cloths . ½ and 6 ells.
Subs. . 3*d.*
Ulnage . ½*d.*

The 18th day of the same month.

Of John of Raghton 2½ white cloths	10*d.*
Of Agnes of Monkegate ½ a 'russet' cloth . . .	2*d.*
Of Robert Plomer one white cloth	4*d.*
Of Thomas of Fereby[1] ½ a white cloth	2*d.*
Of John Bokeland 6 ells of 'blewe'	1*d.*

Sum: Cloths . 4½ and 6 ells.
Subs. . 19*d.*
Ulnage . 2½*d.*

The 20th day of the same month.

Of Roger of Royston ½ a 'grene' cloth	2*d.*
Of John of Kyrkeham one white cloth and one 'blewe' cloth	8*d.*
Of Joan Hukester ½ a 'russet' cloth	2*d.*
Of Alice of Mounketon 3 ells of 'grene' and 3 ells of red .	2*d.*

Sum: Cloths . 3 and 6 ells.
Subs. . 14*d.*
Ulnage . 1¾*d.*

The 21st day of the same month.

Of Andrew Jonour 1 'sangwyn' cloth	4*d.*
Of Joan Hukester ½ a 'grene' cloth	2*d.*
Of Agnes Hukester 6 ells of 'meld'	1*d.*
Of Wandesford for 6 ells of red	1*d.*
Of Alice Hukester for 6 ells of 'meld'	1*d.*

Sum: Cloths . 2 and 5 ells.
Subs. . 9*d.*
Ulnage . 1½*d.*

The 22d day of same month.

Of Geoffry Kereton 1 'grene' cloth and ½ a 'russet' cloth	6*d.*
John of Kyrkeham 1 red and 1 'blewe' cloth . .	8*d.*
Joan Hukster for 3 ells of 'morrey'	½*d.*

Sum: Cloths . 3½ and 3 ells.
Subs. . 14½*d.*
Ulnage . 2*d.*

23d of the same month.

Of John Morelay 5 'blewe' and 1½ 'plunket' cloth .	2*s.* 2*d.*
Henry Lakynsnyther[2] 2 'blewe' and ½ a white cloth .	10*d.*

[1] Thomas of Ferriby, "mercer," was elected a freeman in Feb., 1359-60.

[2] Henry Lakensnyder was admitted a freeman, as son of his father, Arnald Lakensnyder, in 1380-1.

Thomas Houeden 1 'blewe' and 1 white cloth	. .	8d.
Joan Semester for 6 ells of red	.	1d.
Margaret Nuthyll ½ a 'meld' cloth	.	2d.

Sum: Cloths . 11½ and 6 ells.
Subs. . 3s. 11d.
Ulnage . 6d.

On the 24th of the same month.

Of John Laxton[1] 1 'blewe' and 1 red cloth . .	.	8d.
Nicholas Paraunt[2] ½ a white cloth	.	2d.
John Webster ½ a 'russet' cloth	.	2d.
William Saule ½ a 'plunket' cloth	.	2d.

Sum: Cloths . 3½
Subs. . 14d.
Ulnage . 1¾d.

On the 25th day of the same month.

Of John of Thornton[3] for ½ a white cloth . .	.	2d.
Robert Tothe ½ a white cloth	.	2d.
Thomas Wenchelay ½ a 'russet' cloth . . .	.	2d.
John of Threpland[4] for 1 white and 1 'blewe' cloth .	.	8d.
Elena Hewyk for 3 ells of 'blewe' . . .	.	½d.

Sum: Cloths . 3½ and 3 ells.
Subs. . 14½d.
Ulnage . 2d.

The 26th day of the same month.

Of Thomas A'skham[5] 2 red and 1 'blewe' . .	.	12d.
John Braythewayte[6] ½ a 'meld' cloth . . .	.	2d.
Joan of Burton for 6 ells of 'grene' . . .	.	1d.
Joan of Mounkegate for 6 ells of 'russet' . .	.	1d.
John Chartyrs[7] ½ a 'grene' cloth	.	2d.
Agnes Wellom ½ a 'grene' cloth	.	2d.

Sum: Cloths . 4
Subs. . 20d.
Ulnage . 2½d.

[1] John of Laxton, "mercer," was admitted a freeman in 1384–5.

[2] Nicholas Parant, "draper," was admitted a freeman in 1381–2, and was, apparently, one of the Chamberlains of the city in 1396–7.

[3] John of Thorneton, "draper," was admitted a freeman in 1366–7, and, apparently, was a Chamberlain in 1380–1.

[4] John of Threpeland, "merchant," was admitted a freeman in 1382–3. He and his wife, Katharine, and John, his son, admitted to Corpus Christi Guild in 1408.

[5] Thomas of Askham, "draper," was admitted a freeman in 1381–2; his son, Thomas Askham, "lytster," was admitted, "per patrem," in 1415–6.

[6] John of Brathwaite was elected a Chamberlain of York in 1371–2. His daughter, Alice, married John of Raghton (see note, p. 47). John of Braythewayte was Lord Mayor of York in 1393. By deed dated 1449 Alice de la Pole, of York, widow, founded an obit in the church of St. Martin, Conynstreet, for the souls of her father, John Braythewayte, Marione, his wife, John Raghton, her first husband, Edmund de la Pole, her second husband, and also of John Raghton, her son, as well as her own soul after her decease.

[7] A John del Chartres, "littester," was admitted a freeman in 1385–6.

The 28th day of the same month.

Of John of Thorneton 4 ' grene meld ' cloths, 4 red ' meld '
cloths, 2 ' taude ' cloths, 1½ of ' plonket ' cloth, 1 ' redd '
cloth, ½ a ' blewe ' cloth, and ½ a ' sangwyn ' cloth   . 4s. 6d.

Robert Sharples[1] 1 ' blewe ' cloth . . . . .   4d.

John of Brydelyngton[2] ½ a cloth of ' bake ' [sic blake], ½ a red
cloth, and ½ a white cloth . . . .   6d.

Hugh Chartres[3] 1 white cloth . . . .   4d.

Agnes of Wellome ½ a red cloth . . . .   2d.

     Sum: Cloths .   17½
            Subs.   .   5s. 10d.
            Ulnage .   [obliterated] 8¾d. (?)

The 29th day of the same month.

Of John Stevenson ½ a white cloth . . .   2d.

John Wreth ½ a white cloth . . . . .   2d.

Agnes Bakester ½ a ' russet ' cloth . . . .   2d.

John of Topeclyff[4] 2 ' russet ' cloths and 1 white cloth .   12d.

Martin Lonegard ½ a ' plunket ' cloth . . .   2d.

     Sum: Cloths .   5
            Subs.   .   20d.
            Ulnage .   2½d.

The 30th day of the same month.

Of John of Houeden[5] ½ a ' russet ' cloth . . .   2d.

John Symeson ½ a white cloth . . . .   2d.

Agnes Cuteler, 6 ells of ' grene ' . . . .   1d.

     Sum: Cloths .   1 and 6 ells.
            Subs.   .   5d.
            Ulnage .   ¾d.

The first day of October.

Andrew Joynour ½ a ' russet ' cloth and ½ a ' blewe ' cloth .   4d.

Robert Warde[6] for 1½ white cloth . . . .   6d.

Of the same Robert for 6½ ' russet ' cloths and 1 ' scarlet ' cloth   2s. 8d.

John Elsewyk ½ a red cloth . . . .   2d.

John of Spilesby ½ a white cloth . . . .   2d.

Patrick Hossear 12 ells of red and ½ a ' russet ' cloth .   4d.

---

[1] Robert Sharples, " draper," was admitted a freeman in 1377–8.

[2] John of Briddlyngton, " wever," was admitted a freeman in 1386–7.

[3] A Hugh of Chartres, " taillour," was admitted a freeman in 1357–8, but a Hugh Charters is mentioned as " Hugh Charters, junr., draper," in 1416–7, whose son, Thomas, was admitted a freeman " per patrem " in the latter year.

[4] John of Topcliff, " marchaunt," was admitted a freeman in 1383–4, and was appointed a Chamberlain in 1386–7.

[5] John of Houden, seemingly the man mentioned in the text, was Lord Mayor of York in 1384–5.

[6] A Robert Warde, " webster," was made a freeman in 1380–1; a Thomas Warde, son of Robert Warde, " mercator," was admitted in 1405–6, and a John Warde, son of Robert Warde, mercer, was admitted " per patrem " in 1401–2. It seems as though " merchant " and " mercer " were both sometimes translations of " mercator " (?).

Sum: Cloths . 10½ and 12 ells.
   Subs. . 3s. 2d.
   Ulnage . 6d.
   Scarlet . 1 cloth 6d.
   Ulnage . ½d.

The 2d day of the same month.

Of Albreda of Burton for ½ a 'plunket' cloth . . .	2d.
Robert Hobsthort 6 ells of russet	1d.
Robert of Kyrkeby[1] for ½ a cloth of 'ray' . . .	2d.
John of Hamerton[2] ½ a white cloth	2d.
Mabbot [sic] for 6 ells of russet	1d.
William Walker ½ a white cloth	2d.
Robert Brokett[3] ½ a 'plunkett' cloth . . .	2d.

   Sum: Cloths . 2½ and 6 ells.
     Subs. . 2s.
     Ulnage . 1½d.

The 3d day of the same month.

Of Marjory of Kyllynghay ½ a russet cloth . . .	2d.
Alice of Couton ½ a white cloth	2d.
Hugh of Chartyrs for 2 'plunket' cloths . . .	8d.
Thomas Horneby[4] 2 'melde' and 1 cloth of 'taude'. .	10d.
Thomas Pultrer ½ a 'plunkett' cloth , . . .	2d.

   Sum: Cloths . 6
     Subs. . 2s.
     Ulnage . 3d.

The 4th day of the same month.

Of Thomas Horneby 1 cloth of 'cogsall' and 1 'meld' cloth	8d.

   Sum: Cloths . 2
     Subs. . 8d.
     Ulnage . 1d.

The 5th day of the same month.

Of Alice Hukester ½ a white cloth	2d.
John of Walde ½ a white cloth	2d.
John of Calthorn ½ a white cloth	2d.

   Sum: Cloths . 1½
     Subs. . 6d.
     Ulnage . ¾d.

The 6th day of the same month.

Of John of Thorneton 4 'blewe', 3 red, 1 'russet,' and 1 'grene' cloths	3s.

   Sum: Cloths . 9
     Subs. . 3s.
     Ulnage . 4½d.

[1] Robert of Kirkeby, " merchant," was admitted a freeman in 1389-90, and was one of the two Sheriffs, according to Drake, in 1406. His daughter, Agnes, married William Bowes, merchant, eldest son of William Bowes. Her husband was Lord Mayor of York in 1441-2.

[2] A John of Hamerton, " webster," was admitted a freeman in 1364-5.

[3] A Robert Broket, " draper," was admitted a freeman in 1389-90.

[4] A Thomas of Horneby, " tailliour," was elected a freeman in 1372-3.

The 7th day of the same month.

Of John Brathwayt 3 'blewe,' 2½ 'grene,' ½ of 'morrey,' 2½
red, ½ white, and 1 'blake' cloths . . . . 3s. 4d.
William Fouler[1] ½ a cloth of 'motley' . . . . 2d.

Sum: Cloths . 10½
Subs. . 3s. 6d.
Ulnage . 5¼d.

The 8th day of the same month.

Of John of Somerby[2] ½ a red cloth . . . . . 2d.
William Fouleford[3] ½ a 'plunket' cloth . . . . 2d.
Beatrice Warde ½ a 'meld' cloth . . . . . 2d.
Agnes of Wellom ½ a 'meld' cloth . . . . . 2d.
Joan of Dryghous 5 ells of 'plunket' . . . . 1d.
Joan of Burton 6 ells of white . . . . . 1d.

Sum: Cloths . 2 and 11 ells.
Subs. . 10d.
Ulnage . 1½d.

The 9th day of the same month.

Of Thomas of Thuayte[4] ½ a 'russet' cloth . . . . 2d.
Margaret Hukester ½ a 'meld' cloth . . . . 2d.
Thomas Taillour ½ a white cloth . . . . . 2d.
John Qweldale 1 'blewe' and 1 'plunket' cloth . . 8d.

Sum: Cloths . 3½
Subs. . 14d.
Ulnage . 1¾d.

The 10th day of the same month.

Of John of Lynton for ½ a 'russet' cloth . . . 2d.
John Lame[5] for ½ a 'melde' cloth . . . 2d.
William Webester for 6 ells of 'blewe' . . . 1d.
Margaret of Lapyngton 6 ells of 'melde' . . . 1d.

Sum: Cloths . 1 and 12 ells.
Subs. . 6d.
Ulnage . 1d.

The 12th day of the same month.

Of Thomas Brasebreg[6] 1 white, and ½ a 'russet' cloth . 6d.
John Rumby 1 'plunket' cloth . . . . . 4d.

Sum: Cloths . 2½
Subs. . 10d.
Ulnage . 1d.

The 13th day of the same month.

Of Thomas Hornby 3 cloths of 'rede melde' . . . 12d.

[1] William Foughler, "draper," was admitted a freeman 1384–5.
[2] John of Somerby, "taillour," was admitted a freeman 1378–9.
[3] William of Fullford, "webster," was admitted a freeman 1376–7.
[4] A Thomas of Thwayte, "webster," was admitted a freeman 1349–50.
[5] John Lambe, "coverlytwever," admitted a freeman 1378–9.
[6] Thomas of Bracebrigg, "wever," was admitted a freeman in 1391–2,
"because he is exonerated from the Liberty and from the Aldermanship."

John Candeler 1 white cloth . . . . . . 4d.
Adam of Collome 1½ white cloth . . . . . 6d.

    Sum: Cloths . 5½
      Subs. . 22d.
      Ulnage . 2¾d.

The 14th day of the same month.

Of John of Raghton for 2 'blewe' cloths . . . 8d.
Adam Sporier 1 white cloth . . . . . . 4d.

    Sum: Cloths . 3
      Subs. . 12d.
      Ulnage . 1½d.

The 15th day of the same month.

Of Joan of Calthorn for 9 ells of 'plunket' . . . 1½d.
Robert Sarplys 1 'russet' cloth and 1 red cloth . . 8d.
The same Robert for 24 'duzen' of 'narrow clothe,' containing
6 cloths of assize . . . . 2s.

    Sum: Cloths . 8 and 9 ells.
      Subs. . 2s. 9½d.
      Ulnage . 4¼d.

The 16th day of the same month.

Of Hugh of Chartrys 1 white and ½ a 'russet' cloth . 6d.
Richard Wyrsthop 1 'cogsall' cloth . . . . 4d.
Thomas Curour' 1 white cloth . . . . 4d.
Nicholas Peraunt ½ a 'blake' cloth . . . . 2d.
John Candeler 6 ells of white cloth . . . . 1d.

    Sum: Cloths . 4 and 6 ells.
      Subs. . 17d.
      Ulnage . 2¼d.

The 17th day of the same month.

Of John Taillour 6 ells of white cloth . . . . 1d.
Alice of Langton ½ a 'russet' cloth . . . . 2d.
Joan of Brereton 6 ells of 'meld' cloth . . . . 1d.
Alice of Ellerton 6 ells of 'grene' cloth . . . . 1d.
William Redhode[1] 1½ 'russet' cloth . . . . 6d.

    Sum: Cloths . 2½ and 5 ells.
      Subs. . 11d.
      Ulnage . 1¾d.

The 19th day of the same month.

Of William Fouler 1 'plunket' cloth, ½ a 'sangwyn,' ½ a
red, and ½ a white cloth . . . . . . 10d.
Richard Howe[2] 1 'blewe' and 1 white cloth . . . 8d.
Robert of Rypon[3] 1 white and 1 'plunket' cloth . . 8d.

---

[1] A William Redhode, " mercer," was admitted a freeman in 1352–3, and the same man, apparently, was a Chamberlain in 1376–7. In 1385–6 Richard Redhode, " draper," described as " serviens " of William Redhode, was admitted a freeman.

[2] Richard of the Howe, " littester," was elected a freeman in 1384–5.

[3] Robert of Ripon, " merchant," was elected a freeman in 1385–6.

Joan Hoperton ½ a white cloth .   .   .   .   .   2d.
Joan of Flaxton ½ a white cloth .   .   .   .   .   2d.

          Sum: Cloths . 7½
                  Subs.   . 2s. 6d.
                  Ulnage .   3¾d.

The 20th day of the same month.

Of Richard Irenmanger 3 white, 4 'russet' and 1½ 'plunket'
   cloths .   .   .   .   .   . 2s. 10d.
Thomas Horneby 1 red and 1 'meld' cloth .   .   8d.
Nicholas Peraunt 1 'blewe' cloth .   .   .   4d.
Hugh of Stoketon[1] 1 red cloth .   .   .   4d.
Joan of Burton ½ a 'russet' cloth .   .   2d.
Alice of Neweton 7 ells of 'plunket' .   .   1d.

          Sum: Cloths . 13 and 7 ells.
                  Subs.   . 4s. 5d.
                  Ulnage . 6¾d.

The 21st day of the same month.

Of John of Thorneton 3 'blewe,' 2½ 'grene,' ½ a 'blak,' and
  2 red cloths .   .   .   .   .   . 2s. 8d.
Thomas of Gare[2] 8 'blewe,' 4 red cloths, 1 'blake,' 2 'russet,'
  and 13 duzen containing 3 cloths and 6 ells of a cloth of
  assize of 'melde clothe' .   .   .   . 6s. 1d.
William Redhod 1 'blewe' cloth .   .   .   4d.
Robert of Lokton[3] 2 red and 3 'blewe' cloths .   20d.
Richard of Lawe 2 'blewe' and 2 white cloths .   16d.
John Sherman ½ a white cloth .   .   .   2d.

          Sum: Cloths . 36½ and 6 ells.
                  Subs.   . 12s. 3d.
                  Ulnage . 18½d.

The 22d of the same month.

Of John Brathewayt ½ a red, ½ a 'blak,' and ½ a 'blewe' . 6d.
William Scauesby[4] 2 red, 2 'blak,' and 3 'grene,' 1 'russet,'
  1 'plunket,' and ½ white cloth .   .   . 3s. 2d.
Thomas Askham 2 'blewe,' 1 'grene,' 1 'blak,' and 1 red cloth 20d.
John of Thorneton 3 'blewe,' 1 'grene,' and 1½ red cloth . 22d.
Walter Bell 1 'blak,' 1 'russet,' 2 'blewe,' and 1 red cloth . 20d.
Emmota Qweythand 1 'meld,' ½ white, and ½ a 'russet' cloth 8d.

---

[1] Hugh of Stokton, "draper," entered in 1391–2, into residence (*intravit moram*) in the City till Pentecost in the 20th year [of Ric. II] on the penalty of the forfeiture of his freemanship. In 1395–6 we learn that he was " reconciled," paid 9s. to the Chamber and had a day fixed for his residence in the City, viz., the feast of the Purification, in the 23rd year, under penalty of the forfeiture of his freemanship.

[2] Thomas of the Gare, son of William of the Gare, " mercer," was admitted a freeman in 1383–4. According to a note (p. 10) in the Register of Corpus Christi Guild, published by the Surtees Society, he was bailiff in 1394–5, M.P. in 1419, and Lord Mayor in 1420.

[3] Robert of Lokton, " draper," was admitted a freeman in 1385–6.

[4] William of Scauceby, " draper," was admitted a freeman in 1380–1, and was a Chamberlain of the City in 1392–3 and Sheriff of York in 1398.

Agnes Nyghtgale for 7 ells of ' plunket ' . . . . 1*d.*
Richard of Santon 16½ ' meld ' cloths . . . . 5*s.* 6*d.*
John of Thorneton 3½ ' meld,' ½ of ' plunket,' 1½ of red, and
 1½ ' blewe ' cloths . . . . 2*s.* 4*d.*

Sum: Cloths . 52 and 7 ells.
Subs. . 17*s.* 5*d.*
Ulnage . 2*s.* 1¼*d.*

The 23d day of the same month.

Of William of Merton 3 red, 4 ' blewe,' 3 ' grene,' 1 ' blak,' ½ of
 ' russet,' 1 of white, and 1 of ' plunkett ' . . . 4*s.* 6*d.*
Richard Redehode 5 ' blewe,' 3 red, 2 ' blak,' 2 ' russet,' 1
 ' morroy,' and 1 ' plunket ' . . . . . 4*s.* 8*d.*

Sum: Cloths . 52 and 7 ells.
Subs. . 17*s.* 5*d.*
Ulnage . 2*s.* 1¼*d.*

The 24th of the same month.

Of Hugh of Stokton 2 ' blewe,' 1 red, and 1 ' grene ' cloth . 16*d.*
William Fouler 2 ' blewe ' and 1 ' plunkett ' . . . 12*d.*
Richard of Worsthop 1½ of ' plunkett ' . . . . 6*d.*
Hugh of Chartres 1 ' blewe ' and 1 red cloth . . . 8*d.*
William Plater ½ a ' russet ' cloth . . . . . 2*d.*
Hogekyn of Crome 3 white, 2 ' blewe,' and 1 ' plunkett ' cloth 2*s.*
William at ye tonend for 8 ells of ' plunket ' . . 1¼*d.*

Sum: Cloths . 17 and 8 ells.
Subs. . 5*s.* 9½*d.*
Ulnage . 8¾*d.*

The 26th day of the same month.

Of John Taillour ½ a ' russet ' cloth and 7 ells of white . 3*d.*
Alice of Langton ½ a ' russet ' . . . . . 2*d.*
Joan of Brereton 7 ells of ' meld ' and 7 ells of white . . 2*d.*
Alice Sporear 7 ells of ' meld ' . . . . . 1*d.*
Joan Hukester 7 ells of white . . . . . 1*d.*
Alice of Otryngton ½ a ' blew ' cloth . . . . 2*d.*
Agnes of Wellom 6 ells of ' grene ' . . . . . 1*d.*
John of Raghton 4 ' blewe ' cloths . . . . . 16*d.*
William Redhode 1½ ' russet ' cloth . . . . 6*d.*

Sum: Cloths . 8½ and 2 ells.
Subs. . 2*s.* 10*d.*
Ulnage . 4½*d.*

The 27th day of the same month.

Of Robert Broket ½ a ' plonket ' cloth . . . . 2*d.*
Marjory of Bank ½ a ' russet ' . . . . . 2*d.*
Agnes of Monton 6 ells of ' melde '. . . . . 1*d.*
Adam of Notton 6 ells of ' russet ' . . . . . 1*d.*
Agnes of Melby 3 ells of ' blewe ' . . . . . ½*d.*
Joan Fethyr 3 ells of ' grene ' . . . . . ½*d.*

Sum: Cloths . 1½ and 5 ells.
Subs. . 7*d.*
Ulnage . ¾*d.*

The 28th day of the same month.

Of John of Thorneton 4 red, 4 'redemelde,' 3 'blake,' 3½
'blewe,' and 2 'grene' . . . . . . 5s. 6d.
Richard of Santon[1] 1 white, 1 'blak,' 1 'blewe,' ½ a cloth of
'plunket,' 1 red, and 1 'redemelde' . . . . 22d.

Sum: Cloths . 22
Subs. . 7s. 4d.
Ulnage . 11d.

The 29th day of the same month.

Of John of Braythwayt 2 'grene,' 1 'blewe,' 1 'blak,' and
1 red . . . . 20d.
Nicholas Baynbryg 6 white, 2 'russet,' 1 'grene,' and 5 duzen
straytes, containing 1 cloth and 6 ells of a cloth of assize 3s. 5d.

Sum: Cloths . 15 and 6 ells.
Subs. . 5s. 1d.
Ulnage . 7¾d.

The 30th day of the same month.

Of William of Wyrsthopp 6 'blewe,' 8 red, 4 'sangwyn,'
3 'morrey,' 3 'plunket,' 2 'taude,' 2 'blak,' 2½ 'grene'
cloths . . . . 10s. 2d.
Richard of Wyrsthop 1½ 'taude' and ½ a red cloth . . 8d.
William Appylby[2] 1½ 'blewe' cloth . . . . 6d.
Margaret of Griseley 3 ells of red . . . . . ½d.
Mabbot 6 ells of 'melde' . . . . . . 1d.

Sum: Cloths . 34 and 9 ells.
Subs. . 11s. 5½d.
Ulnage . 17¾d.

The 31st day of the same month.

Of Thomas Askham 1 'blewe' cloth, 1 red cloth, and 1 'blak'
cloth . . . . 12d.
George Askham ½ a 'blewe' cloth and ½ a 'plunket' cloth 4d.
Robert Lofthous 1 red cloth and 1 'blak' cloth . . 8d.
William Skawesby 2½ 'blewe' cloths, 2 'grene' cloths, and
2 red cloths . . . . 2s. 2d.

Sum: Cloths . 12½
Subs. . 4s. 2d.
Ulnage . 6¼d.

The 2d day of November.

Of Thomas of Gare 5 'blewe moteley' cloths and 2 'grene
moteley,' and 1 'russet moteley' . . . . 2s. 8d.
Nicholas Peraunt ½ a 'russet' cloth . . . . 2d.
Adam of Stokes for ½ a cloth of the same . . . 2d.
Laurence Lyttester[3] ½ a cloth and 6 ells of 'blewe' . . 3d.

---

[1] A Richard of Santon, "mercer," was admitted a freeman in 1344–5, and
was, perhaps, the Richard of Santon who was a Chamberlain in 1379–80.
There was also a Richard of Santon, "draper," admitted in 1334–5.

[2] A William of Appleby was a Chamberlain of York in 1355–6.

[3] Laurence Littester, of Conyngstreet, was a Chamberlain of York in
1394–5.

Sum: Cloths . 9½ and 6 ells.
   Subs. . 3s. 3d.
   Ulnage . 5d.

The 3d day of the same month.

Of John Ireard 1 'russet' cloth . . . . . 4d.
Albreda of Burton ½ a cloth . . . . . 2d.
Alicia Otryngton 10 ells of 'morrey' . . . . 1½d.
Thomas of Jedeword 7 ells of red . . . . . 1d.
John of Warulby 2 red cloths, 2 'blewe' cloths, 2 'sang-wyn' cloths, 2 white cloths, 1 'grene' cloth, and 1 'plunket' cloth . . . . 3s. 4d.

Sum: Cloths . 12 and 4 ells.
   Subs. . 4s. 0½d.
   Ulnage . 6d.

The 4th day of the same month.

Of John Bowth 1 red cloth . . . . . . 4d.
John of Salesby[1] ½ a red cloth . . . . . 2d.
John Sessay 3 red cloths, 2 'blewe' cloths, and 2 white cloths 2s.4d.
John of Lyndessay[2] 3 white cloths, ½ a 'plunket' cloth, 2 'russet' cloths, and 1 'blewe' cloth. . . . 2s.2d.

Sum: Cloths . 15
   Subs. . 5s.
   Ulnage . 7½d.

The 5th day of the same month.

Of John of Cawod 2 'blewe' cloths and 2 'plunket' cloths . 16d.
William Flemyng[3] 1 white cloth and 1 'russet' cloth . . 8d.
Richard of Calton 1 'melde' cloth . . . . 4d.
Richard of Wyrsthop ½ a red cloth and ½ a 'melde' cloth . 4d.
Robert Sarplys 1 red cloth . . . . . . 4d.

Sum: Cloths . 9
   Subs. . 3s.
   Ulnage . 4½d.

The 6th day of the same month.

Of Thomas Hagthorp 1 'ray' cloth . . . . 4d.
William Mareshall ½ a 'melde' cloth . . . . 2d.
Mabbot ½ a 'blewe' cloth . . . . . . 2d.
John Eleswyk 7 ells of 'blewe' . . . . . 1d.
Alice Clethyrowe ½ a 'melde' cloth . . . . 2d.
Agnes Barbour ½ a white cloth . . . . . 2d.
Margaret of Elvyngton 6 ells of 'blewe' . . . . 1d.
John of Brathwayt ½ a 'meld' cloth and ½ a white cloth . 4d.

Sum: Cloths . 4½
   Subs. . 18d.
   Ulnage . 2¼d.

[1] John of Saleby, "wever," was admitted a freeman in 1382–3.

[2] A John of Lyndesay, son of Robert of Lyndesay, was admitted "per patrem" a freeman in 1379–80, and was a Chamberlain in 1385–6.

[3] William Flemyng, "mercer," was admitted a freeman in 1393–4.

The 7th day of the same month.

Of John Sessay 3 white cloths, 2 'plunket' cloths, 1 'sangwyn' cloth, and 2 red cloths . . . . . . 2s. 8d.

Robert of Lokton 2 'grene' cloths, 1 'blewe' cloth, and 2 red cloths . . . . 20d.

Sum: Cloths . 13
     Subs. . 4s. 4d.
     Ulnage . 6½d.

The 9th day of the same month.

Of Thomas Horneby 2 'grene-melde' cloths, and 1 'sangwyn' cloth . . . . 12d.

Richard of Santon 1 'blewe melde' cloth . . . 4d.

Thomas Askham 1 'grene' cloth and ½ a red cloth . 6d.

Thomas Frere ½ a 'russet' cloth . . . . . 2d.

Sum: Cloths . 6
     Subs. . 2s.
     Ulnage . 3d.

The 10th day of the same month.

Of Agnes of Selby ½ a 'russet' cloth . . . . 2d.

Alice Leleman ½ a 'meld' cloth . . . . . 2d.

Gilbert Shereman ½ a 'russet' cloth . . . . 2d.

Cicilia of Dreyhous 6 ells of 'russet' . . . . 1d.

Sum: Cloths . 1½ and 6 ells.
     Subs. . 7d.
     Ulnage . 1d.

The 11th day of the same month.

Of Thomas Horneby 1 'taude' cloth . . . . 4d.

Thomas Esyngwald[1] ½ a 'russet' cloth . . . . 2d.

Thomas Jedeword 3 ells of 'blak' . . . . . ½d.

Sum: Cloths . 1½ and 3 ells.
     Subs. . 6½d.
     Ulnage . ¾d.

The 12th day of the same month.

Of Joan Coke 6 ells of 'blewe' . . . . . 1d.

John Taillour 6 ells of 'russet' . . . . . 1d.

Alice of Ricall ½ a 'russet' cloth . . . . . 2d.

Sum: Cloths . ½ a cloth and 12 ells.
     Subs. . 4d.
     Ulnage . ½d.

The 13th day of the same month.

Of Thomas of Catton 1 'russet' cloth . . . . 4d.

John of Cetryngton ½ a 'cogesall' cloth . . . 2d.

Thomas of Grysley 1 'blewe' cloth . . . . 4d.

Thomas of [sic] Palmer 1 'sangwyn' cloth . . . 4d.

Thomas of Garton[2] 6 ells of white . . . . . 1d.

[1] A Thomas of Esyngwald, " shereman," was admitted a freeman in 1382–3; he was, perhaps, the Thomas of Esyngwald who was a Chamberlain in 1405–6.

[2] A Thomas of Garton, " mercer," was admitted a freeman in 1353–4.

Joan of Brereton 7 ells of ' russet '   .   .   .   .   1d.

Sum: Cloths . 4
Subs.   . 16d.
Ulnage . 2d.

The 14th day of the same month.

Of John Elsewyk ½ a red cloth   .   .   .   .   .   2d.
John Qweldale 7 ells of ' blewe ' and 7 ells of ' russet '   .   2d.
John of Sessay 2 white cloths, 1 ' sangwyn ' cloth, and 1
  ' blewe ' cloth .   .   .   .   16d.
William Skawesby 2 red cloths, 1 ' blewe ' cloth, 1 ' grene ' cloth,
  and 1 ' blake ' cloth .   .   .   .   .   .   20d.
Richard of Santon 3 ' melde ' cloths   .   .   .   .   2d.

Sum: Cloths . 10
Subs.   . 3s. 6d.
Ulnage . 5¼d.

The 16th day of the same month.

Of Thomas Holme[1] 6 red cloths, 2 ' blak ' cloths, 5 ' morey '
cloths, 6 ' sangwyn ' cloths, 7 ' blewe ' cloths, 1 white
cloth, 1 ' motley ' white cloth, ½ a cloth of ' grene motley,'
1 ' blewe motley ' cloth, and 1 ' grene motley ' cloth   .   10s.

Sum: Cloths . 31
Subs.   . 11s. 4d.
Ulnage . 17d.

The 17th day of the same month.

Of Richard of Ulleston 8 ' sangwyn.' cloths, 6 red cloths,
4 ' russet ' cloths, 8 ' blewe ' cloths, 4 white cloths, and 4
' morrey ' cloths   .   .   .   .   .   .   11s. 4d.

Sum: Cloths . 34
Subs.   . 11s. 4d.
Ulnage . 17d.

The 18th day of the same month.

Of John Kyrkeham 6 ' plunket ' cloths, 9 ' blewe ' cloths, 8 red
cloths, 3 white cloths, 1 ' blak ' cloth, 4 ' morrey ' cloths,
and 2 ' grene ' cloths .   .   .   .   11s.

Sum: Cloths . 33
Subs.   . 11s.
Ulnage . . 16½d.

The 19th day of the same month.

Of John Brathwayt 3 ' cogsale ' cloths, 1 ' grene ' cloth,
1 ' blewe ' cloth, 1 red cloth, 1 ' plunket ' cloth, and 1 cloth
of ' plunket-meld '   .   .   .   . 2s. 8d.

Sum: Cloths . 8
Subs.   . 2s. 8d.
Ulnage . 4d.

---

[1] A Thomas of Howom, of Beverley, " mercer," was admitted a freeman
in 1373–4.

The 20th day of the same month.

Of John Percy[1] 6 red cloths, 5 ' blewe ' cloths, 2 ' plunket '
cloths, 1 ' blewe ' cloth, 1 ' morrey ' cloth, and 1 ' blak '
cloth . . . . 5s. 4d.

Sum: Cloths . 16
Subs. . 5s. 4d.
Ulnage . 8d.

The 21st day of the same month.

Of John of Foston[2] ½ a ' russet ' cloth . . . . 2d.
John Eleswyk ½ a red cloth . . . . . . 2d.
Joan of Moreby ½ a ' russet ' cloth . . . . . 2d.
Alice of Tollerton 6 ells of white . . . . . 1d.
Agnes of Blyth 1 ' taude ' cloth . . . . . 4d.

Sum: Cloths . 2½ and 6 ells.
Subs. . 11d.
Ulnage . 1½d.

The 23d day of the same month.

Of Robert of Fulford for 6 ells of white . . . 1d.
Richard of Manfeld 7 ells of red . . . . . 1d.
Alice of Yeversley 3 ells of ' grene ' . . . . ½d.

Sum: Cloths . ½ a cloth and 3 ells.
Subs. . 2½d.
Ulnage . ½d.

The 24th day of the same month.

Of Cicilia of Shapton ½ a ' blewe ' cloth . . . . 2d.
Gilbert Sherman ½ a ' plunket ' cloth . . . . 2d.
Alice of Crosby ½ a ' russet ' cloth . . . . . 2d.

Sum: Cloths . 1½
Subs. . 6d.
Ulnage . ¾d.

The 25th day of the same month.

Of Thomas of Myre 24 ' duzen of a narrowe cloth ' containing 6 cloths of assize . . . . 2s.
John de Dent[3] 8 white cloths, 2 ' plunket ' cloths, 2 ' russet '
cloths, and 1½ ' blewe ' . . . . 4s.

Sum: Cloths . 19½
Subs. . 6s. 6d.
Ulnage . 9¾d.

The 26th day of the same month.

Of William of Merton 1½ ' grene ' cloth and 1½ red cloth . 12d.
William Struge 1 red cloth and ½ a ' blewe ' cloth . . 6d.

Sum: Cloths . 4½
Subs. . 18d.
Ulnage . 2¼d.

[1] John Perceay, " mercer," was admitted a freeman in 1389–90.
[2] John of Foston, " mercer," was admitted a freeman in 1362–3.
[3] John de Dent, " mercer," was admitted a freeman in 1390–1.

The 27th day of the same month.

Of John Copeland[1] ½ a 'russet' cloth . . . . 2d.
Richard Redehode 1½ 'grene' cloth . . . . 6d.

        Sum: Cloths . 2
             Subs. . 8d.
             Ulnage . 1d.

The 28th day of the same month.

Of Nicholas Baynbryg 1 'plunket' cloth, 1 white cloth, and
1 'blewe' cloth . . . . 12d.
Thomas Couper 1 'melde' cloth . . . . . 4d.
John Raghton ½ a white cloth . . . . . 2d.

        Sum: Cloths . 4½
             Subs. . 18d.
             Ulnage . 2¼d.

The 30th day of the same month.

Of John of Thorneton 1 'blewe' cloth, 1 red cloth, ½ a 'melde'
cloth . . . . 10d.
Thomas Hosear 3 ells of 'grene' . . . . . ½d.
Cicilia Elvngton 6 ells of 'melde' . . . . . 1d.
Joan of Shapton 3 ells of red . . . . . ½d.

        Sum: Cloths . 2½ and 12 ells.
             Subs. . 12d.
             Ulnage . 1½d.

The 1st day of December.

Of Thomas Horneby 1 'taude' cloth . . . . 4d.
Robert of Lofthous 1½ red cloth . . . . . 6d.
John of Raghton 1½ 'blewe' cloth . . . . . 6d.
John of Berewyk 3 ells of 'taude' . . . . . ½d.

        Sum: Cloths . 4 and 3 ells.
             Subs. . 16½d.
             Ulnage . 2d.

The 2d day of the same month.

Of Robert Newbyman 2 white cloths, 2 'plunket' cloths,
1 'sangwyn' cloth, and 2 'blewe' cloths . . . 2s. 4d.

        Sum: Cloths . 7
             Subs. . 2s. 4d.
             Ulnage . 3½d.

The 3d day of the same month.

Of John of Raghton 1 'blewe' cloth, 1 white cloth, and 1 red
cloth . . . . 12d.

        Sum: Cloths . 3
             Subs. . 12d.
             Ulnage . 1½d.

The 4th day of the same month.

Of Thomas Askham 1 red cloth and ½ a 'grene' cloth . 6d.

        Sum: Cloths . 1½
             Subs. . 6d.
             Ulnage . ¾d.

---

[1] John of Coupland, "taillour," was admitted a freeman in 1360–1.

The 5th day of the same month.

Of William Redehode ½ a 'russet' cloth . . . . 2d.
Isabell Rumby ½ a 'plunket' cloth . . . . 2d.

Sum: Cloths . 1
Subs. . 4d.
Ulnage . ½d.

The 7th day of the same month.

Of John of Chartris 1 'melde' cloth . . . . 4d.
John Adamson ½ a white cloth . . . . . 2d.

Sum: Cloths . 1½
Subs. . 6d.
Ulnage . ¾d.

The 8th day of the same month.

Of John of Thorneton 3 'grene' cloths, 2 'blak' cloths, 1 red
cloth, 1 'meld' cloth, and 1 white cloth . . . 2s. 8d.

Sum: Cloths . 8
Subs. . 2s. 8d.
Ulnage . 4d.

The 9th day of the same month.

Of Robert Clerk 7 ells of 'melde' . . . . 1d.
William of Heton 7 ells of 'melde' . . . . 1d.
Margaret of Gysealay (?) 6 ells of 'russet' . . . 1d.
The wife of William Horneby[1] 5 'russet' cloths, 3 'blewe'
cloths, and 2 white cloths . . . . . 3s. 4d.
Richard of Calton ½ a 'melde' cloth . . . . 2d.
Thomas Frere ½ a 'russet' cloth . . . . 2d.

Sum: Cloths . 11½ and 7 ells.
Subs. . 3s. 11d.
Ulnage . 6d.

The 10th day of the same month.

Of Margaret of Ryseley 6 ells of white . . . . 1d.
Alice of Otryngton ½ a 'russet' cloth . . . . 2d.
Cicilia of Dryenhous 3 ells of 'melde' . . . . ½d.
Edward Shereman ½ a 'plunket' cloth . . . . 2d.

Sum: Cloths . 1 and 20 ells.
Subs. . 5½d.
Ulnage . ¾d.

The 2d day of January.

Of Robert of Rypon 4 white cloths and 2 'russet' cloths . 2s.
John Bukeland 1 red cloth and 1 'russet' cloth . . 8d.
John Lyndesey 2 red cloths, 1 'blak' cloth, and ½ a 'russet' cloth 14d.
John of Dent 1 'russet' cloth . . . . . 4d.

Sum: Cloths . 12½
Subs. . 4s. 2d.
Ulnage . 6¼d.

[1] Perhaps she was the wife of William of Horneby, " merchant," who was admitted a freeman in 1374–5 and was a Chamberlain in 1387–8.

The 7th day of the same month.

Of . . . . . . (?) Shepman wyff 1 ' blewe ' cloth and 1 red cloth   8*d.*

John Panall ½ a red cloth and ½ a ' russet ' cloth .   .   4*d.*

         Sum: Cloths . 3

               Subs. . 12*d.*

               Ulnage . 1½*d.*

The 8th day of the same month.

Of John of Garston 3 white cloths, 2 ' blewe ' cloths, 1 red cloth, and 1 ' sangwyn ' cloth .   .   .   . 2*s.* 4*d.*

         Sum: Cloths . 7

               Subs. . 2*s.* 4*d.*

               Ulnage . 3½*d.*

The 9th day of the same month.

Of Laurence Patyner 1 white cloth .   .   .   . 4*d.*

Richard of Howe 5 white cloths, 4 ' blewe,' 1 ' russet,' 1 ' sang-wyn,' 7 ells of white, and 1 red cloth .   .   . 4*s.* 1*d.*

         Sum: Cloths . 13 and 7 ells.

               Subs. . 4*s.* 6*d.*

               Ulnage . 6¾*d.*

The 11th day of the same month.

Of Albreda of Burton 1 ' blewe ' cloth and ½ a white cloth . 6*d.*

         Sum: Cloths . 1½

               Subs. . 6*d.*

               Ulnage . ¾*d.*

The 12th day of the same month.

Of Joan of Horneby 11 white cloths, 4 ' plunket ' cloths, and 5 ' blewe ' cloths .   .   .   .   . 6*s.* 8*d.*

Robert of Rypon ½ a ' blewe ' cloth .   .   .   . 2*d.*

         Sum: Cloths . 20½

               Subs. . 6*s.* 10*d.*

               Ulnage . 10¼*d.*

The 13th day of the same month.

Of Robert Sarplys ½ a ' blewe ' cloth and ½ a red cloth . 4*d.*

         Sum: Cloths . 1

               Subs. . 4*d.*

               Ulnage . ½*d.*

The 14th day of the same month.

[The and-writing hanges.] Of Alice Otryngton ½ a ' blewe ' cloth and 7 yards of ' russet '   3*d.*

Emota Taillour 3 yds. of red cloth .   .   . ½*d.*

William Foughler 2 ' russet motle ' cloths .   .   . 8*d.*

Agnes Bene 6 yds. of blue cloth .   .   .   . 1*d.*

Robert Galtres 4 yds. of ' russet ' cloth .   .   . ½*d.*

John Shopton 4 yds. of red cloth .   .   .   . ½*d.*

         Sum: Cloths . 3 and 11 ells.

               Subs. . 13½*d.*

               Ulnage . 1¾*d.*

E

The 15th day of January.

Of William Dobson 76 dozens of strait cloth, containing 19 cloths of assize . . . . 6s. 4d.

Thomas Lam 22 dozens of strait cloth, containing 5½ cloths of assize . . . . 22d.

William Coke 50 dozens of strait cloth, containing 12½ cloths of assize . . . . 4s. 2d.

       Sum: Cloths . 37
            Subs. . 12s 4d.
            Ulnage . 18½d.

The 20th day of January.

Of John of Middeham 3 green cloths and 3½ blue cloths of assize . . . . 2s. 2d.

Of the same ½ a 'whitemotle' . . . . . . 2d.

Agnes of Stokton 7 yds. of blue cloth . . . . 1d.

       Sum: Cloths . 7 and 7 ells.
            Subs. . 2s. 5d.
            Ulnage . 3¾d.

The 21st day of January.

Of Joan Spicer ½ a white cloth . . . . . 2d.

       Sum: Cloths . ½ a cloth.
            Subs. . 2d.
            Ulnage . ¼d.

The 22d day of January.

Of John of Laxton 2½ red cloths, 2 blue cloths, ½ a white cloth, ½ a black cloth, and ½ a 'plunket' cloth . . . 2s.

       Sum: Cloths . 6
            Subs. . 2s.
            Ulnage . 3d.

The 23d day of January.

Of John Brathwait 2 blue cloths, 1 red cloth, 1 green cloth, and ½ a white cloth . . . . . . 18d.

Robert Sharplys 1 blue cloth and 1 red cloth . . . 8d.

Robert Broket ½ a red cloth . . . . . . 2d.

       Sum: Cloths . 7
            Subs. . 2s. 4d.
            Ulnage . 3½d.

The 29th day of January.

Of Joan Gar 8 ells of 'russet' cloth . . . . 1d.

John Marshall 6 ells of 'plunket' cloth . . . . 1d.

       Sum: Cloths . 14 ells.
            Subs. . 2d.
            Ulnage . ¼d.

The 30th day of January.

Of William Berwyk 1 dozen strait cloths, containing 6 yds. of a cloth of assize . . . . 1d.

Marion Porter ½ a 'plunket' cloth . . . . . 2d.

Thomas Mire 24 dozens of strait cloth, containing 6 cloths of
    assize .   .   .   .   2s.

        Sum: Cloths . 6½ and 6 ells.
             Subs. . 2s. 3d.
             Ulnage . 3½d.

The 1st day of February.

Of John Barnardcastell 1½ white cloth .   .   .   .   6d.
        Sum: Cloths . 1½
             Subs. . 6d.
             Ulnage . ¾d.

The 3d day of February.

Of Thomas of Gare 32 'motle' cloths .   .   .   10s. 8d.
William Sturge 3 blue cloths, 1 black cloth, 1 red cloth,
    2 green cloths, 1 white cloth, and 2 'plunket' cloths . 3s. 4d.
        Sum: Cloths . 42
             Subs. . 14s.
             Ulnage . 21d.

The 4th day of February.

Of Thomas Askham 2 blue cloths, ½ a 'russet' cloth, 1 and 7
    ells of blue cloth .   .   .   .   15d.
William Scausby 2 red cloths, 1 green cloth, 2 black cloths,
    1 'russet' cloth, 1 blue cloth, and 6 ells of green cloth . 2s. 5d.
        Sum: Cloths . 11
             Subs. . 3s. 8d.
             Ulnage . 5½d.

The 5th day of February.

Of John Kirkeby 1 'grene motle' cloth and ½ a cloth of
    'russet motley' .   .   .   .   .   .   6d.
John Shereman ½ a white cloth .   .   .   .   .   2d.
George of Thorp[1] 1 red cloth . .   .   .   .   .   4d.
Thomas Horneby 1 black cloth .   .   .   .   .   4d.
        Sum: Cloths . 4
             Subs. . 16d.
             Ulnage . 2d.

The 6th day of February.

Of John of Thornton 7 white cloths .   .   . 2s. 4d.
Alice Hurste ½ a 'redemelle' cloth . .   .   .   2d.
Thomas Askham 1 blue cloth and 1 red cloth .   . 8d.
George of Thorp 2 green oloths .   .   .   .   8d.
Agnes of Bilton 8 ells of 'russet' cloth .   .   .   1d.
Alan of Hampton 3 red cloths, 3 blue cloths, 2 green cloths,
    and 1 'sangwyn' cloth .   .   .   .   .   3s.
Joan of Shilyngton ½ a 'russet' cloth .   .   .   2d.
        Sum: Cloths . 21 and 8 ells.
             Subs. . 7s. 1d.
             Ulnage . 5¾d.

---

[1] George of Thorp, "draper," was admitted a freeman in 1392–3.

The 8th day of February.

Of John of Knaythe $\frac{1}{2}$ a white cloth	2d.
Agnes Porter 4 ells of ' russet ' cloth	$\frac{1}{2}d.$
John Pult[erer] 8 ells of cloth	1d.
Joan Fulforth 12 (?) ells of white cloth	$1\frac{1}{2}d.$
William of Spofforth[1] 3 ells of ' russet ' cloth . . .	$\frac{1}{2}d.$

Sum: Cloths . 1 and 12 ells.
　　　Subs. . $5\frac{1}{2}d.$
　　　Ulnage . $\frac{3}{4}d.$

The 9th day of February.

Of John of Bedale[2] 50 dozens strait ' russet ' cloths, containing $12\frac{1}{2}$ cloths of assize	4s. 2d.
John Peeke 6 ells of white cloth	1d.
The wife of William Tundewe 6 ells of ' murray ' cloth .	1d.

Sum: Cloths . 13
　　　Subs. . 4s. 4d.
　　　Ulnage . $6\frac{1}{2}d.$

The 10th day of February.

Of William Hemyngburgh[3] $\frac{1}{2}$ a white cloth . . .	2d.
Robert Lofthous $1\frac{1}{2}$ blue cloth, 1 green cloth, 1 red cloth, and 8 ells of white cloth	$15\frac{1}{4}d.$

Sum: Cloths . 4 and 8 ells.
　　　Subs. . $17\frac{1}{4}d.$
　　　Ulnage . $2\frac{1}{4}d.$

[At this point the following total is given in the margin of the roll:]
　　　　　Cloths . $162\frac{1}{2}$ and 6 ells.
　　　　　Subs. . 54s. 2d.
　　　　　Ulnage . 6s. $4\frac{3}{4}d.$

The 11th day of February.

Of Richard Trane $1\frac{1}{2}$ red cloth and 1 ' sangwyn ' cloth .	10d.

Sum: Cloths . $2\frac{1}{2}$
　　　Subs. . 10d.
　　　Ulnage . $1\frac{1}{4}d.$

The 12th day of February.

Of Thomas Couper for $\frac{1}{2}$ a ' melle ' cloth . . .	2d.
Walter Bakster 6 ells of blue cloth	1d.
Richard of Calton $\frac{1}{2}$ a ' murray ' cloth	2d.
William Atte-Toune-end 8 dozens of strait ' plunket ' cloths, containing 6 ells of a cloth of assize	1d.

Sum: Cloths . 1 and 12 yds.
　　　Subs. . 6d.
　　　Ulnage . $\frac{3}{4}d.$

---

[1] William of Spofford, " textor," was admitted a freeman in 1378.

[2] John of Bedall, " marchaunt," was admitted a freeman in 1384-5, and a John of Bedall, " mercer," was a Chamberlain in 1399-1400, probably the same person. He was Mayor in 1417-8.

[3] William of Hemyngburgh, " walker," was admitted a freeman in 1375-6.

The 13th day of February.

Of Robert of Gaynesford 2 ' plunket ' cloths, 2 white cloths,
 1 ' russet ' cloth, and 2 blue cloths   .   .   .   . 2s. 4d.
Thomas of Bracebrigge 2 white cloths   .   .   .   . 8d.

            Sum: Cloths . 9
                 Subs.   . 3s.
                 Ulnage . 4½d.

The 15th day of February.

Of Robert of Gaynesford 2 blue cloths, 1 ' sangwyn ' cloth, and
 ½ a green cloth   .   .   .   . 14d.

            Sum: Cloths . 3
                 Subs.   . 14d.
                 Ulnage . 1½d.

The 16th day of February.

Of John Tothe 6 blue cloths, 6 ' plunket ' cloths, 8 red cloths,
 7 green cloths, 1 black cloth, 6 ' sangwyn ' cloths, and
 4 ' morray ' cloths   .   .   .   .   .   . 12s. 8d.

            Sum: Cloths . 38
                 Subs.   . 12s. 8d.
                 Ulnage . 19d.

The 17th day of February.

Of Albreda of Burton 1 white cloth   .   .   .   .   . 4d.
Walter Wharrum 1 white cloth   .   .   .   . 4d.
Margaret of Hoby 3 ells of white cloth   .   .   . ½d.

            Sum: Cloths . 2 and 3 ells.
                 Subs.   . 8½d.
                 Ulnage . 1d.

The 18th day of February.

Of Mariota Bouthe 1 mell cloth   .   .   .   .   . 4d.
William Pounfrayt[1] 2 red cloths, 1 green cloth, 1 black cloth,
 and 2 blue cloths   .   .   .   . 2s.

            Sum: Cloths . 7
                 Subs.   . 2s. 4d.
                 Ulnage . 3½d.

The 19th day of February.

Of John of Raghton 3 white cloths, 1½ and 7 ells of red cloth   19d.

            Sum: Cloths . 4½ and 7 ells.
                 Subs.   . 19d.
                 Ulnage . 2½d.

The 23d day of February.

Of Isabella of Rotherham 2 ' plunket ' cloths, 2 blue cloths,
 2 white cloths, 1 ' russet ' cloth, and 1 ' sangwyn ' cloth . 2s. 8d.

            Sum: Cloths . 8
                 Subs.   . 2s. 8d.
                 Ulnage . 4d.

[1] William of Pounfrayt, junr., " draper," was admitted a freeman in 1370–1,
and was, apparently, a Chamberlain in 1376–7.

The 25th day of February.

Of John Elsewyk 1 red cloth . . . . . . 4d.
John Porter 6 ells of strait cloth, containing 3 ells of a cloth
of assize . . . . ½d.
Thomas Wodhouse[1] ½ a blue cloth . . . . . 2d.
John Raghton ½ a white cloth . . . . . 2d.
Thomas Galtris ½ a cloth . . . . . . 2d.
Richard Redehode 2 red cloths, 2 green cloths, and 2 blue
cloths . . . . 2s.

Sum: Cloths . 8½ and 3 ells.
Subs. . 2s. 10½d.
Ulnage . 4¼d.

The 27th day of February.

Of John Godebarne ½ a white cloth . . . . 2d.
John of Newby 5 red cloths, 6 blue cloths, 2 white cloths, 2
green cloths, and 2 'plunket' cloths . . . . 5s. 8d.

Sum: Cloths . 17½
Subs. . 5s. 10d.
Ulnage . 8¾d.

[Under the sewing of this membrane the following totals are
given:]   [Sum]: 106 cloths and 7 ells.
Subs. . 36s. 7¼d.
Ulnage . 4s. 5¼d.

The first day of March.

Of Edmund Staue [or Stane] ½ a white cloth . . . 2d.
Emmota of Wistowe 1 white cloth . . . . 4d.
Thomas Bracebrigge ½ a 'russet' cloth . . . . 2d.
John Taillour ½ a 'russet' cloth . . . . . 2d.
Agnes Skipwith 3 ells of 'russet' cloth . . . . ½d.
Agnes Stokton 3 ells of white cloth . . . . ½d.

Sum: Cloths . 2½ and 6 ells.
Subs. . 11d.
Ulnage . 1½d.

The third day of March.

Of John Hillom 4 blue cloths, 3 red cloths, 2 'murray' cloths,
2 'plunket' cloths, 2 green cloths, and 3 'sangwynne'
cloths . . . . 5s. 4d.
Robert Coke 3 white cloths and 2 'russet' cloths . . 20d.
John of Laxton 2 blue cloths, 2 green cloths, and 1 red cloth. 20d.

Sum: Cloths . 26
Subs. . 8s. 8d.
Ulnage . 13d.

The 4th day of March.

Of John Rumby 1 'plunket' cloth . . . . . 4d.
Thomas Couper 1 'russet' cloth . . . . . 4d.
John of Raghton 1 'russet' cloth . . . . . 4d.
Thomas Horneby ½ a black cloth . . . . . 2d.

[1] Thomas of Wodehouses, "shereman," was admitted a freeman in 1382-3.

Thomas Esyngwold ½ a 'russet' cloth . . . . 2d.
John Elsewyk ½ a red cloth . . . . . . 2d.
    Sum: Cloths . 4½
      Subs. . 18d.
      Ulnage . 2¼d.
    The 5th day of March.
Of John Clif[1] 7 ells of 'russet' cloth . . . . 1d.
William Foughler 1 'plunket' cloth . . . . 4d.
    Sum: Cloths . 1 and 7 ells.
      Subs. . 5d.
      Ulnage . ¾d.
    The 8th day of March.
Of Joan Brome 1 'plunket' cloth . . . . . 4d.
Richard Horneby 1 blue cloth and ½ a white cloth . . 6d.
John Bywell 5½ 'medle' cloths . . . . . 22d.
    Sum: Cloths . 8
      Subs. . 2s. 8d.
      Ulnage . 4d.
    The 9th day of March.
Of Henry Lakirsuyther 3 white cloths and 2 'plunket' cloths 22d.
The wife of John Shereman 7 ells of white cloth . . 1d.
John of Grantham[2] 2 'russet' cloths and 1 white cloth . 12d.
Joan of Moreton ½ a white cloth and 4 ells of 'russet' cloth . 2½d.
    Sum: Cloths . 9 and 11 ells.
      Subs. . 3s. 1½d.
      Ulnage . 4¾d.
    The 10th day of March.
Of Thomas Bracebrigg 6 blue cloths, 4 'sangwyn' cloths,
 3 black cloths, 2 'plunket' cloths, 4 green cloths, and
 1 white cloth . . . . 6s. 8d.
Thomas Shereman ½ a white cloth . . . . . 2d.
    Sum: Cloths . 20½
      Subs. . 6s. 10d.
      Ulnage . 10¼d.
    The 11th day of March.
Of John Neuby 4 blue cloths, 4 red cloths, 2 'sangwyn' cloths,
 2 green cloths, and 1 'plunket' cloth . . . . 4s. 4d.
    Sum: Cloths . 13
      Subs. . 4s. 4d.
      Ulnage . 6½d.
    The 12th day of March.
Of John Rumby ½ a 'plunket' cloth . . . . 2d.
John Wynkyll 1 blue cloth . . . . . . 4d.

---

[1] A John of the Clyff, "chapman," was admitted a freeman in 1362–3, and a John of Clyff, "tailliour," in 1369–70.

[2] Thomas of Grantham, "mercer," son of John of Grantham, junr., was admitted a freeman in 1390–1, and a John of Grantham, "mercer," was admitted a freeman in 1355–6.

John of Raghton 2½ white cloths . . . . . 10d.
William Fulforth 7 ells of blue cloth . . . . 1d.
>   Sum: Cloths . 4 and 7 ells.
>   Subs. . 17d.
>   Ulnage . 2¼d.

The 13th day of March.

Of William Skauseby 5 blue cloths, 6 red cloths, and 2 green
cloths . . . . 4s. 4d.
>   Sum: Cloths . 13 cloths.
>   Subs. . 4s. 4d.
>   Ulnage . 6½d.

The 14th day of March.

Of Nicholas Wardmann 6 white cloths, 5 red cloths, 4 ' sangwyn ' cloths, 4 ' murray ' cloths, 5 green cloths, 3 ' plunket ' cloths, and 2 black cloths . . . . . 10s.
Alice of Selby 1½ blue cloth . . . . . . 6d.
John Bukland 3 blue cloths and 4 white cloths . . . 2s. 4d.
>   Sum: Cloths . 38½
>   Subs. . 12s. 10d.
>   Ulnage . 19d.

The 15th day of March.

Of Alice of Selby 2 ' plunket ' cloths, and 3 ' russet ' cloths . 20d.
Cecilia of Drynghouse ½ a white cloth and 8 ells of blue cloth . 3d.
John of Darneton 1 dozen of strait cloths, containing 6 ells
of a cloth of assize . . . . 1d.
Alice of Stylyngton 4 ells of white cloth . . . . ½d.
William of Bedale ½ a 'russet' cloth and 7 ells of white cloth 3d.
Alice of Kirkeby 6 ells of green cloth . . . . 1d.
Nicholas Parant 1 blue cloth . . . . . . 4d.
>   Sum: Cloths . 8 and 6 ells.
>   Subs. . 2s. 8½d.
>   Ulnage . 3¼d.

The 16th day of March.

Of John Bydell 4 white cloths and 2 blue cloths . . . 2s.
Henry of Preston[1] 5 blue cloths, 6 red cloths, 5 ' sangwyn '
cloths, 4 'plunket' cloths, 3 green cloths, and 1 white cloth 8s.
John Yarom[2] 8 blue cloths, 7 red cloths, 6 ' sangwyn ' cloths,
7 ' murray ' cloths, 3 ' plunket ' cloths, and 2 white cloths 13s. 8d.
>   Sum: Cloths . 61.
>   Subs. . 23s. 8d.
>   Ulnage . 2s. 11½d.

The 17th day of March.

Of Thomas of Fenton[3] 3 blue cloths, 3 ' sangwyn ' cloths, 2 red
cloths, 1 green cloth, and 1 white cloth . . . 3s. 4d.

---

[1] Henry of Preston, " mercer," was admitted a freeman in 1379-80, and
was probably the Chamberlain of that name in 1398-9.

[2] John of Yarom, " taillour," was admitted a freeman in 1340-1.

[3] Thomas of Fenton, " mercer," was admitted a freeman in 1391-2.

Thomas of Royston 1 'murray' cloth and 2 'plunket' cloths   12*d*.
Richard Redehode 5 blue cloths, 5 red cloths, 3 green cloths,
  1½ white cloth, 2 black cloths, and 2 'murray' cloths . 6*s*. 2*d*.

> Sum: Cloths . 31½
>   Subs. . 10*s*. 6*d*.
>   Ulnage . 15½*d*.

The 18th day of March.

Of John of Brathwayt 4 blue cloths, 4 red cloths, 3 green
cloths, 2 black cloths, and 1½ white cloth . .   4*s*. 10*d*.
John of Thornton 6 blue cloths, 4 green cloths, 2 'plunket'
cloths, 3 black cloths, 3 'sangwyn' cloths, 3 white cloths,
and 2 'murray' cloths . . . . . . 7*s*. 4*d*.
Richard Haukeswell[1] 7 blue cloths, 6 red cloths, 5 green cloths,
2 white cloths, 3 'sangwyn' cloths, and 2 'plunket'
cloths . . . . 8*s*. 4*d*.

> Sum: Cloths . 61½
>   Subs. . 20*s*. 6*d*.
>   Ulnage . 2*s*. 6¾*d*.

The 19th day of March.

Of Thomas of Holme[2] 8 blue cloths, 6 red cloths, 5 'medle'
cloths, 6 green cloths, and 5 'sangwyn' cloths . .   10*s*.
William Skauseby 2 red cloths, 1 green cloth, and ½ a black
cloth . . . . 18*d*.
John Braythwayte 2 green cloths, 2 red cloths, and ½ a white
cloth . . . . 18*d*.
Richard Redehode 1 blue cloth . . . . . 4*d*.
Robert of Rypon 3 blue cloths and 1 white cloth . . 16*d*.
Thomas Askham 3 blue cloths, 2 red cloths, and 2 green
cloths . . . . 2*s*. 4*d*.

> Sum: Cloths . 51
>   Subs. . 17*s*.
>   Ulnage . 2*s*. 1½*d*.

The 21st day of March.

Of Nicholas Perant ½ a blue cloth . . . . . 2*d*.
Agnes of Wellom 7 ells of 'melle' cloth . . . . 1*d*.
Thomas Sherman ½ a 'russet' cloth . . . . 2*d*.
Agnes Kelfeld 9 ells of white cloth . . . . 1½*d*.
John of Laxton 2 blue cloths, 1 green cloth, and 1 red cloth   16*d*.

> Sum: Cloths . 5½ and 3 ells.
>   Subs. . 22½*d*.
>   Ulnage . 2¾*d*.

The 22d day of March.

Of Robert Porter ½ a white cloth . . . . . 2*d*.
John of Elsewyk 6 ells of 'melle' cloth . . . . 1*d*.
Joan of Moreton 3 ells of red cloth . . . . ½*d*.

---

[1] Richard of Haukeswell, " mercer," was admitted a freeman in 1383–4.

[2] Thomas of Houom (*sic*), brother of Robert of Houom, " mercer," was admitted a freeman in 1352–3, and was the same man, I take it, who was one of the two Mayors in 1371–2, and Mayor the two following years.

Sum: Cloths . ½ a cloth and 7 ells.
     Subs. . 3½d.
     Ulnage . ½d.

The 23d day of March.

Of Robert of Tothe 2 red cloths and 2 blue cloths   .   . 16d.

Thomas of Thornton 1 blue cloth .   .   .   . 4d.

Thomas Neuland[1] 6 blue cloths, 5 red cloths, 4 'sangwyn' cloths; 5 green cloths, and 3 white cloths .   .   . 7s. 8d.

Sum: Cloths . 28
     Subs. . 9s. 4d.
     Ulnage . 14d.

The 24th day of March.

Of Robert of Duffeld[2] 3 blue cloths, 1 'russet' cloth, and 7 ells of blue cloth .   .   .   .   .   . 17d.

Margaret of Stylyngton ½ a 'russet' cloth .   .   . 2d.

William Playt[er] 7 ells of white cloth .   .   . 1d.

William Sage 10 white cloths, 2 'russet' cloths, 1½ 'plunket' cloth . . . . 4s. 6d.

William of Wegan 2 blue cloths, 1 white cloth, and 1 'plunket' cloth . . . . 16d.

Sum: Cloths . 22½ and 1 ell.
     Subs. . 7s. 6d.
     Ulnage . 11¼d.

The 25th day of March.

Of John Wawne[3] 3 blue cloths, 1 'plunket' cloth, and 1 white cloth .   .   .   .   . 20d.

John of Bolton[4] 3 blue cloths, 3 'sangwyn' cloths, 2 'russet' cloths, and ½ a white cloth. .   .   . 2s. 10d.

Sum: Cloths . 13½
     Subs. . 4s. 6d.
     Ulnage . 6¾d.

The 26th day of March.

Of John of Raghton 2 blue cloths and 2 'plunket' cloths . 16d.

William Appilby 1 'motle' cloth .   .   .   . 4d.

Roger Pomfrayte 2½ blue cloths .   .   .   . 10d.

Thomas of Gare 4 blue cloths, ½ a white cloth, 4 green cloths, 3 'sangwyn' cloths, and 25 dozen strait cloths, containing 6 cloths and 6 ells of a cloth of assize . . 5s. 11d.

Sum: Cloths . 25 and 6 ells.
     Subs. . 8s. 5d.
     Ulnage . 12¾d.

---

[1] Thomas of Neuland, " mercer," was admitted a freeman in 1390–1.

[2] Robert of Duffeld, " convereour," was admitted a freeman in 1381–2.

[3] John of Waghen, " chapman," was admitted a freeman in 1392–3, and he seems to have been a Chamberlain in 1411–2.

[4] John of Bolton, " mercer," was admitted a freeman in 1372–3.

The 28th day of March.

Of John of Raghton 3 blue cloths and 3 white cloths . 2s.
John of Laxton 1 'russet' cloth . . . . . 4d.
Thomas of Gare 5 blue cloths, 3 'sangwyn' cloths, 3 green
   cloths, 2½ 'plunket' cloths, and 24 dozen strait cloths,
   containing 6 cloths of assize . . . . . 6s. 6d.

        Sum: Cloths . 26½
             Subsidy . 8s. 10d.
             Ulnage . 12¼d.

The 29th day of March.

Of John Pule 1 dozen strait cloths, containing 6 yds. of a
   cloth of assize . . . . 1d.
John Osbaldewyke 1 blue cloth . . . . . 4d.
Hugh Taillour ½ a 'plunket' cloth . . . . . 2d.
John Middelton 1½ blue cloth . . . . . 6d.
John of Threpeland 3 blue cloths and 2 'plunket' cloths . 20d.
William Sage 3 blue cloths and 3 white cloths . . . 2s.

        Sum: Cloths . 14 and 6 ells.
             Subs. . 4s. 9d.
             Ulnage . 7¼d.

The 30th day of March.

Of Robert Ward 7 blue cloths, 5 red cloths, 3 green cloths,
   3 'sangwyn' cloths and 23 dozen strait cloths, containing
   5 cloths and 3 quarters of a cloth of assize . . 7s. 11d.

        Sum: Cloths . 23 and ¾ths.
             Subs. . 7s. 11d.
             Ulnage 11¾d.

The 1st day of April.

Of William Hillum 4 white cloths and 1 'plunket' cloth . 20d.
Alice of Monkton 8 ells of white cloth . . . . 1d.
Joan Taillour 6 ells of blue cloth . . . . . 1d.
Henry Wyman[1] 8 blue cloths, 8 red cloths, 4 'sangwyn'
   cloths, 5 green cloths, 5 white cloths, and 4 'plunket'
   cloths . . . . 11s. 4d.

        Sum: Cloths . 39½ and 1 ell.
             Subs. . 13s. 2d.
             Ulnage . 19¾d.

The second day of April.

Of John Hedwyke 2 red cloths and 1 and ½ blue cloth . 14d.
William Palmer 18 dozen strait cloths, containing 4½ cloths
   of assize . . . . 18d.
William Coupeland ½ a blue cloth . . . . . 2d.
Agnes of Wellom ½ a 'meldle' cloth . . . . 2d.

        Sum: Cloths . 9
             Subs. . 3s.
             Ulnage . 4½d.

[1] A Henry Wyman, "merchant," was admitted a freeman in 1385–6, and
was Mayor in 1405–6, 1406–7, and 1407–8, but he was a "goldsmith" by trade.

The third day of April.

Of William Leseham 10 blue cloths, 10 red cloths, 8 green
cloths, 8 'sangwyn' cloths, 5 white cloths, 3 'russet'
cloths, and 42 dozen of strait cloths, containing 10½ cloths
of assize, 4 black cloths, and 5 'plunket' cloths .   21s. 2d.

Sum:	Cloths .	63½
	Subs. .	21s. 2d.
	Ulnage .	2s. 7¾d.

The 5th day of April.

Of Robert Ward 6½ white cloths and 4 dozens of strait cloths,
containing 1 cloth of assize . . . . . 2s. 6d.
Nicholas Wardmanne 1½ white cloth . . . . 6d.
Thomas of Holme 4 'russet' cloths . . . . 16d.
Richard Yrenmaker 5 blue cloths, 4 'sangwyn' cloths, 5 red
cloths, 4 green cloths, and 1 'plunket' cloth . . 6s. 4d.

Sum:	Cloths .	32
	Subs. .	10s. 8d.
	Ulnage .	16d.

The 6th day of April.

Of John of Bolton 4 blue cloths, 4 red cloths, 2 'sangwyn'
cloths, and 2 blue cloths . . . . . 4s. 2d.

Sum:	Cloths .	12½
	Subs. .	4s. 2d.
	Ulnage .	6½d.

The 7th day of April.

Of Robert of Rypon 1 white cloth . . . . . 4d.
John of Raghton 1 'russet' cloth and ½ a blue cloth . . 6d.
Thomas Emlay[1] 6 ells of 'blankett' cloth . . . 1d.

Sum:	Cloths .	2½ and 10 ells.
	Subs. .	11½d.
	Ulnage .	1½d.

The 8th day of April.

Of Thomas Smyth 6 blue cloths, 5 'sangwyn' cloths, 5 green
cloths, 4 red cloths, 1 'plunket' cloth, and 1½ 'russet'
cloth . . . . 7s. 6d.

Sum:	Cloths .	22½
	Subs. .	7s. 6d.
	Ulnage .	11¼d.

The 12th day of April.

Of Albreda of Burton 6 ells of 'russet' cloth . . . 1d.
John of Grantham ½ a white cloth . . . . 2d.
Joan of Burton 6 ells of white cloth . . . . 1d.
Robert Ward 3 'sangwyn' cloths, 2 blue cloths, and 7 dozens
of strait cloths, containing 1 cloth and ¾ths of a cloth of
assize . . . . 2s. 3d.

---

[1] A Thomas of Emlay, "tailliour," was admitted a freeman in 1367–8.

Sum: Cloths . 7½ and 5½ ells.
    Subs. . 2s. 7d.
    Ulnage . 3¼d.

The 13th day of April.

Of John Percy 5 blue cloths, 3 green cloths, 6 red cloths, and
4 'sangwyn' cloths . . . . 6s.
Sum: Cloths . 18
    Subs. . 6s.
    Ulnage . 9d.

The 15th day of April.

Of John of Sessay 2 blue cloths, 2 red cloths, 1 green cloth,
and 7 ells of green cloth . . . . . . 21d.
Alice of Selby 6 ells of 'russet' cloth . . . . 1d.
Thomas Sherman 1 blue cloth and ½ a red cloth . . 6d.
Hugh of Chartres 1 'paly' cloth . . . . . 4d.
Alice of Rufford ½ a white cloth . . . . . 2d.
Sum: Cloths . 8½
    Subs. . 2s. 10d.
    Ulnage . 3¼d.

The 16th day of April.

Of Richard Redhode 1½ blue cloth and ½ a 'russet' cloth . 8d.
John of Raghton 3 white cloths . . . . 12d.
Alice of Warton ½ a 'russet' cloth . . . . 2d.
Sum: Cloths . 5½
    Subs. . 22d.
    Ulnage . 2¾d.

The 18th day of April.

Of William of Brigge[1] ½ a red cloth . . . . . 2d.
Thomas Walker ½ a white cloth . . . . . 2d.
John Furnour 8 'russet' cloths, 5 'plunket' cloths, 8 blue
cloths, 4 white cloths, 5 green cloths, and 1½ red cloth 10s. 6d.
The wife of John Bouthe ½ a 'russet' cloth . . . 2d.
William Tankyrlay 1½ blue cloth . . . . . 6d.
Sum: Cloths . 34½
    Subs. . 11s. 6d.
    Ulnage . 17¼d.

The 20th day of April.

Of Cuthbert Walker ½ a blue cloth . . . . 2d.
Agnes of Castell 7 ells of blue cloth . . . . 1d.
Richard Tarte[2] 2 blue cloths and 2 white cloths . . 16d.
Sum: Cloths . 4½ and 7 ells.
    Subs. . 19d.
    Ulnage . 2½d.

The 21st day of April.

Of Richard Redehode 2 blue cloths, 2 red cloths, and 2 green
cloths . . . . 2s.

---

[1] William of Brigg, " draper," was admitted a freeman in 1392–3.
[2] Richard Tart, " draper," was admitted a freeman in 1392–3.

Nicholas Perant 1 green cloth . . . . . 4*d.*
Alice of Topecliff ½ a ' russet ' cloth . . . . 2*d.*
John of Raghton 1 white cloth . . . . . 4*d.*

Sum: Cloths . 8½
Subs. . 2s. 10*d.*
Ulnage . 4¼*d.*

The 22d day of April.

Of Alan Hampton 5 blue cloths, 3 red cloths, 4 green cloths,
and 3 white cloths . . . . 5s.

Sum: Cloths . 15
Subs. . 5s.
Ulnage . 7½*d.*

The 23d day of April.

Of William Sturge 3 red cloths, 2 blue cloths, 3 green cloths,
and ½ a black cloth . . . . . . .2s.10*d.*
William Coupeland 1 red cloth . . . . . 4*d.*
Isabella of Petresfeld 2 white cloths, 2 ' russet ' cloths, and
1 red cloth . . . . 20*d.*
Joan of Cawod ½ a white cloth . . . . . 2*d.*

Sum: Cloths . 15
Subs. . 5s.
Ulnage . 7½*d.*

The 25th day of April.

Of John of Stylyngton[1] ½ a white cloth . . . . 2*d.*
Thomas Turnour ½ a white cloth . . . . . 2*d.*
Alice of Topcliff 2½ blue cloths . . . . . 10*d.*

Sum: Cloths . 3½
Subs. . 14*d.*
Ulnage . 1¾*d.*

The 26th day of April.

Of John of Laxton 2 blue cloths, 2 green cloths, 2 red cloths 2s.
Thomas of Catton[2] 1 ' medle ' cloth . . . . 4*d.*

Sum: Cloths . 7
Subs. . 2s. 4*d.*
Ulnage . 3½*d.*

The 27th day of April.

Of John of Awus ½ a white cloth . . . . . 2*d.*
Matilda Lavendre 6 ells of white cloth . . . . 1*d.*

Sum: Cloths . ½ and 6 ells.
Subs. . 3*d.*
Ulnage . ¼*d.*

[1] John of Stelyngton, " mercer," was admitted a freeman in 1362–3. He
was a Chamberlain in 1383–4, and Robert of Stillyngton, " mercer," son of
John of Stillyngton, " mercer," was admitted a freeman, as son of his father
in 1401–2.

[2] A Thomas of Catton, " mercer," was admitted a freeman in 1342–3, and
a Thomas of Catton, " webster," in 1362–3. The latter is probably the man
referred to in the ulnage roll.

The 28th day of April.

Of Thomas of Jedworth 10 ells of blue cloth . . . 1½d.
John of Thorneton, 6 blue cloths, 4 black cloths, 8 red cloths,
  6 green cloths, 4 'murray' cloths, and 2 white cloths . 10s.

Sum: Cloths . 30 and 10 ells.
Subs. . 10s. 1½d.
Ulnage . 15¼d.

The last day of April.

Of William Fowler 1 'russet motley' cloth, 1 'paly' cloth,
  and 1 'grene' cloth . . . . 12d.

Sum: Cloths . 3
Subs. . 12d.
Ulnage . 1½d.

The first day of May.

Of John Brathwayt 4 red cloths, 4 blue cloths, 4 green cloths,
  4 blue cloths, 2 red cloths, two green cloths, and ½ a black
  cloth . . . . 6s. 10d.

Sum: Cloths . 20½
Subs. . 6s. 10d.
Ulnage . 10¼d.

The 3d day of May.

Of Richard of Santon 4 blue cloths, 4 red cloths, 3 green
  cloths, 3 'cogsale' cloths, 2 black cloths, and 1½ white
  cloth . . . . 5s. 10d.
Richard of Worssope 1 red cloth, 1 green cloth, and 1 'meld'
  cloth . . . . 12d.
Robert Scharplys 2 red cloths, 2 green cloths, and 1 blue cloth 20d.
John of Raghton 1 'russet' cloth . . . . . 4d.

Sum: Cloths . 26½
Subs. . 8s. 10d.
Ulnage . 13¼d.

The 4th day of the same month.

Of Thomas of Donnyngton[1] 9 ells of white . . . 1½d.
Richard of Storowr ½ a 'sangwyn' cloth . . . 2d.
Sissel of Shopton 6 ells of 'russet' and 7 ells of blue . . 2d.
Thomas Blade-smethe ½ a white cloth . . . . 2d.
William of Dell 3 blue cloths, 3 red cloths, and 2 green cloths 2s. 8d.
William Skawsby 1½ red cloth . . . . 6d.
Joan Taillour 7 ells of green . . . . . 1d.
Joan of Monkton ½ a white cloth . . . . 2d.

Sum: Cloths . 12 and 3 ells.
Subs. . 4s. 0½d.
Ulnage . 6d.

The 5th day of the same month.

Joan of Bradlay ½ a 'grene mellyd' cloth . . . 2d.
John Webster ½ white cloth . . . . . 2d.
Alice of Selby ¼ a white cloth . . . . . 2d.
Thomas Cowper 1 red cloth . . . . . 4d.

---

[1] A Thomas of Donyngton, "mercer," was admitted a freeman in 1348-9.

Thomas of Horneby 4 'meld' cloths . . . . 16*d.*
Richard of Santon 1 red cloth . . . . . 4*d.*
Richard Redhode 2 blue cloths, 2 red cloths, and 1 green
cloth . . . . 20*d.*

Sum: Cloths . 12½
Subs. . 4*s.* 2*d.*
Ulnage . 6¼*d.*

The 6th day of the same month.

Of John Wrenkyll 5 'blew' cloths and 5 red cloths, 4 'sang-
wyn' cloths, 4 'grene' cloths, and 1 'plunket' cloth . 6*s.* 4*d.*
Adam of Helpby ½ a 'paly' cloth . . . . . 2*d.*
Richard of Calton ½ 'taud' cloth . . . . . 1*d.*
John Taillour 6 ells of 'grene' . . . . . 1*d.*
John Kays 7 ells of red . . . . 1*d.*
John Webster 3 ells of blue . . . . . . ½*d.*
Annota [? Avota] of Welyngton ½ a 'russet' cloth . . 2*d.*
John Tomson 7 ells of white . . . . . . 1*d.*
Richard Tarte 2 'blew' cloths . . . . . 8*d.*

Sum: Cloths . 23 and 10 ells.
Subs. . 7*s.* 9½*d.*
Ulnage . 11¾*d.*

The 7th day of the same month.

Of Robert of Lowther 10 'blew' cloths, 10 red cloths, 5 'sangwyn' cloths, 5 green cloths, 6 'moray' cloths, and 4
'plunket' cloths . . . . 13*s.* 6*d.*
John Holbeke[1] 4 red cloths, 3 'sangwyn' cloths, 3 'blewe'
cloths, and 1 'blake' cloth . . . . . 3*s.* 8*d.*

Sum: Cloths . 51
Subs. . 17*s.*
Ulnage . 2*s.* 1½*d.*

The 8th day of the same month.

Of Richard Irynmangare 2 blue cloths . . . . 8*d.*
Androw [*sic*] Jonowr 3 'russet' cloths . . . 12*d.*
Thomas Denyas 3 red cloths, 1 blue cloth, and 1 'russet' cloth 20*d.*
Alan Hamerton 3 'russet' cloths and 1½ 'blewe' cloth . 18*d.*

Sum: Cloths . 14½
Subs. . 4*s.* 10*d.*
Ulnage . 7¼*d.*

The 10th day of the same month.

Of Thomas of Dam ½ a 'sangwyn' cloth . . . 2*d.*
Edward Scherman ½ a red cloth . . . . . 2*d.*
Henry Wyman 3 'blewe' cloths, 2 red cloths, 1½ 'plunket'
cloth, and 1 white cloth . . . . . 2*s.* 6*d.*

Sum: Cloths . 8½
Subs. . 2*s.* 10*d.*
Ulnage . 4¼*d.*

---

[1] John of Holbek, "webster," was admitted a freeman in 1369–70, and
was a Chamberlain in 1390–1; and Thomas Holbek, "son of John Holbek,
citizen and merchant of York," was admitted a freeman in 1408–9.

The 11th day of the same month.

Of William Smythe 1 'russet' cloth . . . . 4d.

William Cowpland ½ a 'meld' cloth . . . . 2d.

Joan of Lynton 3 ells of white . . . . . ½d.

Sum: Cloths . 1½ and 3 ells.

Subs. . 6½d.

Ulnage . 1d.

The 12th day of the same month.

Of John Percy 1 blue cloth and 1 'russet' cloth . . 8d.

Thomas Denyas 2 'russet' cloths and 2 red cloths . . 16d.

William of Hale[1] 2 'blewe' cloths . . . . . 8d.

John of Therplande for 50 'duzen narrow' cloths, containing 12½ cloths of assize . . . . 4s. 2d.

Roger of Barton[2] 2 red cloths, 2 'sangwyn' cloths and 2½ 'blewe' cloths . . . . 2s. 2d.

Sum: Cloths . 27

Subs. . 9s.

Ulnage . 13½d.

The 15th day of the same month.

Of Thomas Gare 2 red cloths, 2 'blew' cloths, 2 'sangwyn' cloths, and 6 'duzen narrowe' cloths, containing 1½ cloth of assize . . . . 2s. 6d.

Thomas Bracebrege 4 white cloths . . . . . 16d.

John of Crawyn 7 white cloths and 2 'russet' cloths . 3s.

Sum: Cloths . 20½

Subs. . 6s. 10d.

Ulnage . 10¼d.

The 17th day of the same month.

Of John Webster ½ a red cloth . . . . . . 2d.

Richard Redhode 2 'grene' cloths and 2 red cloths . . 16d.

Adam of Stoke 8 'blew' cloths, 2 'russet' cloths, and 1 'plunket' cloth . . . . 3s. 8d.

Annota of Kelfeld ½ a white cloth . . . . . 2d.

John of Braythwayte 5 'meld' cloths . . . . 20d.

John of Bedale 4 'blewe' cloths, 3 red cloths, 3 'sangwyn' cloths, and 2 'grene' cloths . . . . . 4s.

Of William At-ye-ton-ende 1 'duzen narrow clothys,' containing 6 yards of a cloth of assize . . . . 1d.

Sum: Cloths . 33 and 6 ells.

Subs. . 11s. 1d.

Ulnage . 16¾d.

The 18th day of the same month.

Of John Lyster[3] for 7 ells of white . . . . . 1d.

---

[1] William of the Hale, "littester," was admitted a freeman in 1383-4.

[2] Roger of Barton, "mercer," was admitted a freeman in 1383-4, and his son, William, described as "William Barton, son of Roger Barton, of York, mercer," was admitted in 1411-2.

[3] John Littester, "mercer," was admitted a freeman in 1383-4.

F

William Merton 3 red cloths, 2 'grene' cloths, 1½ 'blewe'
cloths .   .   .   . *2s. 2d.*

> Sum: Cloths . 6½ and 7 ells.
> Subs. . *2s. 3d.*
> Ulnage . 3½*d.*

The 19th day of the same month.

Of Thomas Askham 2 red cloths and 2 'grene' cloths . . 16*d.*

> Sum: Cloths . 4
> Subs. . *2s. 3d.*
> Ulnage . 2*d.*

The 20th day of the same month.

Of . . . . . . of Burton 7 ells of white .   .   .   .   . 1*d.*
John Bywell[1] 2 red cloths .   .   .   .   . 8*d.*
Robert of Pothowe[2] 1 red cloth and 1 white cloth . . 8*d.*

> Sum: Cloths . 4 and 7 ells.
> Subs. . 17*d.*
> Ulnage . 2¼*d.*

The 21st day of the same month.

Of Richard Worsope 1 'grene' cloth and 1 red cloth . . 8*d.*
William of Thorneton ½ a 'grene' cloth .   .   . 2*d.*
John Marschall 1 'blewe' cloth .   .   .   . 4*d.*
William of Deyhton[3] 2 white cloths .   .   . 8*d.*

> Sum: Cloths . 5½
> Subs. . 22*d.*
> Ulnage . 2¾*d.*

The 22d day of the same month.

Of John of Thorneton 2 'blew' cloths and 3 red cloths . 20*d.*
John of Braythwayte 1½ red cloth .   .   .   . 6*d.*

> Sum: Cloths . 6½
> Subs. . *2s. 2d.*
> Ulnage . 3¼*d.*

The 24th day of the same month.

Of Robert Lofthous 2 red cloths and 2 'grene' cloths . 16*d.*
William of Danby[4] 1 white cloth and ½ a 'russet' cloth . 6*d.*
Thomas Cowper ½ a 'grene' cloth .   .   .   . 2*d.*
John of Wylton[5] 7 ells of 'plonket' .   .   . 1*d.*
Richard Redhode 6 ells of 'plunket' .   .   . 1*d.*

> Sum: Cloths . 6½
> Subs. . *2s. 2d.*
> Ulnage . 3¼*d.*

The 25th day of the same month.

Of Margaret of Lynton 7 ells of white .   .   . 1*d.*

---

[1] John of Bywell, " draper," was admitted a freeman in 1385–6.

[2] Robert of Pouthow, " mercer," was admitted a freeman in 1346–7.

[3] William of Dyghton, " taillour," was admitted a freeman in 1389–90.

[4] William of Danby, " mercer," was elected a freeman in 1391–2.

[5] John son of John of Wyllton, " merchant," was admitted a freeman in 1371–2.

John of Thorneton 2 red cloths and 1 'grene' cloth .   .   12d.
        Sum: Cloths .   7 ells.
             Subs.   .   13d.
             Ulnage .   1d.

The 31st day of the same month.

Of William Sturge 1 blue cloth, 1 red cloth, and 1 'grene'
cloth and 9 ells .   .   .   .   .   .   13½d.
        Sum: Cloths .   3 and 9 ells.
             Subs.   .   13d.
             Ulnage .   1¾d.

The 1st day of June.

Of . . . . . . of Burton ½ a white cloth .   .   .   .   2d.
John Walkar ½ a 'plunket' cloth .   .   .   .   2d.
        Sum: Cloths .   1
             Subs.   .   4d.
             Ulnage .   ½d.

The 2d day of the same month.

Of Matilda Trompe 2 'russet' cloths .   .   .   .   8d.
Beatrice Ward 1 red cloth .   .   .   .   .   .   4d.
        Sum: Cloths .   3
             Subs.   .   12d.
             Ulnage .   1½d.

The 8th day of the same month.

Of Sissota of Drynghows ½ a 'meld' cloth .   .   .   2d.
John Bakester ½ a 'blewe' cloth .   .   .   .   .   2d.
        Sum: Cloths .   1
             Subs.   .   4d.
             Ulnage .   ½d.

The 9th day of the same month.

Of John Walker ½ a white cloth .   .   .   .   2d.
Joan of Burton ½ a white cloth .   .   .   .   2d.
        Sum: Cloths .   1
             Subs.   .   4d.
             Ulnage .   ½d.

The 10th day of the same month.

Of Ibota Bumby 2 'plunket' cloths .   .   .   .   8d.
John Paschelawe 1 'plunket' cloth .   .   .   .   4d.
John Candeler 3½ white cloths .   .   .   .   .   14d.
        Sum: Cloths .   6½
             Subs.   .   2s. 2d.
             Ulnage .   3¼d.

The 11th day of the same month.

Of William of Brege ½ a 'blewe' cloth .   .   .   .   2d.
Thomas Couper 1 'blewe' cloth .   .   .   .   .   4d.
        Sum: Cloths .   1½
             Subs.   .   6d.
             Ulnage .   ¾d.

The 14th day of the same month.

Of William Fowler ½ a white cloth . . . . 2d.
    Sum: Cloths . ½ a cloth.
      Subs. . 2d.
      Ulnage . ¼d.

The 15th day of the same month.

Of William At-ton-ende 1 ' duzen narrow ' cloths, containing
¼th of a cloth of assize . . . . . . 1d.
John of Wyton 6 ells of red . . . . . . 1d.
William Skawsby 3 red cloths and 2 ' grene ' cloths . 20d.
    Sum: Cloths . 5 and ¼th and 6 ells.
      Subs. . 22d.
      Ulnage . 3¼d.

The 16th day of the same month.

Of John Dobson ½ a white cloth . . . . . 2d.
John of Braythwayte 3 red cloths, 2 ' grene ' cloths, and 2
' blewe ' cloths . . . . 2s. 4d.
    Sum: Cloths . 7½
      Subs. . 2s. 6d.
      Ulnage . 3¾d

The 17th day of the same month.

Of Richard Santon, 4 red cloths, 3 ' blewe ' cloths, 3 ' grene '
cloths, and 2 ' blak ' cloths . . . . . 4s.
Richard Redhode 3 red cloths, 3 ' blew ' cloths, 3 ' grenne '
[sic], and ½ a ' blak ' cloth . . . . . . 3s. 2d.
    Sum: Cloths . 21½
      Subs. . 7s. 2d.
      Ulnage . 10¾d.

The 19th of the same month.

Of John Chapman 2 red cloths and 1 ' grene ' cloth . . 12d.
    Sum: Cloths . 3
      Subs. . 12d.
      Ulnage . 1½d.

The 21st day of the same month.

Of Robert Broket 1 red cloth . . . . . 4d.
    Sum: Cloths . 1
      Subs. . 4d.
      Ulnage . ½d.

The 22d day of the same month.

Of Ibbota of Roythram 2 ' blew ' cloths . . . . 8d.
Thomas Askham 1 ' blewe ' cloth . . . . . 4d.
John Mordoke 1 white cloth . . . . . . 4d.
    Sum: Cloths . 4
      Subs. . 16d.
      Ulnage . 2d.

The 2d day of July.

Of William Etton ½ a white cloth . . . . . 2d.

John of Wyton 6 ells of 'plonket' . . . . . 1d.
John Walkar ½ a white cloth . . . . . . 2d.
                    Sum: Cloths . 1 and 6 ells.
                          Subs. . 5d.
                          Ulnage . ¾d.

The 3d day of the same month.

Of John Hebson 7 ells of white cloth . . . . 1d.
Joan of Wenkborne ½ a white cloth . . . . 2d.
John Pataner 1 white cloth . . . . . . 4d.
                    Sum: Cloths . 1½ and 7 ells.
                          Subs. . 7d.
                          Ulnage . 1d.

The 4th day of the same month.

Of Annota of Ricall ½ a 'plunket' cloth . . . 2d.
Edward Smart[1] ½ a white cloth . . . . . 2d.
Joan Coke 7 ells of red . . . . . . 1d.
                    Sum: Cloths . 1 and 7 ells.
                          Subs. . 5d.
                          Ulnage . ¾d.

The 5th day of the same month.

Of William Bell 3 red cloths, 3 'grene' cloths, and 2 blue
cloths . . . . 2s. 8d.
John of Thornton 6 red cloths, 4 blue cloths, 4 'grene' cloths,
2 black cloths, and 1½ 'plunket' cloth . . 5s. 10d.
                    Sum: Cloths . 24½
                          Subs. . 8s. 6d.
                          Ulnage . 12¼d.

The 6th day of the same month.

Of Richard Redhod 2 'blewe' cloths, 2 'grene' cloths, and
½ a red cloth . . . . 18d.
                    Sum: Cloths . 4½
                          Subs. . 18d.
                          Ulnage . 2¼d.

The 7th day of the same month.

Of William Skawsby 3 red cloths, 2 black cloths, and 2 'grene'
cloths . . . . 2s. 4d.
John of Laxton 4 red cloths, 3 'blewe' cloths, and 3 'grene'
cloths . . . . 3s. 4d.
John Scherman 7 ells of 'plonket' . . . . . 1d.
                    Sum: Cloths . 17 and 7 ells.
                          Subs. . 5s. 9d.
                          Ulnage . 8¾d.

The 8th day of the same month.

Of William of Marton 5 red cloths, 4 'blewe' cloths, 4 'grene'
cloths, 2 black cloths, and 1 white cloth . . . 5s. 4d.

---

[1] An Edward Smert, "shereman," was admitted a freeman in 1388-9.

John Howden 30 ' duzen narrow clothe,' containing 7½ cloths
    of assize . . . . *2s.* 6*d.*
John of Raghton 1 ' blewe ' cloth . . . . . 4*d.*

Sum: Cloths . 14½
Subs. . 8*s.* 2*d.*
Ulnage . 12¼*d.*

The 9th day of the same month.

Of Robert of Ganysforth 1 ' blew ' cloth, 3 white cloths, and
    2 ' plonket ' cloths . . . . 3*s.*

Sum: Cloths . 9
Subs. . 3*s.*
Ulnage . 4½*d.*

The 10th day of the same month.

Of Byrkyn-syde[1] ½ a ' plonket ' cloth . . . 2*d.*
Thomas Essynwald ½ a ' grene ' cloth . . . . 2*d.*

Sum: Cloths . 1
Subs. . 4*d.*
Ulnage . ½*d.*

The 12th day of the same month.

Of William Bardysay 7 ells of ' plonket ' . . . . 1*d.*
William of Lee 4 white cloths, 3 ' plonket ' cloths, 2 ' russet '
    cloths, 1½ ' blewe ' cloth . . . . . . 3*s.* 6*d.*

Sum: Cloths . 10½ and 7 ells.
Subs. . 3*s.* 7*d.*
Ulnage . 5¾*d.*

The 13th day of the same month.

Of William Evon ½ a white cloth . . . . . 2*d.*
Annota of Kelfeld ½ a ' grene ' cloth . . . . 2*d.*
Joan of Lynton ½ a white cloth . . . . . 2*d.*

Sum: Cloths . 1½
Subs. . 6*d.*
Ulnage . ¾*d.*

The 14th day of the same month.

Of Richard of Santon 3 red cloths, 2 ' grene ' cloths, and
    2 ' blew ' cloths . . . . 2*s.* 4*d.*
William of Marton 1 ' blewe ' cloth . . . . 4*d.*

Sum: Cloths . 8
Subs. . 2*s.* 8*d.*
Ulnage . 4*d.*

The 16th day of the same month.

Of Nicholas of Skelton 9 ' blewe ' cloths, 5 white cloths, and
    2 ' russet ' cloths . . . . 5*s.* 4*d.*
Joan of Bredelyngton ½ a white cloth . . . . 2*d.*

Sum: Cloths . 16½
Subs. . 5*s.* 6*d.*
Ulnage . 8¼*d.*

---

[1] The Christian name is omitted. A William of Birkenside, " tailor," was
admitted a freeman in 1355–6.

The 17th day of the same month.

Of John of Brathwayte 9 ' blewe ' cloths, 5 white cloths, and
3 ' plonket ' cloths . . . . 5s 8d.

    Sum: Cloths . 17
       Subs. . 5s. 8d.
       Ulnage . 8½d.

The 19th day of the same month.

Of Thomas Dawery 4 ' blew ' cloths, 4 ' plonket ' cloths, and
2 ' blew ' cloths . . . . 3s. 4d.
Adam Welfore 2 ' blewe ' cloths . . . . . 8d.

    Sum: Cloths . 12
       Subs. . 4s.
       Ulnage . 6d.

The 20th day of the same month.

Of John of Wenslaw 1 ' plunket ' cloth and 1 red cloth 8d.

    Sum: Cloths . 2
       Subs. . 8d.
       Ulnage . 1d.

The 21st day of the same month.

Of Laurence of Leverton 1 ' plunket ' cloth, 1 ' blew ' cloth,
½ a red cloth, and ½ a ' russet ' cloth . . . . 14d.

    Sum: Cloths . 3½
       Subs. . 14d.
       Ulnage . 1¾d.

The 22d day of the same month.

Of John Fowler 1 ' grene ' cloth . . . . 4d.

    Sum: Cloths . 1
       Subs. . 4d.
       Ulnage . ½d.

The 23d day of the same month.

Of Sissota of Drynghows 7 ells of ' plunket ' and 6 ells of
' blewe ' . . . . 2d.
Alan Wolman 1½ ' russet ' cloth . . . . . 6d.

    Sum: Cloths . 2
       Subs. . 8d.
       Ulnage . 1d.

The 24th day of the same month.

Of Elena of Skorburgh ½ a black cloth . . . . 2d.
Joan of Buton [sic] 7 ells of ' grene ' . . . . 1d.
John of Brydelyngton ½ a black cloth . . . . 2d.

    Sum: Cloths . 1 and 7 ells.
       Subs. . 5d.
       Ulnage . ¾d.

The 27th of the same month.

Of John of Braythwayte 4 red cloths, 3 ' blewe ' cloths, 4
' grene ' cloths, and 2 black cloths . . . . 4s. 4d.

Alice Wayfarar ½ a 'checary' cloth . . . . 2*d.*
William Bardnay ½ a 'russet' cloth . . . . 2*d.*
John Pataner ½ a 'plonket' cloth . . . . . 2*d.*
The wife of Adam of Wehgale 1 'duzen' of 'ray,' containing
  ½ a cloth of assize . . . . 2*d.*

> Sum: Cloths . 15
>   Subs. . 5*s.*
>   Ulnage . 7½*d.*

The 30th day of the same month.

Of John Thorneton 4 red cloths, 3 'grene' cloths, 3½ 'blew'
  cloths, and 2 'blak' cloths . . . . . 4*s.* 2*d.*
Thomas Askham 2 red cloths, 2 'blewe' cloths, and 2½
  'grene' cloths . . . . 2*s.* 2*d.*
Richard Redhode 1 'blew' cloth . . . . . 4*d.*
Joan of Welton 6 ells of red . . . . . . 1*d.*

> Sum: Cloths . 20 and 6 ells.
>   Subs. . 6*s.* 9*d.*
>   Ulnage . 10¼*d.*

The 31st day of the same month.

Of Robert Warde 5 red cloths, 4 white cloths, 3 'russet' cloths,
  and 24 'duzen narrow clothe,' containing 6 cloths of assize 6*s.*

> Sum: Cloths . 18
>   Subs. . 6*s.*
>   Ulnage . 9*d.*

The last day [*sic*] of the same month.

Thomas of Gare 3 'blewe' cloths, 2 red cloths, and 10 'duzen
  narrow clothe,' containing 2½ cloths . . . . 2*s.* 6*d.*

> Sum: Cloths . 7½
>   Subs. . 2*s.* 6*d.*
>   Ulnage . 3¾*d.*

The 2d day of August.

Of William Skawby 5 'blewe' cloths, 3 'grene' cloths, 3 red
  cloths, 1 'plonket' cloth, 1 white cloth, 1 'sangwyn'
  cloth, 1 'meld' cloth, and 1 'russet' cloth . . 5*s.* 4*d.*
Edward Smart ½ a 'blewe' cloth . . . . . 2*d.*
Joan of Dalton 6 ells of 'russet' . . . . . 1*d.*

> Sum: Cloths . 16½ and 6 ells.
>   Subs. . 5*s.* 7*d.*
>   Ulnage . 8¼*d.*

The 4th day of the same month.

Of William Sturge 2 'blew' cloths, 2 red cloths, and ½ a
  'grene' cloth . . . . 18*d.*
Gilbert Scherman 2 'blewe' cloths and 1 'morray' cloth 12*d.*

> Sum: Cloths . 7½
>   Subs. . 2*s.* 6*d.*
>   Ulnage . 3¾*d.*

The 5th day of the same month.

Of the wife of Richard of Tawnton[1] 10 'blew' cloths, 9½ white cloths, 3 'russet' cloths, 2½ 'plonket' cloths, and 1 'cog-sale' cloth . . . . 8s. 8d.

Hyllum[2] 6 'blew' cloths, 5 white cloths, and 3 'plonket' cloths . . . . 4s. 8d.

John . . . . . . [blotted] 5 red cloths, 5 'blewe' cloths, 4 'sang-wyn' cloths, and 4 'morray' cloths . . . . 6s.

Robert of Selby 2 'blewe' cloths and 2 'plunket' cloths . 16d.

      Sum: Cloths . 62
           Subs. . 20s. 8d.
           Ulnage . 2s. 7d.

The 7th day of the same month.

Of Thomas Howden 2 'blewe' cloths and 1 'plunket' cloth. 12d.

      Sum: Cloths . 3
           Subs. . 12d.
           Ulnage . 1½d.

The 8th day of the same month.

Of William Bell 3 red cloths, 2 'blew' cloths, and 2 'grene' cloths . . . . 2s. 4d.

John Osbaldwyke[3] 36 'duzen narow clothe,' containing 10 cloths of assize . . . . 3s.

      Sum: Cloths . 16
           Subs. . 5s. 4d.
           Ulnage . 8d.

The 9th day of the same month.

Of William Redhode 2 red cloths, 2 white cloths, 1 black cloth, and 1 'grene' cloth . . . . 2s.

John of Braythwayte 5 'blew' cloths, 2 white cloths, and 3 'plonket' cloths . . . . 3s. 4d.

      Sum: Cloths . 16
           Subs. . 6s. 4d.
           Ulnage . 8d.

The 10th day of the same month.

Of Robert Wrenche 6 white cloths, 4 'russet' cloths, and 2 'plonket' cloths . . . . 4s.

Thomas Doncaster-man[4] 3 white cloths, 2 'blew' cloths, and 1 'plonket' cloth . . . . 2s.

      Sum: Cloths . 18
           Subs. . 6s.
           Ulnage . 9d.

[1] A Richard of Taunton, "litester," was admitted a freeman in 1349–50, and the same man, apparently, was a Chamberlain 1366–7. Perhaps "uxor" means widow in this case.

[2] The Christian name is not given.

[3] John of Osbaldwyk, "marchaunt," was admitted a freeman in 1385–6, and a John of Osbaldwyk, junr., "mercer," in 1389–90.

[4] Thomas of Doncaster, "mercer," was admitted a freeman in 1375–6, and styled "Thomas of Doncastre, mercer," was a Chamberlain in 1395–6, and Sheriff in 1399–1400.

12th day of the same month.

Of William de Hedon[1] 6 'blewe' cloths, 1 'russet' cloth,
3 white cloths, and 2 'plonket' .　.　.　.　.　4s.

Robert Ganysforthe for 10 'blewe' cloths, 5 white, and
5 'plonket' cloths　.　.　.　.　.　.　. 6s. 8d.

Sum: Cloths . 32
Subs. . 10s. 8d.
Ulnage . 2d.

13th day of the same month.

Of Richard Iyrunmangar for 2 'blewe' cloths and 2 white
cloths　.　.　.　.　.　.　.　.　. 16d.

Sum: Cloths . 4
Subs. . 16d.
Ulnage . 1d.

17th day of the same month.

Of John of Braythwayte for ½ a black cloth　.　.　. 2d.

Thomas Bracebrege 3 red cloths and 3 'blew' cloths, 2
'sangwyn' cloths and 2 'grene'　.　.　.　. 2s. 4d.

Mariota Bowthe for 15 'meld' cloths　.　.　. 5s.

William Sturge 1 red cloth and ½ a 'grene' cloth　.　. 6d.

Sum: Cloths . 27
Subs. . 9s.
Ulnage . 13½d.

19th day of the same month.

Of John Fowrnowr 10 'blew' cloths, 10 red, 5 'sangwyn,' and
5½ 'grene'.　.　.　.　.　.　.　.　. 10s. 2d.

John of Cravyn for 6 'blew' cloths, 7 'plonket,' 5 white,
and 1 'russet' cloth .　.　.　.　.　. 6s. 4d.

William Redhod for 2 'blew' cloths　.　.　.　. 8d.

John of Kyrk[2] for 3 'duzon, 1 motle' [motley], containing
1½ cloth of assize　.　.　.　.　.　.　. 6d.

Sum: of Cloths 53
Subs. . 17s. 8d.
Ulnage . 2s. 2½d.

20th day of same month.

Of Edmund Gloffar[3] 8 white cloths, 4 'plonket' cloths, 4
'sangwyn,' and 2 'blew' cloths .　.　.　.　. 6s.

William Hawneby 6 white cloths, 5 'plonket,' and 3 'russet'
cloths　.　.　.　.　.　.　.　.　. 4s. 8d.

Sum: Cloths . 32
Subs. . 10s. 8d.
Ulnage . 16d.

---

[1] William of Hedon, "chapman," was admitted a freeman in 1387-8.

[2] John of the Kyrk, "webster," was admitted a freeman in 1375-6.

[3] Edmund Gloffar (i.e. Glover) was admitted a freeman under the name of
"Edmund of Coddesbroke, glover," in 1373-4, and in the list of Chamberlains
in 1389-90, as "Edmund Glover."

22d day of same month.

Of John of Braythwayte 5 ' blew,' 3 ' plunket ' cloths, and
2 white cloths . . . . 3s. 4d.
William of Wylton for 19 ' blew ' and white and ' russet '
cloths . . . . 6s. 4d.
Richard Redhod for ½ a red cloth . . . . . 2d.
John of Sessay for 4 red, 3 ' sangwyn ' cloths, and 3 ' grene '
cloths . . . . 3s. 4d.

Sum: Cloths . 39½
  Subs. . 13s. 2d.
  Ulnage . 19½d.

24th day of the same month.

Of Robert Bellman for 3 red and 3 ' blew ' cloths . . 2s.
Annota Hokester for ½ a ' meld ' cloth . . . . 2d.
Annota of Stokton for ½ a white cloth . . . . 2d.
William of Morton for 1 ' blew ' cloth and 1 red cloth, ½ a
' russet ' cloth, and ½ a ' grene ' cloth . . . 12d.
Richard of Ulston for 5 white cloths, 5 ' sangwyn ' cloths,
4 ' blew ' cloths, 2 ' plonket ' cloths, and 2 ' grene ' cloths 6s.
Gilbert Scherman for 1 ' sangwyn ' cloth . . 4d.
Richard Redhod for 2 ' grene ' cloths and 1½ red . . 14d.

Sum: Cloths . 32½
  Subs. . 10s. 10d.
  Ulnage . 16¼d.

26th day of the same month.

Of John of Thorneton for 3 ' blewe ' and 3 ' grene ' cloths,
and 4 red cloths, 1 white cloth, and 1 ' plonket ' cloth 4s.
Andrew Jounowr 1 ' blew ' cloth, 1 ' plonket ' cloth, and
1½ white cloth . . . . 14d.
Robert Lofthous for ½ a blue cloth . . . . . 2d.
Robert Ward for 4 ' blew ' cloths and 3 ' grene ' cloths,
3 ' sangwyn ' cloths, 2 ' plonket ' cloths, and 2 white
cloths . . . . 4s. 8d.

Sum: Cloths . 30
  Subs. . 10s.
  Ulnage . 15d.

[Here follow 2 lines obliterated by a fold in the membrane.]

The 27th day of the same month.

Of John Wyman for 3 ' plunket ' cloths, 3 ' grene ' cloths, 3
' blew,' 2 ' plonket,' and 1 ' russet ' cloths . . . 4s.
John of Thorneton for 3 ' blew ' cloths, 4 red cloths, 3
' grene ' cloths, and 1 ' blak ' cloth . . . . 3s. 8d.
Richard of Santon 12 ' blew ' cloths, 2 red cloths, 2 ' grene '
cloths, and 1 black cloth . . . . . 2s. 4d.
John Appylton 2 red cloths, 2 of ' sangwyne,' and 1 ' blew '
cloth . . . . 20d.

Sum: of Cloths. 35
  Subsidy . 11s. 8d.
  Ulnage . 17½d.

The 29th of the same month.

Of John of Braythwayt for 2 'blew' cloths, 2 red cloths,
and 1 'grene' cloth . . . . 20*d*.

Richard Steerowr for 6 red cloths, 6 'blew' cloths, 4 'sangwyn' cloths, 4 'grene' cloths, and 3 'plonket' cloths . 8*s*. 4*d*

Sum: of Cloths . 30

Subsidy . 10*s*.

Ulnage . 15*d*.

The 31st day of the same month.

Of Thomas of Howme for 2 'sangwyn' cloths, 2 'blewe'
cloths, and 2 red cloths . . . . 2*s*.

Adam of Brege for 5 'blew' cloths, 6 red cloths, 4 'sangwyn' cloths, 3 'grene' cloths, and 1 'plonket' cloth . 6*s*. 4*d*.

Thomas Lakynsnythir for 4 'blewe' cloths, 4 red, 4 'sangwyn,' 3 'grene,' and 2 'plonket' . . . . . . 5*s*. 8*d*.

Henry of Leverton for 4 'blewe,' 3 red, and 2 'grene' cloths   3*s*.

John of Newby for 3 'blew,' 4 red, and 2 'sangwyn' cloths .   3*s*.

Thomas Smyth for 4 'blew,' 4 red, 3 'sangwyn,' and 1 'russet'
cloths . . . . 4*s*. 2*d*.

John of Topclyf for 2 'blew,' 2 red, and 3 'sangwyn' cloths 2*s*. 4*d*.

Sum: Cloths . 79½

Subs. . 26*s*. 6*d*.

Ulnage . 3*s*. 3¾*d*.

The 2d day of September.

Of William Baillif for 3 'blew,' 4 red, 3 'sangwyn,' 2 'grene,'
and 2 'russet' cloths . . . . 4*s*. 4*d*.

John of Barnardcastell 5 'blew,' 5 red, 4 'sangwyn,' 4
'grene,' 3 'plonket,' 2 white, and 2 'moray' cloths . 8*s*. 4*d*.

William Appylby 1 'motley' and 1 'plonket' cloth . . 8*d*.

Sum: Cloths . 40

Subs. . 13*s*. 4*d*.

Ulnage . 20*d*.

4th day of the same month.

Of William Hawnby 4 'grene,' 3 'blew,' 4 'sangwyn,' 3
'russet,' and 2 black cloths . . . . . . 5*s*. 4*d*.

Roger of Barton[1] 3 'blew,' 2 white, 2 'russet,' and 2 'sangwyn' cloths . . . . 3*s*.

Hillū [*sic*] 2 'blew' and 2 'plonket' . . . . 16*d*.

Sum: Cloths . 29

Subs. . 9*s*. 8*d*.

Ulnage . 14½*d*.

5th day of the same month.

Of Godfray Upstand[2] 1 red, 1 'blew,' and 1 'plonket' cloth.

Sum: Cloths . 3

Subs. . 12*d*.

Ulnage . 1½*d*.

---

[1] Roger of Barton, " mercer," was admitted a freeman in 1383–4.

[2] Is Godfrey Upstand the same individual as Godfrey van Uppesvall,
" webster," admitted a freeman in 1375–6 ?

6th day of the same month.

Of William Bardsay 3 ells of white cloth . . . ½*d.*
Joan of Ostell 3 ells of ' russet ' . . . . . ½*d.*

      Sum: Cloths . 6 ells.
           Subs. . 1*d.*
           Ulnage . ¼*d.*

7th day of the same month.

Of John Bewyk 3 ' blew,' 3 red, 2 ' sangwyn,' 2 ' plonket,' and
  2 ' grene ' cloths . . . . 4*s.*
Alan Hamerton 6 ' blew,' 6 red, 5 ' sangwyne,' 3 ' grene,' 4
  ' plonket,' and 6 white cloths . . . . . 10*s.*
Sissota of Schopton 6 ells of white cloth . . . 1*d.*

      Sum: Cloths . 42 and 6 ells.
           Subs. . 14*s.* 1*d.*
           Ulnage . 21*d.*

9th day of the same month.

Of Annota of Kelfeld 6 ells of white cloth . . . 1*d.*
Joan [Johanna] of Mylforth for 1 ' duzen narrow' cloths, con-
  taining 6 ells of a cloth of assize . . . . . 1*d.*
Richard of Morlay for 6 ' blew,' 4 red, 3 ' grene,' 4 ' sangwyn,'
  and 3 ' plonket ' cloths . . . . 6*s.* 8*d.*
John Bywell 4 white, 2 'plunket,' and 1 ' russet ' cloths . 2*s.* 4*d.*

      Sum: Cloths . 27 and 12 ells.
           Subs. . 9*s.* 2*d.*
           Ulnage . 13¾*d.*

11th day of same month.

Of Sissota of Schopton for 6 ells of ' blewe ' . . . 1*d.*
Annota of Kelfeld for 6 ells of white cloth . . . 1*d.*
Joan of Milforthe for 1 ' duzen ' of ' narrow qwyt,' contain-
  ing 6 ells of a cloth of assize . . . . . . 1*d.*
John Chartrys ½ a ' sangwyn ' cloth and ½ a ' grene ' cloth . 4*d.*.
Richard of Worssope ½ a cloth of ' moray ' . . . 2*d.*
John de Knapton ½ a white cloth . . . . . 2*d.*

      Sum: Cloths . 2½ and 6 ells.
           Subs. . 11*d.*
           Ulnage . 1½*d.*

13th day of the same month.

Of William of Marson. ½ a ' plonket ' cloth . . . 2*d.*
John of Thorpe for 6 ells of ' russet ' . . . . 1*d.*
William Palmer 2 ' blew,' 4 red, and 3 ' sangwyn ' cloths . 3*s.*
Alice of Petirfeld 4 white and 4 ' blew ' cloths . . 2*s.* 8*d.*
John of Kyrke for ½ a motley cloth . . . . . 2*d.*
Richard Essyngwald 4 ' blewe,' 4 red, 3 ' sangwyn,' 2 ' grene,'
  and 2 ' plonket ' cloths . . . . 5*s.*

      Sum: Cloths . 24½
           Subs. . 11*s.* 1*d.*
           Ulnage . 6¾*d.*

The 15th day of the same month.

Of Richard Chace[1] for 3 ' blew,' 3 red, and 2 ' plonket ' cloths 2s.8d.

Thomas Newland 4 red, 3 ' blewe,' and 2 ' plonket ' cloths .   3s.

Alice Porter for ½ a white cloth . . . . .   2d.

John Askam 2 ' blew,' 2 ' sangwyne,' and 2 red . .   2s.

John Stewynson for ½ a ' russet ' cloth . . . .   2d.

John of Gousse for the ½ a ' russet ' cloth . . .   2d.

Sum: Cloths . 24½

Subs. . 8s. 2d.

Ulnage . 12¼d.

The 17th day of the same month.

Of John of Thorneton 1 ' blew,' 1 red, and 1 ' grene ' cloth .   10d.

William Hawnby 3 ' blew,' 1 red, and ½ a ' grene ' cloth .   10d.

Mariota Bowthe 4 ' cogsale ' cloths, 1 ' grene meld,' and 6 ells
of red . . . .   21d.

Sum: Cloths . 14½ and 6 ells

Subs. . 4s. 11d.

Ulnage . 7½d.

The 20th day of the same month.

Of Mariota Bowthe 2 ' cogsale ' cloths and 2½ cloths of ' grene
meld ' . . . .   18d.

Richard of Santon 1½ cloth of ' taud ' and ½ a ' plonket ' cloth   8d.

William Elmslay 4 ' taud ' cloths and 4 ' meld ' cloths . 2s. 8d.

Thomas Hornby 1 ' meld ' cloth and 1½ ' plonket ' cloth .   10d.

Richard of Chawmbre 1½ ' blew,' 1 ' plonket,' 1 ' russet,' ½ a
white, and 1 ' sangwyn ' cloth . . . . .   20d.

Sum: Cloths . 22

Subs. . 7s. 4d.

Ulnage . 11d.

The 22d day of the same month.

Of Richard of Santon 2¼ cloths . . . . .   9d.

Alice Frere 3 ells of ' blew ' . . . . . .   ½d.

Alice of Foston 6 ells of ' russet ' . . . . .   1d.

Margaret Hokester 4 ells of ' meld ' . . . .   ½d.

Sum: Cloths . 2½ and 5½ ells.

Subs. . 11d.

Ulnage . 1½d.

Of any profits arising from the subsidy of cloths of the half grain he does not render account, because no cloths were exposed for sale there of this kind of cloth, during the period of his account, as he says upon his oath.

Nor does he answer for any profits arising from forfeitures of vendible cloths exposed for sale, not sealed with the seal therefor appointed, because he found nor could find any cloth of this character during the same period, and this he says upon his oath.

---

[1] Richard Chace, " merchant," was admitted a freeman in 1370–1, and Robert Chace, " gentilman, son of Richard Chace, merchaunt," was elected a freeman in 1438–9. Richard and Katharine Chace are mentioned in the " Obituary " of the Corpus Christi Guild in 1415–6.

Nor does he answer for any money arising from the ulnage or subsidy of cloths in the City and suburbs aforesaid from the aforesaid 20th day of July in the 18th year [of the King], on which day the aforesaid John was appointed to the office aforesaid, until the aforesaid 6th day of September in the same year, because then the aforesaid Writ of the King was first delivered to the aforesaid John, seeing that John of Thornton, deputy of Thomas Bromflete,[1] the farmer of the office aforesaid, received the issues and profits therefrom arising during that same time, and took and had them, as he says upon his oath. Of these issues and profits of the subsidy of cloths, of the ulnage and forfeitures of the same, the said John ought to answer.

Sum total: Scarlet cloths, 1.

Cloths of assize without grain, 3,256 and ½ and 2 yards.
Whereof the subsidy [amounts to] £54 6s. 6d.
The ulnage of the same cloths, £6 15s. 9¾d.
Sum total of money received:
£61 2s. 4¾d.

IV.

$$[E. \frac{345}{17}]$$

West-rithing [sic]

Pountfret

Particulars of the Account of William Barker of Tadcaster,[2] Ulnager of the King in the Westrithing, in the County of York, by Writ Patent of the King given on the 4th day of November, in the 19th year [of his reign], to wit, both of the Subsidy and Ulnage there, as well as of the forfeitures of vendible cloths of this kind not sealed with the seals appointed for this purpose, from the aforesaid 4th day of November in the 19th year until the 20th day of November in the 20th year, from which day William of Hoperton is to account.

1395
1396

From Thomas Draper, 16 cloths of assize. Subs. 5s. 4d. Ulnage 8d.
John Lews, 12 whole cloths of assize. Subs. 4s. Ulnage 6d.
Thomas Hadilsey, 14 whole cloths of assize. Subs. 4s. 8d. Ulnage 7d.
Richard Hodgeson, draper, 10 whole cloths of assize. Subs. 3s. 4d. Ulnage 5d.
Isabella, wife of Holinmane, 12 whole cloths of assize. Subs. 4s. Ulnage 6d.
Robert Marbery, 13 whole cloths, etc. Subs. 4s. 4d. Ulnage 6½d.
William Wakfeld, 16 whole cloths, etc. Subs. 5s. 4d. Ulnage 8d.
John Lavyrok, 9 whole cloths, etc. Subs. 3s. Ulnage 4½d.
Thomas Hosyer, 6 pieces of strait cloth, containing 3 quarters of a cloth of assize. Subs. 3d. Ulnage ½d.

---

[1] Thomas Bromflete was appointed ulnager in the counties of York, Northumberland, Cumberland, and Westmorland, May 12th, 1386, by Letters Patent. A Thomas of Brounflete, merchant, was appointed a freeman of York in 1399.

[2] Will 22nd Oct., 1403, proved 8th Nov., 1403. See *Test. Ebor.*, i, 327.

	John Chintok, 6 yds. of a cloth of assize.	Subs.	1d.	Ulnage	$\frac{1}{4}d.$
	John Bank, 6 yds. of cloth, etc.	Subs.	1d.	Ulnage	$\frac{1}{4}d.$
	Thomas Stawinforth, 3 strait cloths, containing 1½ cloth of assize.	Subs.	6d.	Ulnage	$\frac{3}{4}d.$
	Robert Benet, 6 yds. of a cloth of assize.	Subs.	1d.	Ulnage	$\frac{1}{4}d.$
	John Stone, 3 pieces of strait cloth containing ¾ths of a cloth of assize.	Subs.	3d.	Ulnage	$\frac{1}{2}d.$

105¾ cloths, 35s. 3d.—4s. 5½d.

Wak-	Emma Erle, 48 whole cloths, etc.	Subs.	16s.	Ulnage	2s.
feld	Roger Presaw, 26 whole cloths, etc.	Subs.	8s. 8d.	Ulnage	13d.
	John Kent, 24 whole cloths, etc.	Subs.	8s.	Ulnage	12d.
	William Bate, 16 whole cloths, etc.	Subs.	5s. 4d.	Ulnage	8d.
	Richard Burbrigg, 30 whole cloths.	Subs.	10s.	Ulnage	15d.
	Thomas Kendall, 30 strait cloths, each containing ½ a cloth of assize.	Subs.	5s.	Ulnage	$7\frac{1}{2}d.$
	Henry Draper, 29 strait cloths, each containing ½ a cloth of assize.	Subs.	4s.10d.	Ulnage	$7\frac{1}{4}d.$

173½ cloths, 57s. 10d.—7s. 1¾d.

Ledys	William Snell, 52 whole cloths, etc.	Subs.	17s. 4d.	Ulnage	2s.6d.
	John Dykmane, 22 whole cloths, etc.	Subs.	7s. 4d.	Ulnage	11d.
	Thomas Braddforth, 26 whole cloths, etc.	Subs.	8s. 8d.	Ulnage	13d.
	John Tymbulle, 18 whole cloths, etc.	Subs.	6s.	Ulnage	9d.
	The same Thomas, 4 strait cloths, each containing ½ a cloth of assize.	Subs.	8d.	Ulnage	2d.
Wether-	Robert Browne, 12 whole cloths, etc.	Subs.	4s.	Ulnage	6d.
by	Richard Saundourson, 9 whole cloths.	Subs.	3s.	Ulnage	$4\frac{1}{2}d.$
	William Bischop, 6 whole cloths, etc.	Subs.	2s.	Ulnage	3d.
	Thomas Smyth, 6 strait cloths, each containing ½ a cloth of assize.	Subs.	12d.	Ulnage	$1\frac{1}{2}d.$
	William Tilson, 10 strait cloths, each containing ½ a cloth of assize.	Subs.	20d.	Ulnage	$2\frac{1}{2}d.$
	Robert Bischop, 1 strait cloth, containing ½ a cloth of assize.	Subs.	2d.	Ulnage	$\frac{1}{4}d.$

35½ cloths, 11s. 10d.—17¾d.

Don-	William Barbour, 5 whole cloths, etc.	Subs.	20d.	Ulnage	$2\frac{1}{2}d.$
caster	John of Balne, 4 whole cloths, etc.	Subs.	16d.	Ulnage	2d.
	John Chynyngton, 3 whole cloths, etc.	Subs.	12d.	Ulnage	$1\frac{1}{2}d.$
	Richard Ash, 5 whole cloths, etc.	Subs.	20d.	Ulnage	$2\frac{1}{2}d.$
	Robert Elande, 3 whole cloths, etc.	Subs.	12d.	Ulnage	$1\frac{1}{2}d.$
	Adam Partrik, 3 whole cloths, etc.	Subs.	12d.	Ulnage	$1\frac{1}{2}d.$
	William Millot, 3 cloths of assize.	Subs.	12d.	Ulnage	$1\frac{1}{2}d.$
	William Belle, 1 strait cloth, containing ½ a cloth of assize.	Subs.	2d.	Ulnage	$\frac{1}{4}d.$
	Hugh Mathew, ½ a cloth of assize.	Subs.	2d.	Ulnage	$\frac{1}{4}d.$

28 cloths, 9s.

Rodir-	Thomas Bakster, 4 whole cloths, etc.	Subs.	16d.	Ulnage	2d.
ham	Ralph Povay, 3 whole cloths, etc.	Subs.	12d.	Ulnage	$1\frac{1}{2}d.$
	Robert Bugg, 5 whole cloths, etc.	Subs.	20d.	Ulnage	$2\frac{1}{2}d.$
	Robert Lawe, 6 half cloths of a cloth of assize.	Subs.	12d.	Ulnage	$1\frac{1}{2}d.$

	Adam Symson, 6 strait cloths, containing half a cloth of assize	Subs. 12*d.*	Ulnage 1½*d.*
	18 cloths, 6*s.* 9*d.*		
Barnsley	Richard Kersforth, 3 whole cloths, etc.	Subs. 12*d.*	Ulnage 1½*d.*
	Thomas Lotrington, 4 whole cloths, etc.	Subs. 12*d.*	Ulnage 2*d.*
	From the same Thomas, 4 half cloths, etc.	Subs. 8*d.*	Ulnage 1*d.*
	William Pynder, 6 whole cloths, etc.	Subs. 2*s.*	Ulnage 3*d.*
	Thomas Jakson, 12 strait cloths, each containing ½ a cloth of assize.	Subs. 2*s.*	Ulnage 3*d.*
	John Dayvill, 6 strait cloths, each containing ½ a cloth of assize.	Subs. 12*d.*	Ulnage 1½*d.*
	Elena Wyld, 4 half cloths and 6 yds., etc.	Subs. 9*d.*	Ulnage 1½*d.*
	26 cloths and 6 yds., 8*s.* 9½*d.*—13¼*d.*		
Selby	John Escrik, 8 whole cloths, etc.	Subs. 2*s.* 8*d.*	Ulnage 4*d.*
	John Marschall, 6 whole cloths, etc.	Subs. 2*s.*	Ulnage 3*d.*
	Robert Graynham, 8 half cloths, etc.	Subs. 16*d.*	Ulnage 2*d.*
	Thomas Danyell, 4 cloths, etc.	Subs. 16*d.*	Ulnage 2*d.*
	From the same Thomas, ½ a cloth, etc.	Subs. 2*d.*	Ulnage ¼*d.*
	22½ cloths, 7*s.* 6*d.*—11¼*d.*		
Rypon	John Percy, 18 whole cloths, etc.	Subs. 6*s.*	Ulnage 9*d.*
	John Russell, 14 whole cloths, etc.	Subs. 4*s.* 8*d.*	Ulnage 7*d.*
	John Tavyrner, 9 whole cloths, etc.	Subs. 3*d.*	Ulnage 4½*d.*
	John Mymyrsmyth, 16 whole cloths, etc.	Subs. 5*s.* 4*d.*	Ulnage 8*d.*
	John Littister, 28 whole cloths, etc.	Subs. 9*s.* 4*d.*	Ulnage 14*d.*
	William Fulforth, 72 strait cloths, containing 36 cloths of assize.	Subs. 12*s.*	Ulnage 18*d.*
	John Cawode, 60 strait cloths, containing 30 cloths of assize.	Subs. 10*s.*	Ulnage 15*d.*
	William Thornton, 12 strait cloths, containing 6 cloths of assize.	Subs. 2*s.*	Ulnage 3*d.*
	William Draper, 23 strait cloths, 11½ cloths of assize.	Subs. 3*s.* 10*d.*	Ulnage 5¾*d.*
	From the same William, 8 yds. of a cloth of assize.	Subs. 1½*d.*	Ulnage ¼*d.*
	168½ cloths and 8 yds., 56*s.* 3½*d.*—7*s.* 0½*d.*		
Skipton	John Lambe, 8 whole cloths.	Subs. 2*s.* 8*d.*	Ulnage 4*d.*
	Thomas Bischop, 10 strait cloths, containing 5 cloths of assize.	Subs. 20*d.*	Ulnage 2½*d.*
	Thomas Marschall, 6 strait cloths, containing 3 whole cloths of assize.	Subs. 12*d.*	Ulnage 1½*d.*
	Peter Chapman, 8 strait cloths, containing 4 cloths of assize.	Subs. 16*d.*	Ulnage 2*d.*
	John Warrener, 2 strait cloths, containing 1 cloth of assize.	Subs. 4*d.*	Ulnage ½*d.*
	Thomas Parkynson, 7 yds. of a cloth of assize.	Subs. 1¼*d.*	Ulnage ¼*d.*
	21 cloths and 7 yds., 7*s.* 1¼*d.*—10¾*d.*		

Sum Total of Cloths, 1,718½ and 3 yds.

Subs. £11 19*s.* 6¾*d.*
Ulnage 30*s.* 1¼*d.*
Sum total £13 9*s.* 8*d.*

He does not answer for profits arising from the subsidy on scarlet cloths, or cloths of the half grain, because no cloths of this kind were exposed there for sale within the term [of his office].

Nor does he answer for any profit arising from the forfeiture of any cloths of this kind exposed there for sale before the subsidy thereon due was paid and those cloths sealed in the seal ad hoc·appointed.

V.

[E. $\frac{345}{18}$]

West-rithing. PARTICULARS OF THE ACCOUNT OF WILLIAM OF HOPERTON, late collector of the subsidy and ulnage of saleable cloths in the "Westrithing" in the County of York by writ patent of the King

1396 [Ric. II] given on the 20th day of November in His twentieth year, enrolled in the *Originalia* of the same year, to wit, concerning the same subsidy and ulnage there, from the 20th day of November

1397 in the 20th year up to the 21st day of November in His twenty-first year as below.

[Doncaster.]

Receipts Of John Chynyngton for 6 whole cloths of assize, subs. 2s., of ulnage 3d.

money. Thomas Taillour, 2 whole cloths of assize, subs. 8d., ulnage 1d.

William Barbour, 6 strait cloths containing 3 cloths of assize, subs. 12d., ulnage 1½d.

Thomas Kendall, Drapour, 10 strait cloths containing 5 cloths of assize, subs. 20d., ulnage 2½d.

[Rotherham.]

Of Ralph Povay, 2 whole cloths of assize, subs. 8d., ulnage 1d.

Robert Draper for 12 strait cloths containing 6 cloths of assize, subs. 2s , ulnage 3d.

John Taillour, 4 whole cloths of assize, subs. 16d., ulnage 2d.

Robert Hosyer, 6 strait cloths containing 3 cloths of assize, subs. 12d., ulnage 1½d.

[Wakefield.]

Of William Pynder for 6 whole cloths of assize, subs.2s., ulnage 3d.

Emma Erle, 8 whole cloths of assize, subs. 2s. 8d., ulnage 4d.

Robert Kendalle, 8 strait cloths containing 4 cloths of assize, subs. 16d., ulnage 2d.

Roger Presawe, 10 strait cloths containing 5 cloths of assize, subs. 20d., ulnage 2½d.

John Marschall, 10 whole cloths of assize, subs. 3s. 4d., ulnage 5d.

John Dayvyll, 2 strait cloths containing 1 cloth of assize, subs. 4d., ulnage ½d.

Thomas Cartwright, 6 whole cloths of assize, subs. 2s., ulnage 3d.

Thomas Taillour for 3 whole cloths of assize, subs.12d., ulnage 1½d.

John Wellys, 9 whole cloths of assize, subs. 3s., ulnage 4½d.

[Wetherby.]

Of John Kent, 6 strait cloths containing 3 cloths of assize, subs. 12d., ulnage 1½d.

Robert Taillour, 5 whole cloths of assize, subs. 20*d*., ulnage 2½*d*.
John of the Lee, 8 strait cloths containing 4 cloths of assize, subs. 16*d*., ulnage 2*d*.
Geoffrey Walkare, 10 cloths of assize, subs. 3*s*. 4*d*., ulnage 5*d*.
William Tilson, 7 whole cloths of assize, subs. 2*s*. 4*d*., ulnage 3½*d*.
Robert Kendall, 9 whole cloths of assize, subs. 3*s*., ulnage 4½*d*.
Richard Draper, 12 strait cloths containing 6 cloths of assize, subs. 2*s*., ulnage 3*d*.
John Pierson, 8 strait cloths containing 4 cloths of assize, subs. 16*d*., ulnage 2*d*.
Thomas Moldson, 10 strait cloths containing 5 cloths of assize, subs. 20*d*., ulnage 2½*d*.
Robert Taillour, 6 strait cloths containing 3 cloths of assize, subs. 12*d*., ulnage 1½*d*.
John Draper, 9 whole cloths of assize, subs. 3*s*., ulnage 4½*d*.
[Pontefract.]
John Lews, 6 whole cloths of assize, subs. 2*s*., ulnage 3*d*.
Thomas Draper, 10 whole cloths of assize, subs. 3*s*. 4*d*., ulnage 5*d*.
Thomas Kendalle, 20 strait cloths containing 10 cloths of assize.
John Tankirslay, 9 whole cloths of assize, subs. 3*s*., ulnage 4½*d*.
John Hobson, 4 whole cloths of assize, subs. 16*d*., ulnage 2*d*.
Robert Jakson, 3 whole cloths of assize, subs. 12*d*., ulnage 1½*d*.
Richard Friston, 5 whole cloths of assize, subs. 20*d*., ulnage 2½*d*.
Robert Huchonson, 6 whole cloths of assize, subs. 2*s*., ulnage 3*d*.
John Hosyer, 10 whole cloths of assize, subs. 3*s*. 4*d*., ulnage 5*d*.
William Littister, 9 whole cloths of assize, subs. 3*s*., ulnage 4½*d*.
[?]
Of Robert Grayngham, 6 strait cloths containing 3 cloths of assize, subs. 12*d*., ulnage 1½*d*.
Adam Kele, 4 whole cloths of assize, subs. 16*d*., ulnage 2*d*.
Thomas Symson, 3 whole cloths of assize, subs. 12*d*., ulnage 1½*d*.
Richard Taillour, 4 strait cloths containing 2 cloths of assize, subs. 8*d*., ulnage 1*d*.
John Willyamson, 6 strait cloths containing 3 cloths of assize, subs. 12*d*., ulnage 1½*d*.
John Taillour, 2 whole cloths of assize, subs. 8*d*., ulnage 1*d*.
[Leeds ?]
William Snell, 12 whole cloths of assize, subs. 4*s*., ulnage 6*d*.
Roger Draper, 16 strait cloths containing 8 cloths of assize, subs. 2*s*. 8*d*., ulnage 4*d*.
John Scotte, 5 whole cloths of assize, subs. 20*d*., ulnage 2½*d*.
Robert Taillour, 12 strait cloths containing 6 cloths of assize, subs. 2*s*., ulnage 3*d*.
John Neuton, 8 whole cloths of assize, subs. 2*s*. 8*d*., ulnage 4*d*.
Thomas Relle, 6 whole cloths of assize, subs. 2*s*., ulnage 3*d*.
Richard Walkare, 16 whole cloths of assize, subs. 6*s*. 4*d*., ulnage 8*d*.
Robert Littister, 9 whole cloths of assize, subs. 3*s*., ulnage 4½*d*.
Richard Draper, 10 whole cloths of assize, subs. 3*s*. 4*d*., ulnage 5*d*.
Emma Rotore, 4 whole cloths of assize, subs. 16*d*., ulnage 2*d*.

[Ripon.]

Of John Percey, 20 whole cloths of assize, subs. 6s. 8d., ulnage 10d.

John Mynyrsmyth, 12 whole cloths of assize, subs. 4s., ulnage 6d.

William Russelle, 9 whole cloths of assize, subs. 3s., ulnage 4½d.

John Roper, 15 whole cloths of assize, subs. 5s., ulnage 7½d.

Robert Topclyffe, 30 strait cloths containing 15 cloths of assize, subs. 5s., ulnage 7½d.

Thomas Draper, 6 cloths of assize, subs. 2s., ulnage 3d.

John Walkare, 16 strait cloths containing 8 cloths of assize, subs. 2s. 8d., ulnage 4d.

Richard Littister, 13 whole cloths of assize, subs. 4s. 4d., ulnage 6½d.

John Taillour, 6 whole cloths of assize, subs. 2s., ulnage 3d.

John Schermane, 4 whole cloths of assize, subs. 16d., ulnage 2d.

Robert Potmane, 3 whole cloths of assize, subs. 12d., ulnage 1½d.

Of John Lambe, 12 cloths of assize, subs. 4s., ulnage 6d.

John Skipton, 12 strait cloths containing 6 cloths of assize, subs. 2s., ulnage 3d.

William Draper, 3 whole cloths of assize, subs. 12d., ulnage 1½d.

William Littister, 2 whole cloths of assize, subs. 8d., ulnage 1d.

[?]

Of Thomas Smyth, 4 whole cloths of assize, subs. 16d., ulnage 2d.

Richard Balne, 5 whole cloths of assize, subs. 20d., ulnage 2½d.

Walter Forster, 3 whole cloths of assize, subs. 12d., ulnage 1½d.

Edmund Beche, 8 strait cloths containing 4 cloths of assize, subs. 16d., ulnage 2d.

Richard Beeche, 3 whole cloths of assize, subs. 12d., ulnage 1½d.

He does not answer for any profit arising from the subsidy or ulnage of cloths of scarlet in grain, [of those] of half grain, or [of those] in which some grain shall have been intermixed; nor of forfeitures of saleable cloths of this kind there exposed for sale without having the seal appointed for this purpose applied to them during the time of this account because no cloths of this sort were exposed for sale during the time, as he declares upon his oath.

Sum total: Cloths, 484.

Subs., £7 18s. 0d.

Ulnage, 19s. 9d.

Sum of Receipts, £8 17s. 9d.

[Writ dated 21 Nov., 21 Ric. II, to William of Hoperton to deliver up the seals of his office to John Amyas, appointed ulnager.]

VI.

[E. $\frac{345}{20}$]

PARTICULARS OF THE ACCOUNT OF ROBERT FERYBY, late ulnager of the King in the City of York and suburbs of the same, by Writ Patent of our Lord the King the late King [sic] given on the 18th day of April in the 21st year of his reign, containing these particulars to wit, as well concerning the subsidy and ulnage of saleable cloths as

1398

of the forfeitures of cloths of this kind there exposed for sale, not sealed with the seal appointed for this purpose, from the 18th day of April in the 22nd year of the late King up to the 17th day of October, then next following, to wit for one half year, as below:

1399

From John Thornton, for 21 cloths of assize without grain.	Subs. 7s.	Ulnage 10½d.
From John Sessay, 42 cloths of this kind.	Subs. 14s.	Ulnage 21d.
From John Blekynsope, 16 cloths of this kind.	Subs. 5s. 4d.	Ulnage 8d.
From John Lyndsay, 2 cloths, etc.	Subs. 8d.	Ulnage 1d.
From John Laxton, 23 cloths, etc.	Subs. 7s. 8d.	Ulnage 11½d.
From William Charnton, 12 cloths, etc.	Subs. 4s.	Ulnage 6d.
From John Kirk, 2 cloths, etc.	Subs. 8d.	Ulnage 1d.
From Richard Thurby, 8½ cloths, etc.	Subs. 2s. 10d.	Ulnage 4¼d.
From William Sturge, 3 cloths, etc.	Subs. 12d.	Ulnage 1½d.
From Laurence Lyverton,[1] 4 cloths, etc.	Subs. 16d.	Ulnage 2d.
From Thomas Askam, 10 cloths, etc.	Subs. 3s. 4d.	Ulnage 5d.
From Thomas Holme, 23½ cloths, etc.	Subs. 7s. 10d.	Ulnage 11 halfpence and 1 farthing.
From Richard Chandelar, 14½ cloths.	Subs. 4s. 10d.	Ulnage 7¼d.
From John Brydlyngton, 6½ cloths, etc.	Subs. 2s. 2d.	Ulnage 3¼d.
From John Topclyff, 16½ cloths, etc.	Subs. 5s. 6d.	Ulnage 8¼d.
From John Stelyngflet,[2] 16½ cloths, etc.	Subs. 5s. 6d.	Ulnage 8¼d.
From Adam Burton, 10½ cloths, etc.	Subs. 3s. 6d.	Ulnage 5¼d.
From Robert Scardeburgh, 18 cloths, etc.	Subs. 6s.	Ulnage 9d.
From Thomas Qwetyk, 11½ cloths, etc.	Subs. 3s. 10d.	Ulnage 5¾d.
From William Byrkehed, 15 cloths, etc.	Subs. 5s.	Ulnage 7½d.
From William Newby, 3 cloths, etc.	Subs. 12d.	Ulnage 1½d.
From Robert Cooke, 5 cloths, etc.	Subs. 20d.	Ulnage 2½d.
From Hugh Chartyrs, 8 cloths, etc.	Subs. 2s. 8d.	Ulnage 4d.
From Thomas Ruston, 12 cloths, etc.	Subs. 4s.	Ulnage 6d.
From Danby [sic], 7 cloths, etc.	Subs. 2s. 4d.	Ulnage 3½d.
From Robert Talkan, 2½ cloths, etc.	Subs. 10d.	Ulnage 1¼d.
From John Bolton, 15 cloths, etc.	Subs. 5s.	Ulnage 7½d.
From Robert Bugge, 3 cloths, etc.	Subs. 12d.	Ulnage 1½d.
From William del de [?], 5 cloths, etc.	Subs. 20d.	Ulnage 2½d.
From Geoffrey Savage, 9 cloths, etc.	Subs. 2s.	Ulnage 4½d.
From John Crofton, 7 cloths, etc.	Subs. 2s. 4d.	Ulnage 4½d.
From John Holbek, 5 cloths, etc.	Subs. 20d.	Ulnage 2½d.
From William Redhud, 6½ cloths, etc.	Subs. 2s. 2d.	Ulnage 3¼d.
From William Belby, 2 cloths, etc.	Subs. 8d.	Ulnage 1d.
From Threpland [sic], 6 cloths, etc.	Subs. 2s.	Ulnage 3d.
From John Otlay, 2 cloths, etc.	Subs. 8d.	Ulnage 1d.
From Robert Loye, 36½ cloths, etc.	Subs. 12s. 2d.	Ulnage 18¼d.
From John Braywate, 64 cloths, etc.	Subs. 21s. 4d.	Ulnage 2s. 8d.
From Alan Hamerton, 11 cloths, etc.	Subs. 3s. 8d.	Ulnage 5½d.

[1] Laurence of Liverton, "merchant," was admitted freeman of York in 1376.

[2] A John Stillyngflete was a Chamberlain of York in 1408.

From Henry Preston, 6 cloths, etc.	Subs. 2s.	Ulnage	3d.
From Adam Brygg, 13 cloths, etc.	Subs. 4s. 4d.	Ulnage	6½d.
From John Raghton, 7 cloths, etc.	Subs. 2s. 4d.	Ulnage	3½d.
From John Buttyrkyn, 1½ cloth, etc.	Subs. 6d.	Ulnage	¾d.
From Henry Wakefeld, 5 cloths, etc.	Subs. 20d.	Ulnage	2½d.
From Robert Ward, 7 cloths, etc.	Subs. 2s. 4d.	Ulnage	3½d.
From Thomas Horaby, 7 cloths, etc.	Subs. 2s. 4d.	Ulnage	3½d.
From William Merton, 6 cloths, etc.	Subs. 2s.	Ulnage	3d.
From Gilbert Sherman, 8 cloths, etc.	Subs. 2s. 8d.	Ulnage	4d.
From John Webster, 2½ cloths, etc.	Subs. 10d.	Ulnage	1¼d.
From Thomas Doncaster, 14½ cloths, etc.	Subs. 4s. 10d.	Ulnage	7¼d.
From John Percy, 9 cloths, etc.	Subs. 3s.	Ulnage	4½d.
From Richard Marshall, 3 cloths, etc.	Subs. 12d.	Ulnage	1½d.
From John Barnacastell, 17 cloths, etc.	Subs. 5s. 8d.	Ulnage	8½d.

He does not answer for any profit arising from the subsidy or ulnage of Scarlet cloths, nor of those of half grain, nor for the forfeiture of any cloths or pieces of saleable cloths exposed for sale and not stamped with the seal appointed for this purpose, during the time aforesaid, because no cloths or pieces of this kind have, as he says upon his oath, been exposed for sale within the time [of his account].   Sum   of cloths 592.

of subsidy £9 17s. 4d.
of Ulnage   24s. 8d.
Total Receipts £11 2s. 0d.

VII.

[E. $\frac{345}{24}$]

West Riding.

PARTICULARS OF THE ACCOUNT OF THOMAS TREYGOTT,[1] late " approver " of the subsidy and ulnage of vendible cloths, and of the moiety of forfeitures of the same, in the County of York, to wit, from the Feast of St. Michael in the 9th year of Edward the Fourth, late " de facto " King of England, up to the Feast of St. Michael then next following, to wit, for one whole year, from which Feast of St. Michael in the tenth year of the said late King, John Nevyll, Marquis Montagu, is now farmer of this subsidy and ulnage of vendible cloths, in the City of York and Town of Kingeston-on-Hull, as well as in the said County of York, and as by the Original Roll of the same year he remains charged.

1469, 1470

From Thomas Pykborn, of Doncastre, 35½ vendible cloths sealed there, within the time aforesaid, to wit, on each cloth a subsidy of 4d., and ulnage ½d. .	13s. 4d.
Richard Symmes, of Barnsley, subsidy and ulnage of 48¾ of cloths sealed there	33s. 4d.

[1] Thomas Trigott, of South Kirkby, married Joan, daughter of John Suthill, of Dewsbury. See Hunter's *South Yorkshire*.

Milo Parker, of Wakefeld, subsidy and ulnage of 249
   cloths sealed there . . . . . . £4 13s. 4d.
John Lake, of Halyfax, subsidy and ulnage of 853¼
   sealed there . . . . £16 0s. 0d.
Henry Rokley, of Ledes, subsidy and ulnage of 187½
   cloths sealed there . . . . . . 66s. 8d.
Robert Nevyl, of Almondebury, subsidy and ulnage of
   160 cloths sealed there . . . . . 60s.
John Glasyn, of Rypon, subsidy and ulnage of 889
   cloths sealed there . . . . . . £16 13s. 4½d.
Thomas Boteler, of Selby, subsidy and ulnage of 26½
   cloths sealed there . . . . . . 10s.
John Merebek and Thomas Boteler, of Pountfret, subsidy and ulnage of 106 cloths sealed there . 40s.
Sum of Cloths, 2,586.
Sum total of receipts, £48 10s. 0½d.

VIII.

[E. $\frac{345}{24}$

York   THE ACCOUNT OF RALPH BYRNAND, Approver of the Subsidy
and Ulnage of saleable cloths, and of the moiety of the forfeitures
of the same, to wit, from the Feast of Easter in the 11th year of
1471 the reign of King Edward the Fourth, until the Feast of St. Michael,
1473 in the 13th year, To wit, for two and a half whole years as below.

Doncas- From John Taillour and William Wikes [?] and
tre   the other men of the Town of Doncastre, for Subs. and Ulnage
   44½ saleable cloths there sealed during the time   16s. 8¼d.
   aforesaid.

Barnes- Richard Symmys, Christopher Bene, and the
ley   other men of the Town of Barnesley, for 176½ Subs. and Ulnage
   saleable cloths sealed there during the time   66s. 6¾d.
   aforesaid.

Ledes   Henry Rokley, Robert Bene, and the other men
   of the Town of Ledes, for 365½ saleable cloths   £6 13s. 3¾d.
   sold there during the time aforesaid.

Almon- John Nevell, Thomas Bemand, Laurence Key,
desbury   and the other men of the Town of Almondes-   Subs., Ulnage
   bury, for 320 cloths there sealed during the   £6
   time aforesaid.

Brad- John Hopton, William Walker, and the other   Subs., Ulnage
ford   men of the Town of Bradford, 135½ cloths   47s. 0¾d.
   sealed there during the time aforesaid.

Selby   Thomas Botler, Anthony Kydall, and the other   Subs., Ulnage
   men of the Town of Selby, for 26½ cloths,   9s. 11¼d.
   sealed there, during the time aforesaid.

Kynges- Nicholas Eles,[1] Thomas Bure, and the other men   Subs., Ulnage
ton-on-   of Hull, for 295 saleable cloths, sealed there   110s. 7½d.
Hull   during the time aforesaid.

<hr>

[1] Nicholas Elles was Mayor of Hull in 1455 and 1464.

Pount-fret	Ch. Butler, Laurence Bene, and the other men of the Town of Pountfret, for 107½ cloths, sealed there, during the time aforesaid.	Subs., Ulnage 40s. 8¼d.

City of York   And he [the ulnager] is charged in his account with £100 of the subsidy and ulnage of divers saleable cloths in the City of York and the County and Suburbs of the same owing to our Lord the King as shown [by the tenor of letters patent to Him thereof made] received as well by William Holbek, late Mayor and Alderman of the City of York, from the said feast of Easter in the first year until the feast of All Saints now next following, amounting to the sum of £40, from the Feast of All Saints aforesaid in the 11th year until the Feast of the Purification of Blessed Mary the Virgin in the 12th year, amounting to the sum of £35, as [also] by Christopher Marshall, late Mayor of the City aforesaid, from the said Feast of the Purification of Blessed Mary the Virgin in the said 12th year until the 16th day of November in the said 13th year, amounting to the sum of £25, as is contained in the Memoranda of the Records of Michaelmas Term in the 13th year of the King that now is. Roll 25, ex parte King's Remembrances.

Wake-feld	John Hodgeson and William . . . . . , and the other men of the Town of Wakefeld, for 161 saleable cloths sealed there during the time aforesaid.	Subs., Ulnage 60s. 4½d.
Rypon	John Glasyn, Richard Frankysh, and the other men of the Town of Rypon, for 1,597 saleable cloths, sealed there.	Subs., Ulnage £35 11s. 4½d.
Hale-fax	Nicholas Bemond, John Hauldesworth, and the other men of the town of Halefax, for 1,518½ saleable cloths, made during the time aforesaid. Sum of Receipts, £88 6s. 0¾d.	Subs., Ulnage £28 9s. 5¼d.

The same accounts for 18 copper seals, whereof 10 are for the subsidy and 8 for the ulnage received from Thomas Tregott, late Approver of the Subsidy and Ulnage of saleable cloths in the County of York and Kyngeston-on-Hull aforesaid without Indenture.

IX.

[E. $\frac{345}{24}$]

County and City of York.

[This roll is contained in its original leather pouch.]

PARTICULARS OF THE ACCOUNT OF RALPH BIRNAND, Approver of the Subsidy and Ulnage of saleable cloths in the County of York and City of York, from the Feast of St. Michael in the 13th year of the reign of King Edward IV, until the Feast of St. Michael in the 15th year of the same King, To wit, during two whole years, as below:

1473

1475

County of York.

[Ripon] Laurence Bene and the other men of the Town of Rypon, for 1,396½ cloths.	Subs. £23 2s. 1d. Ulnage 57s. 9¼d.	

[Hali- fax]	Nicholas Bemond and the other men of the Town of Halefax, for 1,493½ cloths.	Subs. £24 17s. 10d. Ulnage 12s. 2¾d.
[Almond- bury]	Laurence Key and the other men of the Town of Almondesbury, for 426 cloths.	Subs. £7 2s. 7d. Ulnage 17s. 9½d.
[Brad- ford]	Henry Leventhorp and the other men of the Town of Bradford, for 178½ cloths.	Subs. 59s. 6d. Ulnage 7s. 5¼d.
[Leeds]	Robert Bene and the other men of the Town of Ledys, for 320 cloths.	Subs. 106s. 8d. Ulnage 13s. 4d.
[Ponte- fract]	Laurence Bene and the other men of the Town of Powmfracte, for 213½ cloths.	Subs. 71s. 2d. Ulnage 8s. 10¾d.
[Wake- field]	John Hodgson and William Carson and the other men of the Town of Wakefeld, for 160 cloths.	Subs. 53s. 4d. Ulnage 6s. 8d.
[Barns- ley]	Christopher Bene and the other men of the Town of Barnsley, for 142½ cloths.	Subs. 47s. 6d. Ulnage 5s. 11¼d.
[Don- caster]	John Taillor and the other men of the Town of Doncastre, for 35½ cloths.	Subs. 11s. 10d. Ulnage 16¾d.
[Hull]	Thomas Bury and the other men of Hull, for 426½ cloths.	Subs. £7 2s. 2d. Ulnage 17s. 9¼d.
[Selby]	John Cros and the other men of Selby, for 19 cloths.	Subs. 6s. 4d. Ulnage 9½d.
City of York	William Holbeke, Christopher Marshall, William Scausby, "merchaunt," William Brown, "Sherman," and the other men of the City of York, for 2,346½ cloths.	Subs. £39 2s. 2d. Ulnage £4 17s. 9¼d.

Sum of cloths in the said County of York, 4,802½, whereof the Subsidy is £80 0s. 10d., and the Ulnage £10 0s. 1¼d.

Sum total of receipts, £134 0s. 10½d.

X.

[E. 345/24]

W.R. and Hull.

County of York, King- ston-on- Hull, City of York, 1471

PARTICULARS OF THE ACCOUNT OF RALPH BYRNAND, whom our now Lord the King, Edward IVth, by his Letters Patent, dated at Westminster, the 17th day of June, in His 11th year, as is enrolled in the Original Rolls of the same year, Roll [blank], in the part relating to the Remembrancer of the Treasury, appointed His Approver of the Subsidy and ulnage of saleable cloths in the County of York, Kyngeston-on-Hull, and the precincts of the same, and also within the City of York, and the suburbs of the same, and, to boot, the moiety of forfeitures of saleable cloths exposed for sale and not sealed there with the King's seals appointed for this purpose. To Hold from the Feast of Easter then last past, until the end of 7 years from then next following, according to the form and effect of divers Statutes published thereanent, To wit, of this subsidy and ulnage of the King there, and of the forfeitures aforesaid from the Feast of

1475
1478

St. Michael, in the 15th year until the Feast of Easter falling on the 22nd day of March in the 18th year of the same King, for 2 whole years, a quarter of a year and 43 days. And from the Feast of Easter in the 18 year, Nicholas Leventhorpe,[1] now Approver of the Subsidy and ulnage aforesaid, is thereof charged.

Receipts of Money.

[City of York]	From John Thong, Christopher Marshall, William Scawsby, merchants, John Bramhowe, Chaplain, Vicar of Topclyff, William Brown, "sherman," William Garland, and the other men of the County of York, and suburbs of the same, for 2,288 saleable cloths, To wit, for each cloth for subsidy 4d., and for ulnage ½d.	Subs. £38 2s. 8d. Ulnage £4 15s. 4d.	
[Ripon]	From Laurence Bene, William Bramhowe, chaplain, late Rector of Gillyng, Richard Frankysch, Thomas Bene, John Bishop, and the other men of the Town of Rypon, for 1,385½ saleable cloths, etc. [as above].	Subs. £23 and 22d. Ulnage 57s. 8¾d.	
[Halifax]	From Nicholas Bemond and the other men of the Town of Halefax, for 1,493½ saleable cloths, etc.	Subs. £24 17s. 10d. Ulnage 62s. 2¾d.	
[Almondbury]	From Laurence Key and the other men of the Town of Almondesbury, for 427 saleable cloths, etc.	Subs. £7 2s. 4d. Ulnage 17s. 9½d.	
[Bradford]	From Henry Leventhorp and the other men of the Town of Bradford, for 214 saleable cloths, etc.	Subs. 71s. 4d. Ulnage 8s. 11½d.	
[Leeds]	From Robert Bene and the other men of the Town of Ledys, for 321 saleable cloths, etc.	Subs. 107s. Ulnage 13s. 4½d.	
[Pontefract]	From Laurence Bene and the other men of the Town of Poumfraith, for 213½ saleable cloths, etc.	Subs. 71s. 2d. Ulnage 8s. 10¾d.	
[Wakefield]	From John Hodgeson, Thomas Cokson, and the other men of the Town of Wakefeld, for 160 saleable cloths, etc.	Subs. 53s. 4d. Ulnage 6s. 8d.	
[Barnsley]	From John Litster and Laurence Key and the other men of the Town of Barnsley, for 162½ saleable cloths, etc.	Subs. 47s. 6d. Ulnage 5s. 11d.	
[Doncaster]	From John Taillor and William Wykys and the other men of the Town of Doncastre, for 35½ saleable cloths, etc.	Subs. 11s. 10d. Ulnage 17¾d.	

[1] H.C.H., 487, 2 R. Miscell., Bdle. 856. Nicholas Leventhorp was appointed ulnager in 1478, and described as "late farmer" of the subsidy and ulnage of saleable cloths in the county and city of York and the precincts of the same, and in the town of Kingston-on-Hull, had an allowance made to him for a pension paid to Richard Wilson, serjeant-at-arms, received out of the ulnage. No account to be found.
Bdle. 857, F.L.H. 2258. By letters patent given at Westminster 5th Oct., 1 Hen. VII, Sir Edward Stanley succeeded Nicholas Leventhorpe in the office of ulnager. No account to be found. He appears to have been still holding the office in the 8th year of Henry VII.

	From Thomas Bere, William Wytherwyk,		
[Kingston-on-Hull]	otherwise called Wythornwyk, and the other men of the town of Kingeston-on-Hull, for 426½ saleable cloths, etc.	Subs.	£7 2s. 2d.
		Ulnage	17s. 9¼d.
[Selby]	From John Crosse and the other men of the Town of Selby, for 21½ saleable cloths.	Subs.	7s.
		Ulnage	10½d.

Sum of Cloths, 7,128. Subs. £118 16s. 0d.
Ulnage £14 and 18d.

Moiety of forfeitures He does not answer for any profit arising from the forfeiture of saleable cloths, or pieces of cloth exposed for sale and not sealed with the King's seals appointed thereanent, in the County, Towns, and City aforesaid, or in the precincts and suburbs of the same, to wit, during the aforesaid time of this account, because the Approver has not found and has not been able to find any cloths to be seized there of this sort during the time aforesaid, as in any way he could discover, as he says upon his oath.

Sum of Receipts, £133 13s. 0d.

Receipt of Seals.

The same answers and accounts for 18 copper seals received as a remainder from his last account; whereof 10 are for the subsidy, and 8 for the ulnage, for the due execution of his office as in the end of the same account more fully is contained mention.

Sum of Receipt of Seals, 18. And these are delivered to Nicholas Leventhorp, now the Approver of the Subsidy and Ulnage in the County and Towns aforesaid, for the due exercise of his office. Of the which 18 seals, forsooth, the aforesaid Nicholas Leventhorp, now the Approver of the Subsidy and Ulnage aforesaid, rests chargeable.

Sum of the receipts of seals, 18, which remain in the custody of the aforesaid Ralph Birnand now Approver there for executing his office with.

APPENDIX I.

$$[\text{E. 122, } \frac{55}{11}]$$

ROLL OF ROBERT OF BARTON AND GILBERT OF BEDEFORD, Guardians and Collectors of the Small New Custom of merchandise shipped from the Port of Kyngeston-upon-Hull, from the 4th day of July, in the 32nd year of the reign·of Lord Edward, illustrious King of England, until the Feast of St. Michael next following.

The Ship of John of Faxflete sailed from the Port of Hull the 13th day of July.

Ralph of Durreem, 17 loads of lead, price £45 10s. 0d.   And he paid 11s. 4½d.

Walter de Feroun, ½ a scarlet [cloth], whereon he paid 12d.

The same had 30 stone of cheese, price 16s.,whereon he paid 2¼d.

The same had 5 salmon, price 5s., whereon he paid ¾d.

Sum, 12s. 7½d.

The Ship of Hermann Bukes of Hamburgh sailed from the Port of Hull the 18th day of August.

The same had 4 loads of lead, price £10, whereon he paid 2s. 6d.

The sum is shown [above].

The Ship of John Shirelokes sailed from the Port of Hull the 25th day of August.

Ralph of Dureem [had] 9½ loads of lead, price £21 17s. 0d., whereon he paid 5s. 5½d.

The Sum is shown [above].

The Ship of Thomas of the Hethe sailed from the port of Hull the 30th day of August.

Godfrey of Loveyn [had] 8 quarters of mustard seed price 24s., whereon he paid 3¾d.   The sum is shown [above].

The Ship of William of Hamburgh sailed from the Port of Hull the same day of August.

Baldewyn of Hamburgh [had] half a cloth without grain, whereon he paid 6d.   The Sum is shown above.

Sum of cloth in grain shipped out of the Kingdom at Hull from the 4th day of July in the 32nd year until the Feast of St. Michael next following.

Half a scarlet [cloth], whereon the custom [is] 12d.

Sum of cloth without grain shipped during the same time,

Half a cloth, whereon the custom [is] 6d.

Estimated sum and value of goods and divers merchandise shipped during the same time, £79 12s. 0d., whereon the custom [is] 19s.10¾d. Nothing [in the way] of increment.

Proved sum of the whole custom, 21s. 4¾d.

IMPORTS OF CLOTH AT HULL, IN 1307

$$[\text{K.R. Customs Accounts, } \frac{51}{1}]$$

Kyngeston-on-Hull.

ROLL OF ROBERT OF BARTON AND GILBERT OF BEDDEFORD, Guardians and Collectors of the New Little Custom at Kyngeston-

on-Hull of goods and merchandise there imported, from the Feast
1307-8 of St. Michael, in the First year of the reign of our illustrious Lord
Edward, King of England, the son of King Edward, until the feast
of St. Michael next following.

4 October, the Ship of William Petersone.
William Lumbard, 5 cloths without grain, whereof the custom
[was] 5s.

6 October, the Ship of Henry of Weyland.
John Sone, 2 cloths without grain, custom 2s.

28 December, the Ship of Boydin of Axhill.
Martin of Raceburgh, 43 cloths without grain, custom 43s.

6 January, the Ship of Simon Ingle.
John Cortes of Flanders, 1 cloth without grain, custom 12d.

11 January, the Ship of William Peterson.
Peter of Hadigham, 5 cloths without grain, custom 5s.
William Bayfot, 14 cloths without grain, custom 14s.
Philip Hund, ½ a cloth without grain, custom 6d.

1 March, the Ship of Arnald of Stenebergh.
John of Hunescotes, 32 cloths without grain, custom 32s.
Godfrey Spicenail, 2 cloths mixed with grain, custom 3s. [?].
Godfrey Spicenail, 34 cloths without grain, custom 34s.

5 April, the Ship of Peter Bellard.
Godfrey Spicenail, 7½ cloths without grain, custom 7s. 6d.
William de Castello, 2 cloths without grain, custom 2s.
William de Castello, 1 piece of cloth and 3 " materaz," price
15s., custom 2¼d.

22 April, the Ship of Boydin of Axhill.
Giles de Lys, 1 cloth mixed with grain, custom 18d.
Giles de Lys, 17 cloths without grain, custom 17s.

16 May, the Ship of William Peterson.
Godfrey Spicenail, 7 cloths without grain, custom 7s.
The Ship of John of Westland.
Giles of Lyz, 6 cloths without grain, custom 6s.

10 June, the Ship of Arnald of Stenesbergh.
Arnald of Stenesbergh, 7 cloths without grain, custom 7s.
Robert Stikeling, 1 cloth mixed with grain, custom 18d.
Godfrey de Sass [?], 30 cloths without grain, custom 30s.
Philip Hunde, 4 cloths without grain, custom 4s.
The Ship of Hugh Clayson.
Hugh Clayson, 1 cloth without grain, custom 12d.

15 June, the Ship of Henry Andrewson.
Dyonis son of Reyner, 6 cloths without grain, custom 6s.;
2 cloths mixed with grain, 3s.

22 June, the Ship of Peter Berland.
Peter Berland, 1 piece of cloth, price 20s., custom 3d.

14 Aug., the Ship of Henry Smythewynd.
Henry Smythewynd, 3 pieces of cloth without grain, price 48s.,
custom 7½d.

20 Aug., the Ship of William of York [de Ebor.].
John de Markes, 1 piece of cloth without grain, price 20s.,
custom 3d.

APPENDIX II.

COLLECTORS AND CONTROLLERS OF THE CUSTOMS AT HULL.

[List of dates from the institution of the " New," otherwise " Little Custom," in 1274-5, 3 Edw. I, but unfortunately the names of the Collectors in this year are not recorded in the Roll, and wool and fells only paid the custom.]

1290. 19-20 Edw. I. Guy Baldewyn, Robert Clerk [*clericus*], and Hugh son of Isabel del Gik[1] were the receivers of the New Custom on wool and fells.

1294. 22-23 Edw. I, 21st July. Robert of Barton and John of Hustweyt were appointed the collectors of the New Custom in the port of Kingston-on-Hull, and continued jointly to hold office until Christmas, 1297, when John of Hustweyt was removed.

1294. 22-23 Edw. I. William of Wickkinggeston, clerk,[2] controller.

1297. 26 Edw. I. Richard Oysel appointed one of the collectors of the New Custom in place of John of Hustweyt.

1303. 32 Edw. I. Robert of Barton and Gilbert of Bedeford, the latter taking the place of Richard of Oysel, collectors. They continued in office until the year 1313.

1313. 7-8 Edw. II. Gilbert of Bedeford and Richard of Gretford, collectors.

1314. 8 Edw. II. Robert of Sandale,[3] controller, and attorney of Sir John of Sandale, his lord.

1316. 10 Edw. II, 29 Oct. Robert of Hastanges, warden of the town of Kingston-on-Hull, appointed controller of customs there, to hold the office in the same manner as Robert of Sandale held it.

1320. 13 Edw. II, 1 April. William of Barton, controller, and Richard of Gretford, collector.

1322. 16 Edw. II, 20 July to 30 Sept., 17 Edw. II. Richard of Gretford and John of Barton,[4] collectors.

1322. 16 Edw. II, 6 Nov. Hamo Quarel, controller.

1323. 17 Edw. II, 29 April. William of Barton the elder, appointed controller.

1323. 17 Edw. II, 20 July. Richard of Gretford and John of Barton, collectors.

---

[1] Hugh, son of Isabel of Kyngeston-upon-Hull, is mentioned as a grantor in a deed dated Feb., 1298 (Frost). It looks as if the place-name " Gik " might be really " Wyke," the original name of the town of Hull. Frost says that the first time the name of Kingston-upon-Hull is mentioned is in a writ of *ad quod damnum* dated 1294.

[2] William of Wickkinggeston's name seems to combine the two names of the town. The name was subsequently corrupted into Wiggeston.

[3] Robert of Sandale was warden of Hull in 1313 and 1316, and, probably, in the intervening years; he was also mayor of Hull in 1313.

[4] John of Barton was mayor of Hull in 1336. He was also coroner, but was superseded in that office on account of his other numerous duties.

1324. 18 Edw. II, Michaelmas. Richard de la Pole, collector.

1324. 18–19 Edw. II, Michaelmas. Richard of Gretford, controller, as attorney of Hamo Quarel.

1325. 18–19 Edw. II. Walter Heyward,[1] collector jointly with Richard de la Pole.

1326. 20 Edw. II. Richard de la Pole and Richard of Shakenhurst, collectors.

1327. 20–21 Edw. II. Richard de la Pole and John of Barton mentioned as the " late collectors."

1330. 4 Edw. III, Nov. John of Barton and Henry of Burton, collectors. Robert of Stanford, controller.

1331. 5 Edw. III. Adam of Coppandale and Hugh the Taverner,[2] collectors.

1334. 8 June, 7 Edw. III. John of Barton and Richard Fitzdieu,[3] collectors.

1334. 8 Edw. III. John of Barton and Richard of Lichefeld, collectors.

1341. 15 Edw. III. John of Barton and Hugh of the Clay named as " former collectors." The King hears that they have been " amoved " from their office.

134 . . [?]. Thomas of Melebourn, collector or controller.

1346. 20 Edw. III, 15 Feb. John of Wessenham, Simon of Wessenham, his brother, and Richard of Saleby, farmers of customs, have a grant " of all " the customs of the realm to hold under a certain form. The King orders the collectors at Hull to pay a salary to John of Wessenham.

1348. 21 Edw. III, 20 Jan. John of Wessenham, the King's butler, collector, employing a deputy at Hull to collect custom on wool, cloth and worsted blankets [*lecti*] and coverlets.

1354. 28 Edw. III. John of Northbergh and Walter Box, collectors.

1354. 28 Edw. III. Adam Punde, controller.

1363. 37 Edw. III. Thomas of Wapplynton and John of Middleton,[4] collectors; Geoffrey of Hamby,[5] supervisor.

1377. 51 Edw. III to 4 Ric. II. Robert of Selby,[6] collector.

1380. 3–4 Ric. II. Thomas Flemyng appointed controller, " receiving the accustomed wages, on condition that he execute the office in person."

1382. 5–6 Ric. II. Thomas Waplyngton and Robert of Selby, collectors.

1382. 5–6 Ric. II. Ralph Crust associated as a collector with Robert Selby and Thomas Waplyngton.

---

[1] Possibly Walter Heyward was the same man as Walter Helleward, who was mayor of Hull in 1342 and again in 1349.

[2] Hugh the Taverner was mayor of Hull in 1334 (Pat. Rolls).

[3] Richard Fitzdieu, " marchant," admitted a freeman of York in 1337.

[4] John of Middleton was a bailiff of Hull in 1364.

[5] Geoffrey of Hamby was mayor of Hull in 1353.

[6] Robert of Selby was mayor of Hull in 1365.

1389. 12-13 Ric. II. William Ponde and John Colthorpe, collectors; Thomas Paule, chaplain, controller.

1391. 15 Ric. II. Robert Garton and John Colthorpe,[1] collectors. Symon of Grimesby, controller.

1392 [?]. 16 Ric. II. Walter Frost and William Pounde, customers.

1397. 23 July, 21 Ric. II. William Culham, controller.

1397. 12 Nov., 21 Ric. II. Thomas Percy, controller.

1397. 3 Dec., 21 Ric. II. Simon of Grimsby,[2] controller.

1398. 17 Nov., 21–22 Ric. II. Robert of Garton and Peter Steller, described as "late Customers."

1399. 11 Feb., 22 Ric. II. Thomas Percy, reappointed controller.

1401. 2–3 Henry IV. John Leventhorp and John Tuttebury, collectors. William Pounde, controller.

1402. 4 Henry IV. John Thorp, clerk, and Henry Wyman,[3] collectors

1413. *Ante* 26 April, 1 Henry V. Richard Altham and John Tuttebury, collectors.

1413. 26 April, 1 Henry V. Richard Burton and Robert Middelton, collectors. John Appelby, controller.

1415. Christmas, 3 Henry V. Thomas Sutton, clerk, and Robert Middelton collectors. Thomas Burgh, controller.

1416 6 April, 3 Henry V. John Bedford[4] and Richard Ulverston, clerk, collectors.

1416. Michaelmas, 4 Henry V. Richard Ulverston, clerk, and John Bedford, collectors. Thomas Burgh, controller.

1425. 1 Jan., 3 Henry VI. Thomas Mareshall[5] and John Bedford; collectors. John Grymesby, controller.

1426. July 24, 4 Henry VI. Richard Ulverstone and John Bedford, collectors, and John Thorp, controller.

1426. 31 Oct., 5 Henry VI. John Bedford and Thomas Elyngham, collectors. John Grymesby,[6] controller.

1427. Michaelmas, 6 Henry VI. Nicholas Blakdurn and John Leversegge, collectors. Thomas Sutton, clerk, controller.

1429. 26 Feb., 7 Henry VI. Nicholas Clerk and Thomas Elingham, collectors. Simon Waghen, controller.

1429. Michaelmas, 8 Henry VI. Richard Ulverston, clerk, and John Bedford, collectors. Thomas Burgh, controller.

---

[1] John Colthorp, mayor of Hull, 1389. His will is dated 17 Ric. II, and his wife Alice, his brother Thomas, the vicar of Foston, Simon of Grymesby, and John Liversege were appointed joint exors. thereof (Town's Records).

[2] Simon of Grymesby was mayor of Hull in 1391.

[3] Henry Wyman, seemingly Henry Wyman, "mercator," admitted a freeman of York in 1386.

[4] John Bedford, mayor of Hull 1412 and 1414.

[5] Thomas Mareshall, mayor of Hull 1415.

[6] John Grymesby, mayor of Hull 1424.

H

1431. Michaelmas, 10 Henry VI. Nicholas Clerk and John Bedford, collectors. John Steton, controller.

1432. 20 April, 10 Henry VI. John Bedford and Thomas Marchall, collectors. John Steton, controller.

1439. 8 Feb., 17 Henry VI. Patrick Skipwith and John Bedford, customers.

1453. 6 April, 31 Henry VI. Nicholas Elys[1] and William Eland,[2] collectors of customs. Ralph Babthorp, controller.

1464. 4 Edw. IV. John Dey[3] and John Grene,[4] collectors. William Wythornwyck, controller.

1465. 5 Edw. IV. John Dey and John Brydde, collectors.

1471. 11 Edw. IV. William Swellyngton and Thomas Alcok, collectors.

[1] Nicholas Elys, sheriff of Hull 1444, and mayor 1455.
[2] William Eland, sheriff of Hull 1458.
[3] John Dey or Day, sheriff of Hull 1463.
[4] John Grene, mayor of Hull 1463

Appendix III.

List of Ulnagers.

1327. 1 Edw. III. Nicholas Shirlok.[1]
1348. 22 Edw. III. John Marreys.[2]
1349. 23 Edw. III. Robert of Gloucester,[3] deputy of John Marreys.
1351. 25 Edw. III. Robert of Wandesford, deputy of John Marreys.
1353. 27 Edw. III. Richard of Riseby, deputy of John Marreys.
1361. 35 Edw. III. John of Topcliff of Thurkelby, John of Topcliff of Ripon, and Thomas Lockton of Malton, deputies of John Marreys.
1365. 39 Edw. III. William Hervey, ulnager for England.
1370. 44 Edw. III. John of Acaster.[4]
1373. 47 Edw. III. Richard of Acaster, deputy.
1374. 48 Edw. III. William Hervy, ulnager for England.
1377. 51 Edw. III and 1 Ric. II. John of Pathorn.[5]
       2-3 Ric. II. William Hervy, ulnager of England.
1379. Feb. 8, 2 Ric. II. John Forster, of Drybek, appointed ulnager in the four northern counties.
1379. 2 and 3 Ric. II. Thomas Scorburgh, ulnager in the East Riding.
1380. 12 May, 3 Ric. II. Thomas of Brounflete appointed ulnager in Counties of York, Northumberland, Cumberland, and Westmorland.
1380. 1-4 Ric. II. John of Roucliff, John Pathorn of York, draper, and William Belle, appointed by William Hervy his deputies in the County of York.
1381. Feb. 10, 4 Ric. II. Thomas Forster, of Drybek, and John Pathorn appointed for the four northern counties.

[1] Nicholas Shirlok, the king's yeoman, had a grant made to him for his life on 19 June, 1327, of the office of ulnager of cloths in England, by Letters Patent. His accounts only deal with imported cloths exposed for sale in England.

[2] John Marreys, king's yeoman, was appointed 12 Feb., 1348, for life, ulnager of all kinds of cloth [" kersies " named] in London, York, Winchester, Bristol, etc., and all other places, made in England. Cloths for sale between merchant and merchant to be sealed before being exposed for sale.

[3] Robert of Gloucester, citizen of London.

[4] John of Acaster, probably the man who was mayor of York in several years.

[5] John Pathorn of York, " draper," deputy ulnager for the counties of York, Northumberland, and Westmorland. John, son of Robert of Pathorn, " draper," was admitted a freeman of York in 1363, and was apparently a chamberlain of York city in 1370.

1384. Nov. 16, 8 Ric. II. John Orwell and John Quixley[1] appointed for the four counties.

1384, 5. 8 Ric. II. Simon of Elvyngton[2] and John Munkhill, deputies of William Hervy in the four counties.

1385. 8–9 Ric. II. Thomas Brounflete, John Orwell, and Thomas Forster, deputies.

1394. 17–18 Ric. II. John Thornton and John Raghton for York City.

1394, 5. 17–19 Ric. II. William Skipwith and Richard Agylton.

1396. 19–20 Ric. II. William Barker.[3]

1397. 20–21 Ric. II. William Hoperton.

1398. 21–22 Ric. II. John Amyas.

1398. 6 Oct., 22 Ric. II.* Thomas of Swanlande.

1460. 38 Henry VI and 1 Edw. IV. Thomas Scarbrough.

1461. 1 Edw. IV. John Nevyll, Lord Montague.

1467. 6–7 Edw. IV. Ralph Byrnand.[4]

1469, 70. 9–10 Edw. IV. Thomas Trygott, of South Kirkby, Esquire.

1478. 17–18 Edw. IV. Nicholas Leventhorpe.

1491–2. 7–8 Henry VII. Sir Edw. Stanley.

[1] John Quixley, probably John Quixlay, chamberlain of York in 1371.

[2] A Simon of Elvyngton was admitted a freeman of York in 1377 or 1378.

[3] William Barker of Tadcaster. His will given in *Test. Ebor.*, i, 327, is a very interesting one. He left to the fabric fund of York Minster the cost of carrying " one shipful of stone by water."

[4] Ralph Byrnand of Blaktoft, gent.

Appendix IV.

Specimen of an Indenture made between an Ulnager and the Sheriff.

$$[\text{E. 101, } \frac{345}{15}]$$

This Indenture made at York on the last day of September in the 19th year of the reign of King Richard the Second, Between Robert Conestable, Sheriff of Yorkshire, and William Skipwith, collector of the subsidy and ulnage of saleable cloths and of the forfeitures of the same in the County aforesaid, from the 20th day of July in the 18th year until the 20th day of October in the 19th year. Witnesseth that the same William hath seized and sold, in the manner underwritten from the hands of divers persons divers pieces of cloth exposed for sale before the subsidy thereon was paid and [before] those cloths were sealed with the seal appointed for the purpose: To Wit, 4 dozen and 6 ells of strait cloths which belonged to Thomas Huchunson of Beverley, of the value of 13s. 4d.; 2 dozen of strait cloths belonging to John Cotyngham, value 6s. 10d.; 10 ells of "Tawne" and "Russet" cloth, belonging to Robert Aldegate, value 10s. 2d.; 2 dozen strait cloths belonging to Robert Standen, value 6s.; 4 ells of "Russet" cloth belonging to William of Cotingham of Beverley, value 4s.; 1 dozen strait cloths belonging to the same William, value 3s.; 1 dozen cloths of blanket belonging to Thomas Fle, value 4s. 6d.; 6 ells of blue cloth belonging to William Wath of Selby, value 6s. 8d.; 2 dozen strait cloths belonging to William Estoft, value 6s. 8d. In Witness whereof the aforesaid parties have alternately set their seals. Given the year and place abovesaid.

INDEX.

An asterisk (*) implies that the name occurs more than once on a page.

Abingdon, Stephen of, 6n
Acaster, John of, 115, 115n; Richard of, 115
Adamson, John, 64
Aghen, Richard, 17
Aglion, . . . , 12, 21; Richard, 14, 23, 36
Agylton, Richard, 47, 116
Ailsy, Roger, 35, 36
Ake, William, 35
Akworth John, 40; Richard, 39
Alcok, Bishop John, 33n; Robert, 33, 33n; Thomas, 33, 33n; William, 33n
Aldgate, Robert, 117
Aleynson, Thomas, 42
Alien, 32; aliens' cloth, 33
Alienigenæ, viii
Alkebare, Alkebarowe, Thomas, 25, 36
Allecame, William, 41
Allerton, 42
Almondbury, Almondebury, Almondesbury, 103*, 104, 106
Altham, Richard, 113
Amolonk, John, 27
Amyas, John, 100, 116
Andrew, Junour, 48
Andrewson, Henry, 110
Anlaby, John, 35
Annotson, John, 40
Anson, Thomas, 41
Antays, Thomas, 36
Anton, John, 24
Apelton, Appylton, John, 22, 91
Appelby, Appilby, Appylby, John, 113; William, 58, 58n, 74, 92
Approver, 104, 108
Archer, Robert, 44
Arcybot, John, 46
Arcylot, William, 37
Arnald, John, 11
Ash, Richard, 96
Ashley, Professor, viii, xix, xx
Askham, Askam, George, 58; John, 94; Thomas, 51, 51n, 56, 58, 60, 63, 67*, 73, 82, 84, 88, 101
Aslaby, John, 35
Asliott, Aslot, William, 14, 22
Assheton, Adam of, 42

Assize of measures, xxiii
atte Pole, Richard, 6n; William, 6n
Atthaye, John, 32
At-ton-ende, Atte-Toune-end, At-ye-ton-ende, William, 57, 68, 81, 84
Austin friars, xviii
Awebergh, Thomas, 18
Awus, John of, 78
Axhill, Boydin of, 110*

B . . . , John of, 17
Babthorp, Ralph, 114
Bailiff of Hull, 1n, 7n, 8n, 24
Baillif, William, 92
Bakester, Bakster, Agnes, 52; John, 83; Thomas, 96; Walter, 68
Bakker, John, 14
Balderby, Richard of, 42
Baldewyn, Guy, 111
Balne, John of, 96; Richard, 100
Balster, John, 43
Baltic, The, 5n
Bank, Banke, John, 96; John of, 39; Marjory of, 57
Barber, Barbour, Agnes, 59; Alice, 48; Geoffrey, 44; Thomas, 12, 13, 24; William, 96, 98
Bardewyk, Berwick, Simon of, 6, 6n
Bardney, William, 88
Bardsay, Bardysay, William, 86, 93
Bare, Thomas of, 41
Barker, John, 12; Margaret, 42; William, xxix, 44, 47, 95, 116, 116n
Barkesworth, John, 20
Barnardcastell, Barnacastell, John, 67, 102; John of, 92
Barnsley, Barneslay, Berneslay, xxx, 40, 102, 103, 105, 106
Barnsley Church, Chantry in, xxx
Barton, John of, 48, 111*, 111n, 112*; Mariota of, 49; Master John, 6n; Robert of, vii, viii, xiii, 1, 1n, 2, 3, 4, 5, 109*, 111*; Roger of, 81, 81n, 92, 92n; William, 81n, 111*
Bate, John, 46; Richard, 25*, 45; William, 96
Bateson, Miss, xxviii
Batte, Richard, 14; William, 35
Battey, John, 35

I

PRINTED BY
J. WHITEHEAD AND SON LTD., ALFRED STREET, BOAR LANE,
LEEDS.

www.ingramcontent.com/pod-product-compliance
Ingram Content Group UK Ltd.
Pitfield, Milton Keynes, MK11 3LW, UK
UKHW042156280225
455719UK00001B/364